SECOND EDITION

Introduction to Differential Equations

Richard K. Miller

Department of Mathematics
Iowa State University

Prentice Hall, Englewood Cliffs, New Jersey 07632

Library of Congress Cataloging-in-Publication Data

Miller, Richard K.
    Introduction to differential equations / Richard K. Miller.—2nd ed.
        p.   cm.
    Includes bibliographical references and index.
    ISBN 0-13-478264-X
    1. Differential equations.   I. Title.
    QA371.M56   1991
    515′ .35—dc20   90–19753
                    CIP

Editorial/production: Nicholas Romanelli
Interior and cover design: Meryl Poweski
Manufacturing buyer: Paula Massenaro

 © 1991, 1987 by Prentice-Hall, Inc.
A Division of Simon & Schuster
Englewood Cliffs, NJ 07632

Printed in the United States of America

10 9 8 7 6 5 4 3 2 1

ISBN 0-13-478264-X

Prentice-Hall International (UK) Limited, *London*
Prentice-Hall of Australia Pty, Limited, *Sydney*
Prentice-Hall Canada Inc., *Toronto*
Prentice-Hall Hispanoamericana, S.A., *Mexico*
Prentice-Hall of India Private Limited, *New Delhi*
Prentice-Hall of Japan, Inc., *Tokyo*
Simon & Schuster Asia Pte. Ltd., *Singapore*
Editora Prentice-Hall do Brasil, Ltda, *Rio de Janeiro*

Library of Congress Cataloging-in-Publication Data

Miller, Richard K.
  Introduction to differential equations / Richard K. Miller.—2nd ed.
      p.   cm.
  Includes bibliographical references and index.
  ISBN 0-13-478264-X
  1. Differential equations.   I. Title.
  QA371.M56   1991
  515′ .35—dc20   90–19753
                          CIP

Editorial/production: Nicholas Romanelli
Interior and cover design: Meryl Poweski
Manufacturing buyer: Paula Massenaro

 © 1991, 1987 by Prentice-Hall, Inc.
A Division of Simon & Schuster
Englewood Cliffs, NJ 07632

Printed in the United States of America

10 9 8 7 6 5 4 3 2 1

ISBN   0-13-478264-X

Prentice-Hall International (UK) Limited, *London*
Prentice-Hall of Australia Pty, Limited, *Sydney*
Prentice-Hall Canada Inc., *Toronto*
Prentice-Hall Hispanoamericana, S.A., *Mexico*
Prentice-Hall of India Private Limited, *New Delhi*
Prentice-Hall of Japan, Inc., *Tokyo*
Simon & Schuster Asia Pte. Ltd., *Singapore*
Editora Prentice-Hall do Brasil, Ltda, *Rio de Janeiro*

Contents

Preface

Publication of this second edition of *Introduction to Differential Equations* is a result of the enthusiastic response to the first edition.

This new edition has **numerous changes.** There are over 80 new problems among the exercises. Included in these are routine drill problems, intermediate exercises, challenging theoretical problems and a variety of applied problems. Chapter 1 has been rewritten and streamlined. Examples and arguments in the remainder of the text have been revised and updated. Summaries and review problem sections have been added at the ends of eight more chapters. A number of photos have been added, chosen to enliven the material and its applications for students. All of the revisions were made to realize a more interesting, readable, and exciting text. I am indebted to the reviewers of this edition for their suggestions, and I thank them for their comments.

Written for sophomore–junior students in engineering, the physical or biological sciences, and mathematics, this book contains a complete, clear, and flexible coverage of differential equations. The only **prerequisites** are elementary calculus and some basic knowledge of complex numbers and matrix notation. Students who study Chapter 8, on numerical methods, will also need a basic knowledge of a programming language such as Pascal, Fortran, or Basic, and access to a computer.

The text can be used for a one-semester, two-quarter, or full-year course on the introduction to differential equations. Chapters 1 through 7 have been used at Iowa State University in a four-semester-hour course for sophomore engineers and in a four-semester-hour honors course. Chapters 10 and 11 have been used in a "mathematics for engineers" course at the junior–senior level. Because of time pressure, the selection of topics for such courses must be done carefully. For **maximum flexibility,** the text is organized so that basic topics are in the earlier sections of each chapter; chapters are as independent of each other as possible; and most sections can be covered in a one-hour lecture. In keeping with this philosophy the chapter summaries and chapter review problems emphasize the basic topics in that chapter. On the other hand, the text has a **broad coverage** of standard introductory topics. It covers items that other texts treat incompletely or omit altogether. Your favorite introductory topic is probably included. There is ample material for a full-year course.

Detailed explanations of the theory in each section are supported by numerous worked-out examples. There are many routine drill problems for students to test their understanding of the theory, as well as challenging theoretical and applied problems which extend and complement the text material. There are also many traditional and nontraditional examples of **applications** to mechanical problems, chemical kinetics, economics, business, biology and ecology, control theory, electromagnetic theory, elasticity, acoustics, quantum mechanics, and more. Since I have taught differential equations for more than 25 years and published research papers in engineering journals with engineering co-authors for more than 15 years, these applications are sensible and well motivated. In applications the modeling process is emphasized and the underlying physical assumptions are always pointed out.

Features of this edition:

Chapter 2 introduces sign analysis and many exercises which emphasize error analysis in modeling situations. The Volterra–Lotka predator–prey model is used to introduce phase-plane analysis and the notion of periodic solutions.

Since experience indicates its usefulness, Chapter 3 includes a review of complex numbers. Both linear and *nonlinear* mechanics problems are discussed with realistic motivating examples. A summarizing table for the method of undetermined coefficients has been added to Chapter 3.

The annihilator method has been added to Chapter 4. This method is then used to justify the method of undetermined coefficients.

Surprisingly, some students now get through calculus without even seeing sequences and series. Many other students have time for only a little on this topic, and others who did study the subject do not seem to remember all of the basic facts about series. Hence, Chapter 5 starts with an extensive review of series.

Laplace transforms are treated in Chapter 6. In order for the student to grasp some of the depth and breadth of this topic I include a discussion of delta functions followed by a discussion of their approximation in mechanics labs using impulse hammers, a discussion of control theory, and a discussion of applications of Laplace transforms to integral equations. Transforms are then used to study an integral equation economic growth model.

My experience indicates that almost all students have been exposed to a little matrix theory but most do not have a working command of the topic. Chapter 7 is designed to provide that working command while studying systems of differential equations. That chapter contains an extensive review of basic matrix theory and determinants and then immediately illustrates that theory by applying it to systems of differential equations. About one-third of the chapter is material on matrices, determinants, and eigenvalues–eigenvectors.

Numerical methods are treated in Chapter 8. The chapter goals are to show students how numerical solutions are obtained, to make them aware of the various possible numerical errors, and to bring them to the point where they can effectively use a fourth-order Runge–Kutta program for systems of differential equations. I have added material which will illustrate the nature of round-off errors. The chapter on numerical methods is suitable for self-study and has been used for a one-semester-hour self-study course at Iowa State. The students must have access to a computer; a small personal computer will do.

Chapters 10 and 11 contain an introduction to Fourier series and separation of variables. These two topics can either be integrated or studied separately; each of these possibilities has advantages and disadvantages.

I have chosen to present Fourier series in a separate chapter. This allows a thorough development of Fourier series and their applications to filtering and control theory.

I am grateful to many students and colleagues for their suggestions and criticisms. Special thanks to Drs. R. Bishop, L. Dornhoff and H. Osborn of the University of Illinois, J. Gatica of the University of Iowa, T. Herdman at Virginia Tech, A. Acker of Wichita State University, M. Mousa at the Air Force Institute in Cairo, and B. Cain and J. Mathews at Iowa State University.

Iowa State University   Richard K. Miller

INTRODUCTION TO
DIFFERENTIAL EQUATIONS

CHAPTER ONE

*Introduction*_____

In this chapter we explore some typical and important problems whose solutions depend crucially on questions involving differential equations. We introduce the basic ideas of differential equations and their solutions.

It was a lovely April Sunday evening in Colombia, South America, until the lights went out. Chaos reigns in a modern city when the lights go out! Television went dead, stoves cooled, and the city traffic snarled. Drivers were graphically reminded that traffic lights are powered by electricity. Panicky elevator passengers got an even more graphic reminder of our modern dependence on electric power. On this April Sunday in 1985 over 80% of Colombia's power supplies were knocked out, leaving over 20 million people, most of the southern two thirds of the country, literally in the dark.

The troublemakers were two large oil-filled transformers which exploded and caught fire. The trouble was quickly isolated when protective equipment automatically cut the two transformers out of the power system. What should have been a small problem became a large problem when the flames ionized the air around the transformers causing arcing on nearby high voltage equipment. The resulting power imbalance caused automatic protective devices to trip. Transmission lines and generating equipment began to go out of service like falling dominos. In the space of 90 seconds 83% of Colombia's power was knocked out!

Large power outages can occur anywhere. On a hot July 23, 1987, at 1:19 p.m., 2.8 million people in Tokyo lost their electric power. Many readers may remember the 1977 New York City blackout. The most spectacular power interruption in North America was the 1965 failure which plunged the entire northeastern section of the United States and a significant portion of eastern

Canada into a blackout. This power failure led to a major reassessment of the North American power system and a major program of research on power system reliability. Much progress has been made toward assuring reliability. However, power systems are so complex that complete understanding is probably impossible. Moreover, new technology makes constant reassessment necessary.

The problem is to efficiently match energy input from generating stations with the customer's energy use. This must be done in such a way that the whole network remains synchronized at approximately 60 cycles per second and in such a way that customers' voltage levels stay within acceptable bounds. Major disturbances occur when an important piece of equipment fails. For example, one may lose a generator (i.e., have to take a generator out of service), or a lightning strike might cause a transmission-line fault. A system is considered reliable (or stable) when such disturbances do not result in loss of synchronism. The interconnection of the power system of the United States has increased efficiency and increased the ability of the power system to survive most disturbances. However, it has also increased our vulnerability to occasional catastrophic failures such as the 1965 blackout. In other words, the system does not fail as much as it used to, but when it does, the failure can be a spectacular one. As an example of a potential problem, consider southern Florida. Southern Florida is quite populous. The area imports much of its power from northern Florida and from Georgia. The interconnections to the north are relatively weak. If a large generator were lost, most of the lost power would have to be imported. If a given transmission line could not carry the necessary power, automatic switching equipment will take this transmission line out of service to avoid overloading. This could cause overloading on a second transmission line, and so on. The end result would be *electrical islanding*—that is, separation of southern Florida from the national power network. If islanding occurs while a large amount of power is being imported, the local power system must shed part of its load or else shut down completely. Load shedding must be done rapidly but carefully or the shedding itself will cause instability. Electrical islanding occurs occasionally but so far has not resulted in any large-scale blackouts.

Realistic models of electrical power networks are incredibly complex. The system is divided into three types of components: generators, transmission lines, and loads (see Figure 1.1. and Photo 1). The point where two or more components are connected is termed a *bus*. Knowing the number and characteristics of the components and knowing the location of the buses, the designer can write a system of differential equations that describe the network—the so-called **swing equations** (see Section 1.2). To get a feeling for the complexity of such systems, consider Iowa, a medium-sized state which is, by the standards of southern California or northern Illinois, neither populous nor heavily industrialized. The *Modified Iowa Test System* has 17 generators, 162 buses, and 284 transmission lines, as well as a large number of loads. Hookups to neighboring states are handled in this model by electrical equivalencing methods. (The effects of neighboring states' networks are reasonably well known. Hence the networks of neighboring states can be replaced by simple systems that have

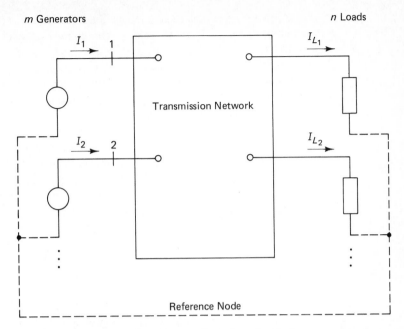

Figure 1.1. Schematic representation of an electrical power network.

Photo 1. High voltage power lines. (Courtesy of Commonwealth Edison Co.)

approximately the same effects.) This test system is sufficiently realistic to be used for planning and design purposes by the local power companies. IEEE, the Institute of Electrical and Electronic Engineers, has set up two relatively small systems for use when testing new methods of analyzing power networks. One of these, the New England Test System, has 10 generators, 39 buses, and 46 transmission lines. The second test system has 20 generators, 118 buses, and 171 transmission lines. The corresponding systems of equations are so large that even modern computers are of limited use when analyzing the systems.

The swing equations, those differential equations which describe a system, are used in the design of reliable, efficient power systems. They can also be used after the fact to determine how a failure occurred and how it might have been prevented. In the case of the 1985 Colombia blackout a transient stability analysis using these equations showed that the system would have remained stable if protective equipment on the transmission lines had been set to trip more quickly.

The design and operation of nuclear reactors (see Photo 2) and the related reactor safety studies provide many examples of the use of systems of differential equations. We shall consider only reactor safety studies, indeed only the one specific problem of reactor stability. The differential equations used to study stability problems are called *kinetic equations*. These equations describe the time behavior of the neutron population in the reactor core. The exact form of the equations varies with the method of construction and the geometry of the reactor. Various approximations are made depending on what question is

Photo 2. Nuclear power station. (Courtesy of Commonwealth Edison Co.)

to be studied. For example, different approximations are usually made for short-term stability problems, long-term stability problems, startup situations, shutdown situations, emergency-shutdown situations, operation at steady power, operation during a change in the power level, and so on. In many situations engineers have found that a model called the **point kinetics model** is adequate (see Section 1.2). The reactivity term and the source term in the point kinetics model can be picked to model a variety of special situations of the type listed above. In many simple situations solutions of the point kinetics equations are known or can be satisfactorily approximated. In other situations the behavior of solutions is only partially understood and is the subject of current research. A more complete analysis of the point kinetics model would be very helpful for the efficient design and operation of reactors.

Our third example of modern uses for differential equations comes from the aircraft industry. Airplanes have become a more and more important part of modern life. With the increased use of aircraft there has been a corresponding increased need to train new pilots and to retrain experienced pilots in the use of new types of aircraft. In response to the problem, engineers have developed flight simulators in which pilots can practice "flying" an aircraft while on the ground. A modern flight simulator has a complete, full-sized mock-up of the cockpit of the given aircraft, including seats, windows, instruments, displays, and controls. This cockpit is mounted on a platform that is powered by hydraulic cylinders (see Photos 3 and 4). The simulator is operated by one or more computers. The flight characteristics of the aircraft have been described by a complex system of differential equations. Typically, 15 or more equations are needed. The master computer is told the aircraft's initial conditions. Moreover, it can sense the pilot's operation of the controls of the aircraft. Given this information, the computer can solve the system of differential equations to determine what the aircraft will do under the given circumstances. The information generated by the computer is used to control the cockpit instruments and displays and to control the motion of the base through its hydraulics. For example, if the pilot puts the aircraft into a climb, the pilot can feel the nose come up and can read the rate of climb on the instrument panel.

Flight simulators have been extremely successful. Since a modern flight simulator will give its pilot an extremely realistic "flight," simulators are used extensively in pilot training programs. The use of simulators for a portion of pilot training has an obvious safety advantage. When simulators are used, there is a decreased need to tie up expensive aircraft in a training program and a corresponding decreased need for maintenance and for expendables such as fuel.

The use of differential equations is essential in the design and operation of a flight simulator. The dynamic characteristics of the aircraft must be accurately modeled by a system of differential equations. These differential equations must then be solved during the operation of the simulator. But just what are differential equations? What does it mean to model something using differential equations? What kind of data is needed to solve a differential equation? How does one solve a differential equation? It is the purpose of this book to answer these questions.

Photo 3. B-52 flight simulator cockpit. (Courtesy of The Singer Company, Link Flight Simulation Division.)

Photo 4. Instrument flight simulator. (Courtesy of The Singer Company, Link Flight Simulation Division.)

1.1 ORDINARY DIFFERENTIAL EQUATIONS

By a **differential equation,** we shall mean any equation involving a function and derivatives of this function. Differential equations are divided into two classes, ordinary and partial. **Ordinary differential equations** contain only functions of a single variable, called the **independent variable,** and derivatives with respect to that variable. **Partial differential equations** contain a function of two or more variables and some partial derivatives of this function. The **order** of a differential equation is the order of the highest derivative contained in the equation. Thus

$$\left(\frac{d^2y}{dx^2}\right)^3 + 4\frac{dy}{dx} + 5y\frac{dy}{dx} + 6y = 0$$

is an ordinary differential equation of order 2. Here y stands for the unknown function and x is the independent variable. Similarly,

$$\text{(1.1)} \qquad \left(\frac{dy}{dx}\right)^2 = (\sin xy + 2)^2$$

is an ordinary differential equation of order 1. Again y stands for the unknown function and x is the independent variable. On the other hand,

$$\frac{\partial^3 u}{\partial x^3} + \frac{\partial u}{\partial x}\frac{\partial^2 u}{\partial t^2} + xtu = 0$$

is a partial differential equation of order 3. Here u stands for an unknown function of x and t. Both t and x are independent variables.

ORDINARY DIFFERENTIAL EQUATION

An nth-order ordinary differential equation is an equation of the form

$$\text{(1.2)} \qquad F(x, y, y', y'', \dots, y^{(n)}) = 0,$$

where prime means derivative with respect to x, that is, $y' = dy/dx$, $y'' = d^2y/dx^2$, and so on.

We shall always assume that (1.2) can be solved for $y^{(n)}$, that is (1.2) can be rewritten in the form

$$\text{(1.3)} \qquad y^{(n)} = f(x, y, y', y'', \dots, y^{(n-1)}).$$

This form of the equation will avoid any possible ambiguities such as in (1.1), where one is really dealing with two different ordinary differential equations,

$$\text{(1.1a)} \qquad \frac{dy}{dx} = \sin xy + 2$$

and

(1.1b)
$$\frac{dy}{dx} = -\sin xy - 2.$$

SOLUTION

By a **solution** of (1.3) on an interval J, we mean a function $y = \varphi(x)$ such that $f(x, \varphi(x), \varphi'(x), \ldots, \varphi^{(n)}(x))$ is defined for all x in J and is equal to $\varphi^{(n)}(x)$ for all x in J.

For example, the first-order ordinary differential equation

(1.4)
$$\frac{dy}{dx} = 2y - 4x$$

has the solution $y = 2x + 1$ in the interval $J = \{x: -\infty < x < \infty\}$. This can be checked by computing $y' = 2$ and $2y - 4x = 2(1 + 2x) - 4x = 2 = y'$. In the same way one can check that

$$y = 1 + 2x + ce^{2x}, \qquad -\infty < x < \infty$$

is also a solution for any constant c.

In a similar manner one can check that the second-order equation

(1.5)
$$y'' + y = 0$$

has the solution $y = \cos x$. Indeed, for any constants c_1 and c_2 the expression $y = c_1 \cos x + c_2 \sin x$ defines a solution. A method for solving this equation will be developed in Chapter 3.

One often wishes to find a solution of a given differential equation that satisfies certain prescribed conditions, called *initial conditions*. For example, Newton's second law of motion implies that a particle of fixed mass M which is moving along a straight line under the influence of a force F will move in such a way that

(1.6)
$$M\frac{d^2x}{dt^2} = F.$$

Here $x(t)$ is the position of the particle at time t. The velocity of the mass at time t will be denoted by $v(t)$. Hence $v(t) = x'(t)$. We assume that the force F is a function of t, x, and v, that is,

(1.7)
$$F = f(t, x, v) = f\left(t, x, \frac{dx}{dt}\right).$$

Assumption (1.7) is a typical situation in such problems. Combining (1.6) and (1.7), we obtain a second-order differential equation for the unknown position x, namely

(1.8)
$$M\frac{d^2x}{dt^2} = f\left(t, x, \frac{dx}{dt}\right).$$

From physics we recall that the motion of the particle is completely determined from (1.8) if the initial position and the initial velocity of the particle are known, that is, if we know

(1.9) $$x(0) = a_0 \quad \text{and} \quad x'(0) = a_1.$$

Conditions (1.9) are the **initial conditions** needed to specify one and only one solution of (1.8). Of course, specifying a solution of (1.8) by using (1.9) is a far cry from actually finding the solution, but it does get us started.

Initial conditions can be specified for the general nth-order equation (1.3). For example, given a first-order differential equation

(1.10) $$y' = f(x, y),$$

an **initial condition** has the form $y(x_0) = a_0$. Equation (1.10) together with the given initial condition determine an **initial value problem,**

(I) $$y' = f(x, y), \qquad y(x_0) = a_0.$$

EXAMPLE 1.1

By giving initial conditions for (1.4) we mean picking numbers x_0 and a_0 and requiring that the solution y satisfy $y(x_0) = a_0$. For example, if we choose $x_0 = 0$ and $a_0 = 1$, the initial value problem is

(1.11) $$\frac{dy}{dx} = 2y - 4x, \qquad y(0) = 1.$$

The solution of (1.11) is $y = 1 + 2x$. This can be verified by checking that both equations in (1.11) are true. The student should do this. ■

For the initial value problem (I) the following basic result is true.

EXISTENCE AND UNIQUENESS THEOREM

Given the initial value problem (I), suppose that f is continuous and has a continuous partial derivative $\partial f / \partial y$ in some rectangle $b < x < c$, $B < y < C$ which contains the point (x_0, a_0). Then (I) has a unique solution $y = \varphi(x)$. This solution will be defined on some interval $a < x < A$ which contains x_0.

The hypotheses of this theorem on the function f are very mild and will usually be satisfied. Those students interested in a proof of this theorem are referred to more advanced books on differential equations (e.g., Simmons, 1972, Chap. 11) and to Problems 24 and 25 of Section 1.2.

A **general solution** of (1.10) is a useful intuitive idea. By a general solution of (1.10) we will mean a solution $y = \Phi(x, c)$, which contains an "arbitrary constant." Different values of c can be specified in order to satisfy different initial conditions. Similarly, a general solution of a second-order differential equation should contain two arbitrary constants which can be specified in order to determine particular solutions and so on for the *n*th order case (1.3). We will not try to be more precise than this just now.

EXAMPLE 1.2   Consider the initial value problem

(1.12) $y' = 2y - 4x, \qquad y(0) = 5.$

A general solution of this equation is $y = 1 + 2x + ce^{2x}$. The initial condition requires that we choose the constant c so that

$$y(0) = 1 + 2 \cdot 0 + ce^{2 \cdot 0} = 5.$$

This means that $1 + c = 5$ or $c = 4$. Hence the unique solution of (1.12) is

$$y = 1 + 2x + 4e^{2x}. \quad \blacksquare$$

A general solution is sometimes exhibited in **implicit form.** By this we mean that we are given an expression

(1.13) $\Phi(x, y, c) = 0,$

where it is understood that (1.13) determines y as a function of x and c in such a way that y solves the differential equation (1.10).

EXAMPLE 1.3   The expression $y^2 - x^2 - c = 0$ determines solutions of the equation $y' = x/y$ in implicit form. To see this we first notice that $y^2 = x^2 + c$ so that

$$y = \sqrt{x^2 + c} \qquad \text{or} \qquad y = -\sqrt{x^2 + c}.$$

Hence

$$\frac{dy}{dx} = \pm \frac{1}{2}(x^2 + c)^{-1/2}(2x) = \frac{x}{\pm\sqrt{x^2 + c}} = \frac{x}{y},$$

as required. $\blacksquare$

1.2   *FURTHER REMARKS*

In addition to the *n*th-order equation discussed in Section 1.1, **systems of differential equations** are important in applications. By a system of *n* equations we mean *n* simultaneous ordinary differential equations containing *n* unknown functions. For example,

(2.1) $\dfrac{du}{dx} = 3u + 4v, \qquad \dfrac{dv}{dx} = -u + 3v + 1$

is a system of two differential equations for the two unknown functions *u* and *v*. The independent variable is *x*. Systems of differential equations can be very complicated when they are meant to describe complicated situations.

The **point kinetics model,** used to describe the behavior of a nuclear reactor, is an important example of a system of equations. To understand the model, a little physics is needed. When fuel atoms split, neutrons and reaction products are produced. Neutrons produced in this way are called *prompt neutrons* since they appear within 10^{-8} second. Certain of the reaction products will decay further and will eventually produce more neutrons. Reaction products that produce further neutrons are called *neutron precursors.* Neutrons produced in this way are called *delayed neutrons.* The delay may be as long as several seconds. The variables used in the usual point kinetics model are the time t, the reactor power $P(t)$, and the effective concentration of delayed neutron precursors $C_i(t)$. There are six delayed neutron precursors. Hence we need $C_i(t)$ for $i = 1, 2, 3, 4, 5, 6$. For a reactor with a single core the point kinetics equations are

$$\frac{dP}{dt} = \frac{\rho(t) - \beta}{l} P(t) + \sum_{i=1}^{6} \lambda_i C_i(t) + S(t),$$

$$\frac{dC_1}{dt} = \frac{\beta_1}{l} P(t) - \lambda_1 C_1(t),$$

(2.2)
$$\frac{dC_2}{dt} = \frac{\beta_2}{l} P(t) - \lambda_2 C_2(t),$$

$$\vdots$$

$$\frac{dC_6}{dt} = \frac{\beta_6}{l} P(t) - \lambda_6 C_6(t).$$

The terms λ_i, β_i, and l are physical constants that can be determined while $\beta = \beta_1 + \beta_2 + \ldots + \beta_6$. The term $\rho(t)$ is the *reactivity.* The term $S(t)$ represents a neutron source external to the reactor. The form of the two terms $\rho(t)$ and $S(t)$ must be varied in order to represent different operating situations.

The **swing equations** are used by engineers to model electrical power networks. If a network contains two generators, the classical form of the swing equations is

(2.3)
$$M_1 \delta_1'' + D_1 \delta_1' = P_1 - g_1 - c_{11} \sin (\delta_1 - \delta_2) - c_{12} \cos (\delta_1 - \delta_2)$$
$$M_2 \delta_2'' + D_2 \delta_2' = P_2 - g_2 - c_{21} \sin (\delta_2 - \delta_1) - c_{22} \cos (\delta_2 - \delta_1).$$

Here δ_1 and δ_2 are the rotor angles of the two generators, P_1 and P_2 are the mechanical power inputs to the generators, M_i and D_i are constants that depend on the given generator, and the terms g_i and c_{ij} are constants that depend on the transmission network and the loadings.

PROBLEMS

In Problems 1–8, classify the equation as an ordinary or partial differential equation. Determine the order.

1. $\dfrac{d^3 y}{dx^3} + 4 \left(\dfrac{dy}{dx} \right)^2 = y.$ **2.** $y' + 2y = \sin x.$

3. $\dfrac{d^2u}{dt^2} + 2t^2\dfrac{du}{dt} + 3t^3u = 0.$

4. $\dfrac{\partial u}{\partial t} + \sqrt{1+u^2}\,\dfrac{\partial u}{\partial x} = 0.$

5. $\sqrt{u} + 3\dfrac{du}{ds} = \dfrac{d^3u}{ds^3}.$

6. $\dfrac{\partial^4 u}{\partial t^4} + 4\dfrac{\partial^2 u}{\partial t\,\partial x} = \dfrac{\partial^5 u}{\partial x^5}.$

7. $\dfrac{\partial z}{\partial t} = \dfrac{\partial^2 z}{\partial x^2} + \dfrac{\partial^2 z}{\partial y^2}.$

8. $(y')^2 + 2xy' + x^2 = 0.$

In Problems 9–13, verify that the expressions given are solutions of the equation.

9. $y' + ky = 0,\ y = ce^{-kx}.$

10. $y'' - 5y' + 6y = 0,\ y_1 = e^{3x},\ y_2 = e^{2x},\ y = c_1y_1 + c_2y_2.$

11. $y'' - 4y = 0,\ y_1 = \cosh 2x,\ y_2 = \sinh 2x,\ y = c_1y_1 + c_2y_2.$

12. $2t^2\dfrac{d^2u}{dt^2} + 3t\dfrac{du}{dt} - u = 0,\ u_1 = \sqrt{t},\ u_2 = \dfrac{1}{t},\ u = c_1u_1 + c_2u_2$ for all $t > 0.$

13. $y' = e^{x-y},\ e^y = e^x + c$ (solution given implicitly).

In Problems 14–18, solve the initial value problem. Use the general solutions given in Problems 9–13.

14. $y' = 3y,\ y(0) = 1.$ **15.** $y' + 3y = 0,\ y(0) = 2.$

16. $y'' - 4y = 0,\ y(0) = 2,\ y'(0) = -1.$ **17.** $y'' - 5y' + 6y = 0,\ y(0) = 0,\ y'(0) = 1.$

18. $z' = e^{x-z},\ z(0) = 3.$

19. Verify that $(y')^3 - y = 0,\ y(0) = 0$ has the two solutions $y \equiv 0$ and $y = (\tfrac{2}{3}x)^{3/2}.$ Why does this not violate the statement of the existence and uniqueness theorem?

20. Suppose that $\Phi(x, y, c) = 0$ determines a general solution of $y' = f(x, y)$ in implicit form. Show that

$$\frac{\partial \Phi}{\partial x}(x, y, c) + \frac{\partial \Phi}{\partial y}(x, y, c)f(x, y) = 0.$$

21. From the three equations

$$\frac{dI}{dx} = 2IS - I, \qquad \frac{dR}{dx} = -3R + I, \qquad S + I + R = 1,$$

determine a system of two differential equations that I and R satisfy.

22. Let $f(y)$ be a continuously differentiable function defined for $-\infty < y < \infty.$ Let $\varphi(x)$ be the unique solution of

$$y' = f(y), \qquad y(0) = a.$$

Define $\psi(x) = \varphi(x - x_0).$ Show that $y = \psi(x)$ is the unique solution of

$$y' = f(y), \qquad y(x_0) = a_0.$$

23. Consider the delay-differential equation

$$y'(x) = y\left(x - \frac{\pi}{2}\right).$$

(a) Solve the equation on $0 < x \leq \pi/2$ given that $y(x) = \sin x$ on $-\pi/2 \leq x \leq 0$.

(b) Verify that $y(x) \equiv 0$ is a solution on $-\infty < x < \infty$.

(c) Does the problem $y'(x) = y(x - \pi/2)$, $y(0) = 0$ have a unique solution?

24. Many students are familiar with *simple iteration* and its use in solving the equation $x = g(x)$. Assume that g is a function defined on an interval $J = [a, b]$ with range in this same interval. Assume that $|g'(x)| < 1$ all x in J. Given any point x_0 in J, we define $x_1 = g(x_0)$, $x_2 = g(x_1)$, etc. Thus

$$x_{n+1} = g(x_n) \qquad \text{for } n = 0, 1, 2, \ldots.$$

It can be shown that there is one and only one solution $\bar{x}$ of the equation $x = g(x)$ on the interval J. Moreover,

$$\lim_{n \to \infty} x_n = \bar{x}.$$

(a) Using simple iteration, show that the equation $x = \frac{1}{2}\sin x$ has a solution on the interval $-\pi < x < \pi$. Given $x_0 = \pi/2$, compute x_n for $n = 1, 2, 3, 4, 5$. (Use a calculator.) Can you guess the value $\bar{x}$ of the solution?

(b) Show that simple iteration can be used to solve $x = 2 \sin x$ in the interval $\pi/2 < x < 2\pi/3$. Compute x_n for $n = 1, 2, 3, 4, 5$ given that $x_0 = 1.85$. *Hint:* Pick $J \subset (\pi/2, 2\pi/3)$.

25. In this problem we discuss how simple iteration (see Problem 24) can be used to solve the initial value problem

(I) $$y' = f(x, y), \qquad y(x_0) = a_0$$

when f and $\partial f/\partial y$ are continuous in a rectangle

$$D = \{(x, y) : |x - x_0| \leq A, |y - a_0| \leq B\}.$$

(a) Show that $y = \varphi(x)$ solves (I) on $x_0 - A \leq x \leq x_0 + A$ if and only if $\varphi(x)$ solves the integral equation

(I$_1$) $$\varphi(x) = a_0 + \int_{x_0}^{x} f(s, \varphi(s))\, ds, \qquad |x - x_0| \leq A.$$

Hint: Integrate (I).

(b) *Picard iteration* for (I$_1$) is the iteration that produces the sequence of functions

$$\varphi_0(x) = a_0,$$

$$\varphi_1(x) = a_0 + \int_{x_0}^{x} f(s, \varphi_0(s))\, ds,$$

$$\varphi_2(x) = a_0 + \int_{x_0}^{x} f(s, \varphi_1(s))\, ds,$$

$$\vdots$$

$$\varphi_{n+1}(x) = a_0 + \int_{x_0}^{x} f(s, \varphi_n(s))\, ds$$

$$\vdots$$

for $|x - x_0| \leq A$. The functions $\varphi_n(x)$ are called the *Picard iterates*. Assume that $|f(x, y)| \leq M$ on D and that $MA < B$. Use mathematical induction to show that the Picard iterates are all defined and continuous on $|x - x_0| \leq A$ and that $|\varphi_n(x) - a_0| \leq B$ for all n and all x in $x_0 - A \leq x \leq x_0 + A$.

(c) In addition to the assumptions in part (b), suppose that

$$\left| \frac{\partial f}{\partial y}(x, y) \right| \leq L$$

for all (x, y) in D. Show that

$$|\varphi_{n+1}(x) - \varphi_n(x)| \leq \left| L \int_{x_0}^{x} |\varphi_n(s) - \varphi_{n-1}(s)| \, ds \right|$$

and that

$$\max_{|x - x_0| \leq A} |\varphi_{n+1}(x) - \varphi_n(x)| \leq LA \left(\max_{|x - x_0| \leq A} |\varphi_n(x) - \varphi_{n-1}(x)| \right)$$

(d) If A is so small that $LA < 1$, it can be shown that the sequence $\varphi_n(x)$ converges to the solution $\varphi(x)$ of (I). Show that there is only one solution of (I_1) on the interval $|x - x_0| \leq A$.

CHAPTER REVIEW

In this chapter some basic ideas and terminology were introduced. The **order** of a differential equation is the order of the highest derivative contained in the equation. A **solution** is a function which satisfies the equation. A **general solution** of an nth-order equation will contain n arbitrary constants. A solution can be specified **explicitly** by a formula or **implicitly** by means of a relation that determines a solution.

Initial conditions are used to specify one and only one solution. The differential equation together with its initial conditions determine an **initial value problem**. **Systems of differential equations** are sets of n differential equations in n unknowns.

HISTORICAL SNAPSHOT

People have long been fascinated by the flight of projectiles, the course of falling bodies, and the movements of the planets and stars. Significant progress on understanding the motion of such objects had to wait on the invention of calculus with its notion of derivatives. The tool for the study of such motions is the subject of differential equations. Sir Isaac Newton (1642–1727) observed that certain important laws of natural science can be phrased in terms of equations involving rates of change (i.e., derivatives). The most famous example of such a natural law is Newton's second law of motion.

Newton's inventions and discoveries began in 1665 when he was 23. By the 1690's such distinguished scientists as Isaac Newton, Gottfried Leibniz (1646–1716), Jacque Bernoulli (1654–1705), Jean Bernoulli (1667–1748), and Christian Huygens (1629–1695) were solving differential equations. Many of the methods which they developed are still in use today. In the eighteenth century such scientific giants as Leonhard Euler (1707–1783), Daniel Bernoulli (1700–1782), and Joseph Lagrange (1736–1813) contributed to the development of the subject. The pace of progress quickened as theoretical and applied science became more

Photo 5. Lift off. (Courtesy of the National Aeronautics and Space Administration.)

important. The pioneering work that led to the development of ordinary differential equations as a branch of modern mathematics is due to A. L. Cauchy (1789–1857), Carl Jacobi (1804–1851), Georg Riemann (1826–1866), William Hamilton (1805–1865), Charles Hermite (1822–1901), Henri Poincaré (1854–1912), Emile Picard (1856–1941), A. M. Lyapunov (1857–1918), George Birkhoff (1884–1944), and others. The demands of modern engineering and the advent of computing machines have stimulated continued progress up to the present day.

Most people are aware that Wolfgang Mozart began his famous musical career while still a child. Many also know that Johann Sebastian Bach was a musical giant and had a family so talented that several dozen Bachs were eminent musicians during the sixteenth through the nineteenth centuries. The history of differential equations includes a similar cast of colorful characters. For example, Jean Baptiste Fourier was the precocious son of a French tailor. He was orphaned at 8, ghost writing sermons at 12, and teaching mathematics at 16. The Bernoullis, a Swiss family, are the most remarkable dynasty in mathematics. The family produced eight prominent mathematicians—three of whom were outstanding. These were Jakob, Jean and Daniel, all mentioned above. In his day, Daniel was as famous as Isaac Newton. The family later went into other scientific fields.

CHAPTER TWO

First-Order Equations

We now turn to the study of first-order ordinary differential equations of the form

(E) $$y' = f(x, y),$$

where f and $\partial f/\partial y$ are defined and continuous for all (x, y) in a rectangle $D = \{(x, y): A_1 < x < A_2 \text{ and } B_1 < y < B_2\}$.

We shall sometimes find a general solution of (E) and we shall sometimes seek to solve (E) subject to an initial condition

(0.1) $$y(x_0) = a_0,$$

where (x_0, a_0) is some specified point of the rectangle D. The **existence and uniqueness theorem** states that the initial value problem consisting of (E) and (0.1) has one and only one solution. A general solution of (E) will have one arbitrary constant. This constant can be specified by one initial condition of the form (0.1).

2.1 SEPARATION OF VARIABLES

The following type of differential equations will be solved in this section.

SEPARABLE DIFFERENTIAL EQUATIONS

Certain first-order differential equations can be rearranged to obtain an equation of the form

(1.1) $$p(x) + q(y)\frac{dy}{dx} = 0.$$

Here $p(x)$ is a function of x only and $q(y)$ is a function of y only. When (E) can be written in the form (1.1) we say that it **separates** or that the equation is **separable.**

For example, the equation

$$\frac{dy}{dx} = \frac{\sin x}{2y + 6}$$

can be written as

$$-\sin x + (2y + 6)\frac{dy}{dx} = 0.$$

This equation is separable. The equation

$$\frac{dy}{dx} = x^2 + x^2 y^2 = x^2(1 + y^2),$$

is separable; indeed, we can write it in the form

$$-x^2 + (1 + y^2)^{-1}\frac{dy}{dx} = 0.$$

Similarly, the equation

$$\frac{dR}{dt} = 3R$$

is separable since it can be written in the form

$$-3 + R^{-1}\frac{dR}{dt} = 0.$$

Let $y = \varphi(x)$ be the solution of (1.1) satisfying the initial condition $y(x_0) = a_0$. Then (1.1) can be written in the form

$$p(x) + q(\varphi(x))\frac{d\varphi(x)}{dx} = 0$$

or

$$p(x) = -q(\varphi(x))\frac{d\varphi(x)}{dx}.$$

Integrating both sides of this equation, we obtain

$$\int_{x_0}^{x} p(s)\,ds = -\int_{x_0}^{x} q(\varphi(s))\varphi'(s)\,ds.$$

Since $\varphi'(x_0) = -p(x_0)/q(\varphi(x_0)) = -p(x_0)/q(a_0)$, if $p(x_0)$ and $q(a_0)$ are both non-zero, then $\varphi'(x_0) \neq 0$. Thus $\varphi(x)$ is either a monotone increasing function of x [if $\varphi'(x_0) > 0$] or a monotone decreasing function of x [if $\varphi'(x) < 0$]. In either case we can use the change of variables $u = \varphi(x)$ in the right hand integral to see that

(1.2) $$\int_{x_0}^{x} p(s)\,ds = -\int_{\varphi(x_0)}^{\varphi(x)} q(u)\,du = -\int_{a_0}^{y} q(u)\,du.$$

Let $P(x)$ and $Q(y)$ be indefinite integrals of $p(x)$ and $q(y)$. Then (1.2) can be written in the form

(1.3) $$P(x) = -Q(y) + c$$

for some constant c.

SOLUTION METHOD FOR SEPARABLE EQUATIONS

Our discussion shows that the separable equation (1.1) can be solved as follows. *Separate the variables* in (1.1) to obtain

$$p(x)\,dx = -q(y)\,dy.$$

Integrate the left-hand side with respect to x and the right-hand side with respect to y. The result (1.3) determines y implicitly as a function of x.

EXAMPLE 1.1   Find a general solution of

$$\frac{dy}{dx} = \frac{2 + \sin x}{3(y-1)^2}.$$

Also, find the solution that satisfies the initial condition $y(0) = 2$.

The differential equation separates. It can be written as

$$3(y-1)^2\,dy = (2 + \sin x)\,dx.$$

Integration of the right-hand side with respect to y and the left-hand side with respect to x gives

(1.4) $$(y-1)^3 = 2x - \cos x + c.$$

We now solve (1.4) for y. A general solution is

$$y = 1 + (2x - \cos x + c)^{1/3}.$$

The initial condition $y = 2$ when $x = 0$ can be used to see that $2 = 1 + (0 - 1 + c)^{1/3}$ or $c = 2$. Hence the solution that satisfies the given initial condition is

$$y = 1 + (2x - \cos x + 2)^{1/3}. \quad \blacksquare$$

Most students find this method of solution relatively easy to understand and to apply. In spite of this, some students have trouble doing separation of variables problems because they are "rusty" with integrals. A quick review of methods of integration from calculus will help solve this problem.

EXAMPLE 1.2   Find the solution of

(1.5)
$$y' = \frac{x^3 y - y}{y^4 - y^2 + 1}, \qquad y(0) = 1.$$

The equation separates. Since $y' = dy/dx$, it can be rewritten as

(1.6)
$$\left(y^3 - y + \frac{1}{y} \right) dy = (x^3 - 1)\, dx.$$

We integrate each side of (1.6) to obtain

(1.7)
$$\frac{y^4}{4} - \frac{y^2}{2} + \log|y| = \frac{x^4}{4} - x + c.$$

It is not possible to explicitly solve for y in terms of the independent variable x and the constant c. However, this expression does implicitly determine a general solution. We use the initial condition $y = 1$ when $x = 0$ in (1.7) to see that

$$\tfrac{1}{4} - \tfrac{1}{2} + 0 = 0 - 0 + c,$$

or $c = -\tfrac{1}{4}$. Thus the solution of (1.5) is the function $y = \varphi(x)$ which satisfies the equation

$$y^4 - 2y^2 + 4 \log|y| = x^4 - 4x - 1,$$

and the condition $\varphi(0) = 1$. $\quad \blacksquare$

As the next example shows, variable names other than x and y can be used. The method of solution is the same.

EXAMPLE 1.3   Solve

$$\frac{dR}{dt} = 2R, \qquad R(0) = -1.$$

On separating variables we obtain $dR/R = 2\,dt$. Hence $\log|R| = 2t + c$,

$$|R| = e^{2t+c} = e^c e^{2t},$$

and

$$R = (\pm e^c)e^{2t}.$$

The expression $\pm e^c$ can be replaced by a new arbitrary constant c_1. From $R = c_1 e^{2t}$ and the initial condition $R(0) = -1$ we see that $c_1 = -1$. ∎

From the calculations in Example 1.3, it is clear that $R = c_1 e^{2t}$ is a candidate for a general solution of

(1.8)
$$\frac{dR}{dt} = 2R.$$

Since $c_1 = \pm e^c$, our method of solution leads to the curious restriction that c_1 can be any positive or any negative number but c_1 is not zero. This restriction is easily removed. When $c_1 = 0$, then $R = c_1 e^{2t} = 0 \cdot e^{2t} \equiv 0$. Moreover, R identically zero is easily seen to be the solution of the initial value problem

$$\frac{dR}{dt} = 2R, \qquad R(0) = 0.$$

$R(t) \equiv 0$ is a **constant solution** or **stationary solution.** Another way to say the same thing is that $R(t) \equiv 0$ is an **equilibrium point** of the differential equation (1.8). The method of separation of variables will normally not find equilibrium points of a differential equation. However, equilibrium points are easily found by a separate analysis once one has been warned to look for them.

EXAMPLE 1.4   Find a general solution of $y' = ky$ when k is a nonzero real constant.
The calculation is almost the same as in Example 1.3. The equation separates to obtain $y^{-1}\,dy = k\,dx$. Hence

$$\log|y| = kx + c, \qquad |y| = e^{kx}e^c,$$

and

(1.9)
$$y = c_1 e^{kx}.$$

Here $c_1 = \pm e^c$. Since $y = 0$ is a constant solution, then $c_1 = 0$ is also permissible. Hence (1.9) is a general solution. ∎

When we derived the method of separation of variables we found that it was necessary to assume that

$$p(x_0) \neq 0 \quad \text{and} \quad q(a_0) \neq 0.$$

It is easy to see why the assumption $q(a_0) \neq 0$ is needed. We recall that in order to apply the existence and uniqueness theorem it is first necessary to rewrite (1.1) in the form

$$\frac{dy}{dx} = -\frac{p(x)}{q(y)}.$$

If $q(a_0) = 0$, the function $f(x, y) = -p(x)/q(y)$ is not even defined when $y = a_0$. Hence we have no particular reason to believe that there will be a solution. The condition that $p(x_0) \neq 0$ is not essential. A discussion of this restriction (and how to remove this restriction) is given in the problem section.

PROBLEMS   In Problems 1–10, find a general solution.

1. $\dfrac{dy}{dx} = \dfrac{x}{y^2}.$ **2.** $\dfrac{dy}{dx} = \dfrac{e^x}{y}.$

3. $y' + e^x y = e^x y^2.$ **4.** $\sin y \dfrac{dy}{dx} = \cos x.$

5. $\dfrac{dy}{dx} = \dfrac{1 + y^2}{\sqrt{1 + x^2}}.$ **6.** $y' = xy^2 - x.$

7. $\dfrac{du}{dt} = \dfrac{1 + u}{1 + t}.$ **8.** $\dfrac{dN}{dt} = 1 + N^2 + t + tN^2.$

9. $y' = (1 - y^2)^{1/2}(1 - x^2)^{1/2}.$ **10.** $\sin x \cos^2 y = y' \cos^2 x.$

In Problems 11–16, solve the initial value Problem.

11. $\dfrac{dy}{dx} + 3y = 6,\ y(0) = 1.$ **12.** $y' = \dfrac{2x^3}{y(1 + x^4)},\ y(0) = -1.$

13. $x^2\, dy = (x^3 - x^2 + x - 1)(y^2 - 3y + 2)\, dx,\ y(1) = 4.$

14. $y' = \dfrac{\sinh x}{\cosh y},\ y(1) = 0.$ **15.** $x\, dy + y^2\, dx = 0,\ y(1) = 0.5.$

16. $\cos x \dfrac{dy}{dx} = y \tan x,\ y\!\left(\dfrac{\pi}{3}\right) = 2.$

17. Solve the problem $x^2 y' = y,\ y(1) = 1$. What is the largest interval where the solution makes sense? Do the same for $x^2 y' = y,\ y(-1) = 1$. Could you have guessed, from looking at the equation, that there might be problems at $x = 0$?

18. (a) Solve $y' = y^2,\ y(x_0) = q_0$ when $q_0 > 0$. Graph the solution. What is the largest interval containing x_0 in which the solution makes sense?

   (b) Repeat the problem when $q_0 < 0$.

   (c) Repeat the problem when $q_0 = 0$.

   The existence and uniqueness theorem states that a solution of (E) and (0.1) exists but does not say anything about the size of the interval where it will be defined. Is it possible to estimate the size of this interval for a general function $f(x, y)$? Explain your reasoning.

19. Solve the problem $y' = y^{1/3},\ y(0) = 0$ by separating variables. Verify that your answer is a solution by substituting it into the equation. Verify that $y \equiv 0$ is also a solution of the problem. Why will separation of variables never find the second solution?

20. Solve $y' = y$, $y(0) = q_0$. Show that the solution has the following limiting behavior:

$$\lim_{x \to +\infty} y(x) = +\infty, \text{ if } q_0 > 0;$$

$$\lim_{x \to \infty} y(x) = -\infty, \text{ if } q_0 < 0; \quad \text{and}$$

$$\lim_{x \to -\infty} y(x) = 0, \text{ for any value of } q_0.$$

21. Solve the initial value problem $y' = y - y^2$, $y(0) = q_0$ when $0 < q_0 < 1$. Show that the solution $y = \varphi(x)$ of this problem has the following limiting behavior:

$$\lim_{x \to \infty} \varphi(x) = 1, \qquad \lim_{x \to -\infty} \varphi(x) = 0.$$

Compute limit $\varphi(x)$ as $x \to \infty$ when $q_0 > 1$. Can you find a solution when $q_0 = 1$? When $q_0 = 0$?

22. Suppose that $r(y)$ is continuously differentiable over the interval $B_1 < y < B_2$ and that $s(x)$ is a positive continuous function over $A_1 < x < A_2$. Given x_0 in (A_1, A_2) and a_0 in (B_1, B_2), consider the initial value problem

$$\frac{dy}{dx} = s(x)r(y), \qquad y(x_0) = a_0.$$

(a) Show that this equation has a solution.

(b) Show that a_0 is an equilibrium point of the differential equation if and only if $r(a_0) = 0$.

23. In Problem 22, let $y = \varphi(x)$ solve the initial value problem on the interval $A_1 < x < A_2$. Prove each of the following statements.

(a) If $r(a_0) = 0$, then $\varphi'(x) = 0$ for all x in (A_1, A_2).

(b) If $r(a_0) > 0$, then $\varphi'(x) > 0$ for all x in (A_1, A_2).

(c) If $r(a_0) < 0$, then $\varphi'(x) < 0$ for all x in (A_1, A_2).

24. Suppose that $p(x)$ is continuous on $A_1 < x < A_2$ and $q(y)$ is continuously differentiable on $B_1 < y < B_2$. Suppose that $q(a_0) \neq 0$ but $p(x_0) = 0$. Let $\varphi(x)$ be the solution of

$$p(x) + q(y)\frac{dy}{dx} = 0, \qquad y(x_0) = a_0$$

on the interval $A_1 < x < A_2$. Suppose that $P'(x) = p(x)$ and $Q'(y) = q(y)$. Prove each of the following statements.

(a) If $p(x)$ is never zero on (x_0, A_2), then $P(x) + Q(y) \equiv C$ is constant over (x_0, A_2).

(b) If $p(x)$ is never zero on (A_1, x_0), then $P(x) + Q(y) \equiv C$ is constant over (A_1, x_0).

(c) If $p(x) = 0$ for all x in the interval (A_1, x_0) or the interval (x_0, A_2), then $P(x) + Q(y) \equiv C$ is constant on the same interval.

25. In Problem 24, suppose that $p(x)$ has at most a finite number of zeros over an interval J. Prove that $P(x) + Q(\varphi(x)) \equiv C$ is constant over J.

2.2 SEPARATION OF VARIABLES: SOME APPLICATIONS

All theory depends on assumptions which are not quite true—that is what makes it theory. The art of successful theorizing is to make the inevitable simplifying assumptions in such a way that the final results are not very sensitive. A "crucial" assumption is one on which the conclusions do depend sensitively, and it is important that crucial assumptions be reasonably realistic. When the results of a theory seem to flow specifically from a special crucial assumption, then if the assumption is dubious, the results are suspect.[1]

This is the opinion of the distinguished economist R. M. Solow. Solow was referring to economic theory; however, his warning applies equally well to any other science. Fortunately, it is not usually too difficult to see what assumptions are crucial in the physical sciences and to decide whether or not these assumptions are reasonably realistic. A good portion of a typical engineer's four years of training is directed to this activity. The scientific community has much less experience in mathematizing the social and the biological sciences. Hence the mathematical theorizing of these sciences must be approached with more care.

The differential equation

$$(2.1) \qquad \frac{dy}{dx} = ky$$

is one of the most important equations encountered in several centuries of experience with differential equations. It will usually be assumed that k is positive. Rather than allowing k to be negative, we shall usually write

$$(2.2) \qquad \frac{dy}{dx} = -ky,$$

where k is assumed to be positive. The method of separation of variables can be applied to (2.1). The result, as was seen in Section 2.1, is a general solution of the form

$$y = ce^{kx}, \qquad -\infty < x < \infty.$$

Different values of c result in different curves in the (x, y) plane. Several such curves are graphed in Figure 2.1. We see that when c is positive the solution curve is monotone increasing (i.e., growing) and tends to positive infinity as x tends to infinity. When c is negative the solution curve has the same general shape except that it is directed downward, that is, it is monotone decreasing. The value $c = 0$ picks out the constant solution $y \equiv 0$. The general

---

[1] R. M. Solow, *Q. J. Econ.*, Vol. 70 (1956), p. 65. Reprinted by permission of the publisher.

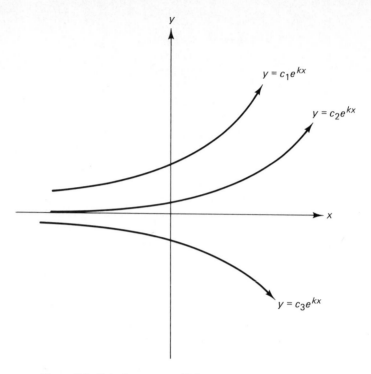

Figure 2.1. Solutions $y = c_i e^{kx}$ for $c_1 > c_2 > 0$ and $c_3 < 0$.

behavior of these solutions can be predicted without solving (2.1). Indeed, for the equation

$$y' = f(x, y),$$

a solution $y = \varphi(x)$ will be increasing when its derivative is positive and decreasing when its derivative is negative. In other words, $y = \varphi(x)$ is increasing when $f(x, y) = f(x, \varphi(x)) > 0$ and decreasing when $f(x, y) < 0$. A constant solution $y \equiv y_0$ occurs if and only if $f(x, y_0) = 0$ for all x. This type of **sign analysis** can be applied to (2.1). For (2.1) we have $f(x, y) = ky$ and $k > 0$. Hence solutions will be increasing when $y > 0$ and decreasing when $y < 0$. The only constant solution is $y \equiv 0$ (see Figure 2.2).

Now consider (2.2) with k assumed to be positive. A general solution, obtained by separation of variables, is

$$y = ce^{-kx}, \qquad -\infty < x < \infty.$$

$ky < 0$	0	$ky > 0$
Region of Decreasing Solutions		Region of Increasing Solutions

Figure 2.2. Sign analysis of $f(x, y) = ky$.

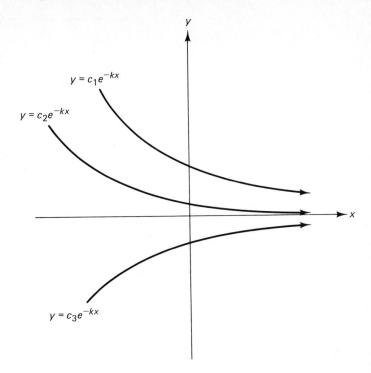

Figure 2.3. Solutions $y = c_i e^{-kx}$ for $c_1 > c_2 > 0$ and $c_3 < 0$.

Again different values of c result in different curves in the (x, y) plane. Several such curves are depicted in Figure 2.3. The curves in Figure 2.3 can be obtained from those in Figure 2.1 by reflection about the y-axis. For $c > 0$ the solutions are decreasing (or decaying) toward zero. For $c < 0$ the solutions are increasing toward zero. Moreover, when $c = 0$ we obtain the constant solution $y \equiv 0$. A sign analysis of $f(x, y) = -ky$ is given in Figure 2.4. Since $-ky < 0$ when $y > 0$, then solutions are decreasing when $y > 0$. Since $-ky > 0$ when $y < 0$, then solutions are increasing when $y < 0$. Moreover, since $-ky = 0$ if and only if $y = 0$, then $y \equiv 0$ is the only constant solution. The information obtained from this sign analysis agrees with the information obtained from the actual solution $y = ce^{-kx}$.

Figure 2.4. Sign analysis of $f(x, y) = -ky$.

SIGN ANALYSIS

The foregoing discussion will be particularly useful when applied to first-order differential equations of the form

(A)
$$\frac{dy}{dx} = F(y),$$

where F is a continuously differential function of y only. The procedure goes as follows:

1. Find all solutions of the equation $F(y) = 0$, and graph these on the number line. These points are the constant solutions of the differential equation (A).
2. The constant solutions found in (1) divide the number line into intervals. On each of these intervals the function $F(y)$ will be either always positive or else always negative. Determine which, and mark each interval as positive or negative.
3. Every solution which starts at an initial y_0 in an interval marked positive must be an increasing function of x. On the other hand, if the interval is marked negative, then the solution will be decreasing.

It has been found that to a very good approximation, radioactive materials decay with time by an amount proportional to the total amount of radioactive material present. Thus if A is the total amount of radioactive material present, then

$$\frac{dA}{dt} = -kA$$

for some positive constant k. The value of the constant k depends on the particular radioactive material under discussion. Since the solution of this differential equation is $A(t) = ce^{-kt}$, then $A(0) = c$ is the amount of material initially present. Hence $A(t) = A(0)e^{-kt}$, where $A(0) \geq 0$. The constant k determines the half-life of the material. The **half-life** is defined as the amount of time τ necessary for one-half of the initial amount of material to disappear, that is, $A(\tau) = A(0)/2$. Hence τ satisfies the equation

(2.3)
$$A(\tau) = A(0)e^{-k\tau} = \frac{A(0)}{2}.$$

If k is known, then τ can be determined from (2.3). If τ is known, then k can be calculated from (2.3). If $A(t)$ is known for some known $t_1 > 0$, then this information can be used to calculate k and τ. The following example illustrates how one does such calculations.

EXAMPLE 2.1   Thorium (^{232}Th), a heavy gray metal, is a radioactive material of atomic weight 232. It occurs most commonly in the mineral thorite. The half-life of ^{232}Th is approximately 1.4×10^{10} years. Compute k for ^{232}Th. If a piece of thorite initially contained 2 grams of ^{232}Th, how many years must elapse before 1.9 grams remain?

To solve this problem, we use (2.3) with $\tau = 1.4 \times 10^{10}$ years. From (2.3) we see that

$$e^{-k\tau} = \tfrac{1}{2} \quad \text{or} \quad -k\tau = \log \tfrac{1}{2} = -\log 2.$$

Hence

$$k = \frac{1}{-\tau}(-\log 2) = \frac{\log 2}{1.4 \times 10^{10}} = \frac{\log 2}{1.4} \times 10^{-10}$$

or

$$k \cong 0.495 \times 10^{-10}.$$

If $A(0) = 2$ grams and t_1 is the time elapsed when 1.9 grams remain, then $A(t) = 2e^{-kt}$ and

$$A(t_1) = 1.9 = 2e^{-kt_1} \quad \text{or} \quad e^{-kt_1} = \frac{1.9}{2}.$$

Hence

$$-kt_1 = \log\left(\frac{1.9}{2}\right) = \log 1.9 - \log 2$$

and

$$t_1 = \frac{\log 1.9 - \log 2}{-k} = (\log 2 - \log 1.9)\frac{1.4}{\log 2} \times 10^{10}$$

$$\cong 0.104 \times 10^{10} \text{ years.} \quad \blacksquare$$

EXAMPLE 2.2
A Dating Game

Radiocarbon dating is a widely used technique for dating archaeological samples. This technique, developed in the late 1940's by W. F. Libby at the University of Chicago, determines dates by estimating the level of carbon 14 in a sample. The radioactive isotope ^{14}C is constantly being formed in the upper atmosphere by bombardment of nitrogen by cosmic rays (neutrons). The isotope is then oxidized to carbon dioxide which mixes with ordinary carbon dioxide (containing ^{12}C atoms). Carbon dioxide is taken up by plants and plants are, in turn, ingested by animals. The atmosphere as well as all living things contain a constant (or nearly constant) proportion of carbon 12 and carbon 14. When an organism dies it ceases to exchange carbon with the environment and thus ceases to take in carbon 14. Since carbon 14 is radioactive with a half-life of 5570 years, the level of this isotope in the organism slowly decreases. The period since death can be determined from the amount of ^{14}C still present in the sample.

In many materials, for example ash or charcoal, scientists believe that they can estimate the initial amount of carbon 14 very precisely. Estimating the amount currently in the sample is, of course, subject to measurement errors. For example, suppose that the amount A_0 of ^{14}C initially in a sample is known precisely, and the amount A_1 of ^{14}C currently in a sample can be estimated to within 1%. Then the problem is to determine how closely one can estimate the age of the wood.

To solve this problem let $A(t) = A_0 e^{-kt}$ be the amount of ^{14}C in the sample at time t. Since the half-life τ satisfies $e^{-k\tau} = 1/2$, then

$$k = \frac{\log 2}{\tau} = \frac{\log 2}{5570}.$$

If the amount of ^{14}C currently in the sample is A_1 and t is its age, then $A_1 = A_0 e^{-kt}$, or

$$t = \frac{\log(A_0/A_1)}{k} = \frac{\log A_0 - \log A_1}{k}.$$

The amount of ^{14}C actually in the sample is between $0.99A_1$ and $1.01A_1$. Let t_1 and t_2 be the age estimates for these two amounts, i.e.,

$$t_1 = \frac{\log(A_0/0.99A_1)}{k} = \frac{\log A_0 - \log A_1 - \log 0.99}{k}$$

and

$$t_2 = \frac{\log(A_0/1.01A_1)}{k} = \frac{\log A_0 - \log A_1 - \log 1.01}{k}.$$

Hence

$$t - t_2 = \frac{\log 1.01}{k} \cong 79.96, \quad \text{and} \quad t_1 - t = -\frac{\log 0.99}{k} \cong 80.76.$$

The actual age of the sample is between 80.76 years more and 79.96 years less than the estimate. This is true no matter how old the sample! A sample estimated to be 5000 years old would be between 4920 and 5081 years old (a reasonably satisfactory error). However, a sample estimated at 100 years would be between 20 and 181 years old (a very unsatisfactory error).

Problem 5 at the end of this section provides another example of this type of problem plus a problem with both the initial and the final amounts subject to error. Of course *both* the initial and the final estimates of amounts of ^{14}C in the sample are, in fact, subject to at least small errors. The following projects develop this topic further.

1. Suppose that the initial amount A_0 can be estimated within $P_0\%$ error and the final amount A_1 within $P_1\%$ error. How closely can one estimate the age of the sample?

2. If ^{14}C is produced at a constant rate $r > 0$ and decays at rate $-kC$, then show that the production of carbon 14 is modeled by the equation $C' = -kC + r$. Solve this equation and use your solution to analyze the long time behavior of $C(t)$. Are solutions eventually nearly constant? Does sign analysis of the differential equation indicate the same conclusion?

Photo 6. Archeologists at work in East Africa. (Courtesy of Dr. John Bower.)

In a favorable environment, we are told, a biological population will grow at a rate proportional to its size. This is expressed mathematically as

(2.4)
$$\frac{dP}{dt} = kP.$$

Growth described by (2.4) is sometimes **simple growth** or **Malthusian growth.** Alternatively, when a population satisfies (2.4) to good approximation, that population is said to be in its **logarithmic growth phase.** Several assumptions are implicit in the model (2.4). First, we must assume that the population is sufficiently large so that the population can be considered continuous (i.e., not restricted to integers). This would probably be true of a population of several million but not of a population of 25. In fact, to avoid this problem, $P(t)$ is often taken to be the population density or to be biomass rather than the number of individuals. Second, we are assuming a homogeneous environment and a homogeneous population which is evenly spread over the living space. Third, we are assuming that there are no limitations to growth, that is, no limitations of food, space, and so on.

Solutions of (2.4) have the form

$$P(t) = P(0)e^{kt}.$$

Since $P(0) \geq 0$ (all populations are nonnegative), then $P(t)$ is increasing when $P(0) > 0$, hence the name *Malthusian growth*. The case $P(0) = 0$ leads to the uninteresting constant solution $P(t) \equiv 0$. The constant k is called the **natural growth rate** of the population. It determines the doubling time—the **doubling time** τ is that time necessary for an initial (positive) population to double. In symbols we see that

(2.5) $P(\tau) = 2P(0) = P(0)e^{k\tau}.$

From (2.5) we can determine k when τ is known or τ when k is known. If $P(0)$ and $P(t_1)$ for some $t_1 > 0$ are known, this information can be used to obtain both k and τ.

EXAMPLE 2.3   A small amount of a certain one-celled organism is placed in a beaker of liquid substrate (food) and is kept stirred. This organism is known to satisfy (2.4) during the initial phase of its growth. If the population density triples in 2 hours, determine the natural growth rate k and the doubling time τ.

Since $P(t) = P(0)e^{kt}$ and since $P(2) = 3P(0)$, then

$$3P(0) = P(0)e^{2k} \quad \text{or} \quad e^{2k} = 3.$$

Hence

$$k = \frac{\log 3}{2} \cong 0.549.$$

Given k, we determine τ from (2.5). Indeed, from (2.5) we see that

$$2 = e^{k\tau} \quad \text{or} \quad \log 2 = k\tau.$$

Hence

$$\tau = \frac{\log 2}{k} = \log 2\left(\frac{2}{\log 3}\right) = \frac{2\log 2}{\log 3}$$

$$\cong 1.262 \text{ hours.} \quad \blacksquare$$

In Example 2.3 the assumption that the population grows according to the simple growth model (2.4) is a *crucial assumption*. Growth of a given one-celled organism may or may not satisfy (2.4). One must know some microbiology in order to decide if this crucial assumption is true. Indeed, for certain species of one-celled organisms one will observe the following behavior. When the organism is first introduced into the substrate the population remains constant for a given length of time. This is called the **lag phase.** The length of this lag phase can vary significantly for different sample populations of the same species. Following the lag phase, the population will grow in the manner predicted by (2.4). The crucial assumption (2.4) cannot be correct for such a species since (2.4) does not predict any lag phase.

Many chemical and biological processes are modeled by using the law of mass action. For this model to be appropriate all reactants must be homogeneous and uniformly distributed. Moreover, any important parameters, such as temperature or pressure, must be held constant.

Let m substances with concentrations $s_1, s_2, s_3, \ldots, s_m$ combine to form a product with concentration p. **The law of mass action** is the statement that dp/dt is proportional to the product of the m concentrations s_i, that is,

$$\frac{dp}{dt} = ks_1 s_2 \ldots s_m.$$

For example, if $m = 1$, then the law of mass action states that $dp/dt = ks_1$. In the special case where the substrate is also the product, we have $s_1 = p$. In this special case the law of mass action reduces to simple growth (2.4), that is, $dp/dt = kp$. This equation has already been discussed. We will now consider a more complicated example of the law of mass action.

We consider the course of an epidemic in a homogeneous population of fixed size. We divide the total population into two groups. Those who have the disease are called infectives, and those who do not have the disease will be called susceptibles. If I is the infective portion of the population and S the susceptible portion, then by assumption $S + I = 1$. We further assume that the dynamics of this epidemic satisfy the law of mass action. Hence

(2.6)
$$\frac{dI}{dt} = kIS, \qquad I + S = 1.$$

From (2.6) we conclude that

(2.7)
$$\frac{dI}{dt} = kI(1 - I).$$

If we can solve (2.7) for $I(t)$, then $S(t)$ will also be known since $S(t) = 1 - I(t)$. [We could equally well solve for $S(t)$. This gives

$$\frac{dS}{dt} = -\frac{dI}{dt} = -kIS = -kS(1 - S)$$

and $I(t) = 1 - S(t)$.] Equation (2.7) is called a **logistic equation.** Its solutions, for $0 < I(0) < 1$, are called **logistic curves.**

Figure 2.5 contains a sign analysis of the function $f(I) = kI(1 - I)$ for $k > 0$. From Figure 2.5 we see that solutions of (2.7) will be decreasing for $I < 0$ and for $I > 1$. Of course, solutions of (2.7) are of physical interest only when $0 \leq$

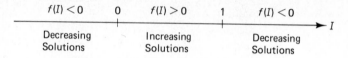

Figure 2.5. Sign analysis of $f(I) = kI(1 - I)$.

$I(t) \leq 1$. Solutions will increase when $0 < I < 1$. There are two constant solutions, namely $I(t) \equiv 0$ and $I(t) \equiv 1$. The solution $I(t) \equiv 0$ corresponds to zero initial infection and hence no epidemic. The solution $I(t) \equiv 1$ corresponds to 100% infection. We separate the variables in (2.7) and obtain

$$(2.8) \qquad \frac{dI}{I(1 - I)} = k \, dt.$$

The term on the left in (2.8) can be decomposed by using *partial fractions*. The student has seen partial fractions in calculus. In this case, constants A and B must be determined so that

$$\frac{1}{I(1 - I)} = \frac{A}{I} + \frac{B}{1 - I}.$$

Multiplication by $I(1 - I)$ yields

$$(2.9) \qquad 1 = A(1 - I) + BI.$$

On putting $I = 0$ in (2.9), we find that $A = 1$, while $I = 1$ in (2.9) gives $B = 1$. Hence (2.8) can be written as

$$\left(\frac{1}{I} + \frac{1}{1 - I}\right) dI = k \, dt.$$

Integration gives

$$\log |I| - \log |1 - I| = kt + c$$

or

$$\log \left|\frac{I}{1 - I}\right| = kt + c.$$

Hence

$$\frac{I}{1 - I} = e^{kt}(\pm e^c) = e^{kt} c_1.$$

This equation can be solved for I. The answer is

$$(2.10) \qquad I(t) = \frac{c_1 e^{kt}}{1 + c_1 e^{kt}}.$$

Given an initial condition $I(0) = I_0$, we see that $I_0 = c_1/(1 + c_1)$ or $c_1 = I_0/(1 - I_0)$. This can be used in (2.10) to obtain

$$(2.11) \qquad I(t) = \frac{[I_0/(1 - I_0)]e^{kt}}{1 + [I_0/(1 - I_0)]e^{kt}} = \frac{I_0 e^{kt}}{1 - I_0 + I_0 e^{kt}}.$$

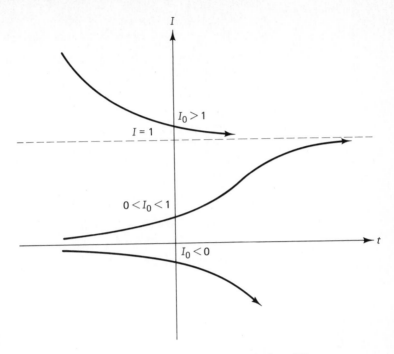

Figure 2.6. Typical solutions of $dI/dt = f(I)$.

The solution $I(t)$ is graphed in Figure 2.6 for some typical values of I_0. The constant solutions $I \equiv 0$ and $I \equiv 1$ cannot be obtained by separation of variables. However, we were already aware of these two special solutions.

For $0 < I_0 < 1$ the solution (2.11) is increasing, as expected. Moreover, since $k > 0$,

$$\lim_{t \to \infty} I(t) = \lim_{t \to \infty} \frac{I_0 e^{kt}}{1 - I_0 + I_0 e^{kt}}$$

$$= \lim_{t \to \infty} \frac{I_0}{(1 - I_0)e^{-kt} + I_0} = \frac{I_0}{I_0} = 1.$$

Hence we see that if the crucial assumption (2.6) is true, the infection will grow and will eventually include, for all practical purposes, the entire population.

PROBLEMS

1. A colony of a certain bacteria is growing in a well-stirred substrate. Let $C(t)$ be the concentration of the bacteria in the solution at time t. It is known that $dC/dt = kC$. If in 1 hour the initial concentration has tripled, find k. Also determine the doubling time.

2. If 4 grams of a radioactive material decays to 1.03 grams in 200 years, how much will be left in 600 years? What is the half-life of this material?

3. Radium ($^{226}_{88}$Ra) has a half-life of about 1600 years. Suppose that a given sample of pitchblende contains 10^{-5} gram of radium. How much radium did this sample con-

tain 5000 years ago? How much will it contain 5000 years from now? What crucial assumption do you make in order to work this problem?

4. A sample of calcium 45 ($^{45}_{20}$Ca) decays to 65.2% of the original amount in 100 days. Find the half-life of this material.

5. Carbon 14 has a half-life of 5570 years.

   (a) If the amount A_0 initially in a sample is known precisely and the amount A_1 currently in the sample can be estimated to within 0.1%, how closely can one estimate the age of the sample?

   (b) If A_0 and A_1 can both be estimated to within 1%, then how closely can one estimate the age of the sample?

6. Solve the problem $y' = by$, $y(x_0) = q_0$ when b is a fixed constant.

7. Find all constant solutions of $y' = \sin y$. In what regions are the solutions of this equation increasing? decreasing?

8. Solve each initial value problem.

   (a) $y' = y(y^2 - 1)$, $y(0) = 2$.   (b) $y' = y(y^2 - 1)$, $y(0) = 1$.

   (c) $y' = y(y^2 - 1)$, $y(0) = 0$.   (d) $p' = 3p(p^2 + 1)$, $p(0) = 1$.

   (e) $dp/dx = 2pr$, $p + r = 5$, $p(0) = 1$.   (f) $R' = -2R + 4$, $R(0) = 0$.

   (g) $dR/dx = 2R - P + Q$, $2P + Q + R = 1$, $P + Q + 2R = 2$, $R(0) = -1$.

9. In $y' = b_0 y$, $y(0) = q_0$ suppose that both q_0 and b_0 must be determined by measurements. Call the measured estimates q_1 and b_1. Let Z be the solution of $Z' = b_1 Z$, $Z(0) = q_1$.

   (a) Suppose that $q_1 = q_0$ while $b_i > 0$ and $|b_0 - b_1| \le \varepsilon$. Find, in terms of ε, the maximum possible error $|y(x) - Z(x)|$ over the interval $0 \le x \le A$. *Hint:* Compute $\partial y/\partial b$ and use the mean value theorem.

   (b) Suppose that $q_1 = q_0$ while $b_0 < -\varepsilon$, $b_1 < 0$ and $|b_0 - b_1| \le \varepsilon$. Find, in terms of ε, the maximum possible error $|y(x) - Z(x)|$ over the interval $0 \le x \le A$. Assume that $A > -(b_0 + \varepsilon)$.

   (c) Suppose that $b_0 = b_1$ while $|q_0 - q_1| \le \varepsilon$. Find the maximum possible error $|y(x) - Z(x)|$ over $0 \le x \le A$.

10. Consider the two problems

$$y' = ay, \qquad y(0) = q_0 > 0$$

   and

$$Z' = aZ - \varepsilon Z^2, \qquad Z(0) = q_0,$$

   where $a > 0$, $\varepsilon > 0$ and ε is small. Compute the limit of $y(x)$ and of $Z(x)$ as $x \to \infty$. Does the small term εZ^2 make a crucial difference in the answer? With $q_0 = 1$, $a = 1$, and $\varepsilon = 0.001$, find $y(2)$ and $Z(2)$. (You will need a calculator.) Does the small term εZ^2 make a crucial difference in the answer?

11. U.S. agencies have dumped some 90,000 barrels of radioactive waste in the Atlantic and Pacific Oceans. The material was mixed with concrete, encased in steel drums, and dumped. The steel eventually rusts. Since concrete is porous, seawater will slowly leach the radioactive material from the concrete. It was assumed that this

material would be so diluted in the sea that no danger could result. However, EPA-funded scientists have found such materials as americium 241 and various isotopes of plutonium sticking to ocean floor sediment near the barrels.

(a) Americium 241 has a half-life of 458 years. How many years will it take before the current amount of ^{241}Am is reduced to 10% of its current amount?

(b) Look up the half-life of plutonium 239 and then answer part (a) for the radio-nuclide.

(c) Repeat part (b) for plutonium 238.

12. An ore sample contains 1 gram of uranium. The uranium in the sample is 99.28% ^{238}U, 0.71% ^{235}U, and 0.01% ^{234}U. Assume that the half-life of ^{238}U is 4.5×10^9 years, that of ^{235}U is 7.3×10^8 years, and that of ^{234}U is 2.5×10^5 years. Assuming that each isotope decays according to a differential equation of the form $A' = -kA$ with appropriate k's, what were the proportions in the sample of these three isotopes of uranium 1 million years ago? What will the proportions of these three isotopes of uranium be 1 million years hence?

13. In 1964, Soviet scientists bombarded plutonium with 113- to 115-MeV neon ions to produce an element of atomic number 104 (call it E104). This isotope of E104 has a half-life of 0.15 second. If initially no E104 is present and if it can be produced at the rate of r micrograms per day, how much will be present after 2 seconds? *Hint:* Show that the amount A of E104 will satisfy an equation of the form $A' = -kA + R$. Find k and R in *correct units*.

14. In 1969, American scientists bombarded ^{249}Cf with carbon 12 nuclei of 71 MeV to produce an isotope of E104 with atomic weight 257. This isotope decays to ^{253}No with a 4.5-second half-life. The ^{253}No decays to stable products with a half-life of 10 seconds. If a sample just removed from the accelerator initially has E_I micrograms of ^{257}E104 and N_I micrograms of ^{253}No, how much of each will be present after 20 seconds? *Hint:* N will satisfy an equation of the form $N' = -k_2N + k_1E$ while $E(t)$ will satisfy an equation $E' = -k_1E$. Determine k_1 and k_2, solve for $E(t)$ and then solve for $N(t)$.

15. The scientists Verhulst (1828) and Peral (1930) proposed the following growth model for a population living in an environment with limited resources (e.g., space, food, sunlight, etc.):

$$\frac{dP}{dt} = kP\left(1 - \frac{P}{K}\right), \qquad P(0) = P_0.$$

Here $k > 0$ is the natural growth rate of the population when resources are unlimited and K is a positive constant called the **carrying capacity** of the environment.

(a) Using sign analysis, find all constant solutions and discuss the general behavior of solutions.

(b) Solve the equation when $0 < P_0 < K$. Compute the limit as $t \to \infty$ of your solution.

(c) Solve the equation when $P_0 > K$. Compute the limit as $t \to \infty$ of your solution.

(d) Discuss why K is called the carrying capacity.

16. Sometimes a population must attain a critical size P_C before it will sustain itself and grow. Given positive constants k, P_C, and P_M with $P_C < P_M$, show that

$$\frac{dP}{dt} = k(P - P_C)(P_M - P)P$$

represents such a situation. Solve this equation when $P(0) = P_0$, where P_0 satisfies

(a) $P_0 < P_C$.   (b) $P_C < P_0 < P_M$.   (c) $P_0 > P_M$.

Also find all constant solutions.

17. Suppose that the population dynamics of a species is governed by the equation

$$\frac{dP}{dt} = k(P_M - P),$$

where $k > 0$ and $P_M > 0$. Using sign analysis, discuss the general behavior of solution for various values of $P(0) = P_0$. Solve the equation when

(a) $k = 2$, $P_M = \pi$, $P_0 = 1$.   (b) $k = 2$, $P_M = \pi$, $P_0 = 5$.

(c) $k = 3$, $P_M = 10$, $P_0 = 1$.   (d) $k = 3$, $P_M = 10$, $P_0 = 10$.

18. (a) If 1 gram of a radionuclide decays to 0.94 gram in 2 years, what is the half-life of this isotope?

(b) After doing part (a) we discover that the amounts given were measured in such a way that 1% errors are possible. Hence 1 ± 0.01 grams decayed to 0.94 ± 0.0094 gram in 2 years. Using these data, what are the longest possible and the shortest possible estimates of the half-life?

19. The water board for a certain city is trying to forecast future needs. There are certain standard ways to forecast water demand. The method they have used is to assume that water use is governed by the equation

$$\frac{dW}{dt} = kW,$$

where W is the water demand in cubic feet per day and t is time measured in days. The current water treatment plant, with a maximum capacity of $\frac{1}{2}$ million cubic feet per day, is obsolete, expensive to operate, and should be replaced. It will take 3 years to design and build a new plant. For political reasons the new plant must be designed to last 15 years.

(a) If water demand was 350,000 cubic feet per day 5 years ago and is now 420,000 cubic feet per day, when should the design of the new plant begin? If design begins immediately, what should the maximum capacity of the new plant be? What is the doubling time for W?

(b) Suppose that the plant was designed and built using the data from part (a). Suppose that the figures 350,000 and 420,000 cubic feet per day were found to be subject to measurement errors of as much as 2% (i.e., $350,000 \pm 7000$ and $420,000 \pm 8400$). Estimate the shortest and longest possible amounts of time that the new plant can operate before its maximum capacity is reached.

2.3 HOMOGENEOUS DIFFERENTIAL EQUATIONS

Many differential equations that are not separable can be reduced to the separable case by a suitable substitution. An important class of differential equations for which a suitable substitution is known is the class of homogeneous differential equations.

A function $h(x, y)$ of two variables x and y is called **homogeneous of degree** n if for all positive λ and all (x, y) where h is defined, we have

$$h(\lambda x, \lambda y) = \lambda^n h(x, y).$$

For example, $h(x, y) = x^3 + 2x^2 y + 3xy^2 + 4y^3$ is homogeneous of degree three. This can be checked by computing

$$\begin{aligned} h(\lambda x, \lambda y) &= (\lambda x)^3 + 2(\lambda x)^2(\lambda y) + 3(\lambda x)(\lambda y)^2 + 4(\lambda y)^3 \\ &= \lambda^3 x^3 + 2\lambda^3 x^2 y + 3\lambda^3 xy^2 + 4\lambda^3 y^3 \\ &= \lambda^3(x^3 + 2x^2 y + 3xy^2 + 4y^3) \\ &= \lambda^3 h(x, y). \end{aligned}$$

The function $h(x, y) = x^2 + xy + 4$ is not homogeneous. To see this, we compute

$$\begin{aligned} h(\lambda x, \lambda y) &= (\lambda x)^2 + (\lambda x)(\lambda y) + 4 \\ &= \lambda^2(x^2 + xy) + 4. \end{aligned}$$

The last expression does not have the form

$$\lambda^n h(x, y) = \lambda^n(x^2 + xy + 4)$$

for any value of n. Similarly,

$$h(x, y) = x^2 \cos\left(\frac{y}{x}\right) + (\log|x| - \log|y|)xy$$

is homogeneous of degree 2,

$$\frac{x^2}{x^2 + 2xy + y^2}$$

is homogeneous of degree 0, and

$$\sqrt[3]{x^4 + 3y^4}$$

is homogeneous of degree $\frac{4}{3}$. We shall be particularly interested in the case where h is homogeneous of degree 0.

HOMOGENEOUS DIFFERENTIAL EQUATIONS

A differential equation

(E) $$y' = f(x, y)$$

is called a **homogeneous differential equation** when f is a homogeneous function of degree 0, that is, when $f(\lambda x, \lambda y) = \lambda^0 f(x, y) = f(x, y)$ for all (x, y) for which f is defined and all $\lambda \neq 0$.

We assume the (E) is a homogeneous differential equation. Let $\lambda = 1/x$ and note that

$$f(x, y) = f(\lambda x, \lambda y) = f\left(1, \frac{y}{x}\right).$$

Hence $f(x, y)$ can be written as a function of y/x, namely $F(y/x) = f(1, y/x)$. Moreover, (E) can be written in the form

(3.1) $$y' = F\left(\frac{y}{x}\right).$$

This suggests making the substitution $v = y/x$. Since we seek y as a function of x, what is really meant by this substitution is

(3.2) $$v(x) = \frac{y(x)}{x} \quad \text{or} \quad y(x) = xv(x).$$

The substitution (3.2) is used in (3.1) as follows:

$$y'(x) = F\left(\frac{y(x)}{x}\right) = F(v(x))$$

and

$$y'(x) = xv'(x) + 1 \cdot v(x) = xv'(x) + v(x).$$

Thus

(3.3) $$xv'(x) + v(x) = F(v(x))$$

or

$$v'(x) = \frac{F(v(x)) - v(x)}{x}.$$

This equation is usually written in simpler and shorter notation as

(3.4) $$\frac{dv}{dx} = \frac{F(v) - v}{x}.$$

The reason for using the transformation (3.2) is that the new equation is separable. Thus (3.4) can be solved using the techniques of Section 2.1.

EXAMPLE 3.1   Solve the initial value problem

(3.5) $$x^2 \frac{dy}{dx} = y^2 - xy + x^2, \qquad y(1) = 2.$$

First we solve for y' in (3.5). This gives $y' = (y^2 - xy + x^2)/x^2$. Since $f(x, y) = (y^2 - xy + x^2)/x^2$ is homogeneous of degree 0, the discussion above applies. We define $v = y/x$ and compute

$$\frac{dy}{dx} = \frac{y^2 - xy + x^2}{x^2} = \left(\frac{y}{x}\right)^2 - \frac{y}{x} + 1 = v^2 - v + 1.$$

Since $y = xv$, then $y' = xv' + v$. Hence (3.5) becomes

$$x\frac{dv}{dx} + v = v^2 - v + 1.$$

We now simplify and solve. This gives

$$x\frac{dv}{dx} = v^2 - 2v + 1 = (v - 1)^2$$

and

$$(v - 1)^{-2}\, dv = x^{-1}\, dx.$$

Integration gives

$$-(v - 1)^{-1} = \log|x| + c$$

or

$$v = 1 - \frac{1}{\log|x| + c}.$$

Since $v = y/x$, a general solution of (3.5) is

$$y = x\left(1 - \frac{1}{\log|x| + c}\right)$$

From $y = 2$ when $x = 1$ we find that $c = -1$. ∎

Note that in working this example we have not gone directly to (3.4). Rather, we have used the substitution $v = y/x$ and worked through the calculation to the new equation. We suggest that the reader do the same. That is, we suggest that the reader remember the method rather than memorizing (3.4).

The word *substitution* and the phrase *change of variables* have the same meaning. We can say "substitute $v = y/x$" or "change variables to $v = y/x$." Students are often unsure how to proceed with a substitution. The idea is always to write the original equation in terms of the new variable or variables and then to simplify if necessary. This is what was done with the substitution (3.2). Thus (3.3) is the original equation, namely (3.1), written in terms of the new variable v.

This method of solution can be summarized as follows:

SOLUTION METHOD—HOMOGENEOUS EQUATIONS

Use the substitution $v = y/x$ in equation (3.1) in order to reduce (E) to

$$\frac{dv}{dx} = \frac{F(v) - v}{x}.$$

Solve this equation for v using separation of variables. Then reverse the substitution to find y.

Note that (3.5) in Example 3.1 can be written in the form

(3.6) $$P(x, y) + Q(x, y)\frac{dy}{dx} = 0,$$

where P and Q are homogeneous functions of the same degree. Then (3.6) can be written in the form

$$\frac{dy}{dx} = -\frac{P(x, y)}{Q(x, y)} = R(x, y).$$

The function R will be homogeneous of degree 0 since

$$R(\lambda x, \lambda y) = -\frac{P(\lambda x, \lambda y)}{Q(\lambda x, \lambda y)} = -\frac{\lambda^n P(x, y)}{\lambda^n Q(x, y)} = R(x, y).$$

Hence the substitution $v = y/x$ can be applied to any equation of the form (3.6) if P and Q are homogeneous functions of the same degree.

EXAMPLE 3.2   Find a general solution of

(3.7) $$y^2 = (xy - x^2)\frac{dy}{dx}.$$

Since y^2 and $xy - x^2$ are both homogeneous of degree 2, the substitution $v = y/x$ can be applied. Write

$$\frac{dy}{dx} = \frac{y^2}{xy - x^2} = \frac{(y/x)^2}{(y/x) - 1} = \frac{v^2}{v - 1}.$$

Since $y = vx$, then $y' = xv' + v$ and

$$x\frac{dv}{dx} + v = \frac{v^2}{v - 1} \quad \text{or} \quad x\frac{dv}{dx} = \frac{v}{v - 1}.$$

We now separate variables to obtain

$$\frac{v - 1}{v}\, dv = x^{-1}\, dx.$$

Integration yields $v - \log|v| = \log|x| + c$ or $v = \log|xv| + c$. Since $v = y/x$, a general solution of (3.7) is given implicitly by

$$\frac{y}{x} - \log|y| = c. \quad \blacksquare$$

One of the main problems in applying this method is to recognize that the given equation is homogeneous. This problem is particularly acute when the variables used are not x and y.

EXAMPLE 3.3   Find the solution of

$$S\frac{dS}{dt} = \frac{t^2 + S^2}{t}, \qquad S(2) = 1.$$

First we solve for dS/dt, that is,

$$\frac{dS}{dt} = \frac{t^2 + S^2}{St}.$$

(3.8)

As a function of t and S the numerator $t^2 + S^2$ is homogeneous of degree 2. Indeed, if we put $P(t, S) = t^2 + S^2$, then

$$
\begin{aligned}
P(\lambda t, \lambda S) &= (\lambda t)^2 + (\lambda S)^2 \\
&= \lambda^2 (t^2 + S^2) \\
&= \lambda^2 P(t, S)
\end{aligned}
$$

Similarly, $Q(t, S) = St$ is homogeneous of degree 2. Hence (3.8) is a homogeneous equation in (t, S). We write it in the form

$$\frac{dS}{dt} = \frac{t}{S} + \frac{S}{t}, \qquad S(2) = 1.$$

Next we substitute $v = S/t$, that is, $v(t) = S(t)/t$ or $S(t) = tv(t)$. Hence $dS/dt = v(t) + t\, dv/dt$ and (3.8), expressed in terms of v and t, is

$$v + t\frac{dv}{dt} = \frac{1}{v} + v.$$

We simplify and solve as follows:

$$t\frac{dv}{dt} = \frac{1}{v},$$

so

$$v\, dv = t^{-1}\, dt$$

and

$$\frac{v^2}{2} = \log|t| + c.$$

Since $v = S/t$, then

$$\frac{S^2}{2t^2} = \log|t| + c$$

or

$$S = \pm t(2 \log|t| + 2c)^{1/2}.$$

From the initial condition $S(2) = 1$ we see that S is positive and t is positive, that is, $S = t(2 \log t + 2c)^{1/2}$. Since $S(2) = 1$, then

$$1 = 2(2 \log 2 + 2c)^{1/2} \quad \text{and} \quad c = \tfrac{1}{8} - \log 2.$$

The solution is

$$
\begin{aligned}
S(t) &= t(2 \log t - 2 \log 2 + \tfrac{1}{4})^{1/2} \\
&= t\left(\log\left(\frac{t}{2}\right)^2 + \frac{1}{4}\right)^{1/2}. \quad \blacksquare
\end{aligned}
$$

Notice that instead of finding a function of y/x as we did in (3.1) one could find a function of x/y and then use the substitution $v = x/y$. Either $v = x/y$ or $v = y/x$ can be used. The choice depends on which substitution leads to the easiest integral.

PROBLEMS

1. Determine which functions are homogeneous. If a function is homogeneous, determine the degree of homogeneity.

   (a) $x^2 + xy$.

   (b) $x^2y + 2xy^2 + xy + 4y^3$.

   (c) $3x^2y + xy^2 - \pi y^3$.

   (d) $\min\left(\dfrac{x}{2}, \dfrac{y}{4}\right)$.

   (e) $\max\left(\dfrac{x}{3}, y\right)$.

   (f) $\min\left(\dfrac{x^2}{2}, \dfrac{xy}{3}, \dfrac{y^2}{\pi}\right)$.

   (g) $x^a y^{1-a}$, where a is a given real number.

   (h) $x^a y^b$, where a and b are given real numbers.

   (i) $(3x^3 + 4y^3)^{1/5}$.

   (j) $(ax^p + by^p)^{1/q}$, where a, b, p, and q are given positive numbers.

   (k) $\log x^2 - 2 \log y$.

   (l) $\dfrac{1}{x^2 + y^2}$.

   (m) $\dfrac{\sqrt{x + y}}{x \log y - x \log x}$.

In Problems 2–9, decide which equations are homogeneous and which are not.

2. $x\dfrac{dy}{dx} + y \sin xy = y\dfrac{dy}{dx}$.

3. $\dfrac{dy}{dx} + \log y = \log x$.

4. $\dfrac{dy}{dx} = \dfrac{\cos xy - 1}{x^2 y^2}$.

5. $(x - y)\dfrac{dy}{dx} = 2y - x$.

6. $\dfrac{dy}{dx} = \dfrac{x^3 + 2xy + y^3}{xy^2 + x^2 y}$.

7. $x\dfrac{dy}{dx} = 2y\dfrac{dy}{dx} + x - y + 3$.

8. $\dfrac{dK}{dt} = -K + t$.

9. $2t \, dN = (N + t) \, dt$.

In Problems 10–20, solve the equation. If no initial condition is given, find a general solution.

10. $x\dfrac{dy}{dx} = 3y - x$.

11. $t\dfrac{dz}{dt} = t + 2z$.

12. $\dfrac{dy}{dt} = \dfrac{y^2 + 2ty}{t^2}$.

13. $(x^2 + y^2) \, dy + 2xy \, dx = 0$.

14. $t\dfrac{dN}{dt} = N + \sqrt{t^2 - N^2}$.

15. $\dfrac{dy}{dx} = \dfrac{y - 6x}{2x - y}$, $y(0) = 1$.

16. $(2x + y) \, dy + (4x + 3y) \, dx = 0$, $y(0) = 2$.

17. $x^2 \dfrac{dy}{dx} - (4x^2 + xy + y^2) = 0$, $y(1) = -1$.

18. $\dfrac{dy}{dx} = \dfrac{x^2 y}{x^3 - y^3}$, $y(1) = 1$.

19. $\dfrac{dN}{dt} = \dfrac{t - N}{t + N}$, $N(0) = 2$.

20. $x \cos\left(\dfrac{y}{x}\right) \dfrac{dy}{dx} + x = y \cos\left(\dfrac{y}{x}\right)$.

21. Let f be continuous for *all* (x, y) and be homogeneous of degree 0.

    (a) Show that $f(x, y)$ is constant along any line in the (x, y) plane which passes through the origin.

    (b) Show that f is a constant function.

22. Let $y' = f(x, y)$ be a homogeneous differential equation and let $F(v) = f(1, v)$. Suppose that F and F' are continuous on $-\infty < v < \infty$. Let $y = \varphi(x)$ be the solution of (E) on $x_0 \leq x < A$ such that $y(x_0) = a_0$ where $x_0 > 0$. Prove each statement.

    (a) If $F(a_0/x_0) > a_0/x_0 > 0$, then $\varphi(x)$ is monotone increasing on $x_0 < x < A$.

    (b) Suppose that $F(v) < v$ on $A < v < B$ and $F(A) = A$, $F(B) = B$. If $Ax_0 < a_0 < Bx_0$, then $Ax < \varphi(x) < Bx$.

    (c) Suppose that $\varphi(x) \equiv a_0$ is a constant solution for $0 < x < \infty$. Then either $a_0 = 0$ or else $y = a$ is a solution for all $a > 0$ or else $y = a$ is a solution for all $a < 0$.

23. Show that if f is homogeneous of degree n, then

$$x \frac{\partial f}{\partial x} + y \frac{\partial f}{\partial y} = nf.$$

24. Can you solve the homogeneous equation

$$x^2 \frac{dy}{dx} = y^2 - xy + x^2$$

subject to the initial condition $y(0) = 2$? What is the difficulty?

MISCELLANEOUS PROBLEMS   In Problems 25–28, obtain a general solution to each equation. Some are homogeneous and some are separable.

25. $(2x - y) \dfrac{dy}{dx} + x = 2y$.

26. $(\sin x)y' + \cos y = 0$.

27. $x \dfrac{dy}{dx} = \sqrt{xy} \dfrac{dy}{dx} + y$.

28. $x^2 \dfrac{dR}{dx} = x(\sqrt{xR} + R)$.

29. (a) Show that the substitution $Z = y + 4x$ changes the equation

    (3.9) $\dfrac{dy}{dx} + 4 = \cos\left(\dfrac{y + 4x}{x}\right) + \dfrac{y + 4x}{x}$

    into the homogeneous equation

$$\frac{dZ}{dx} = \cos\left(\frac{Z}{x}\right) + \frac{Z}{x}.$$

    (b) Find a general solution of (3.9).

In Problems 30–33, solve by first finding a substitution (or substitutions) which will reduce the problem to a separable one. Find a general solution.

30. $\dfrac{dy}{dx} = \sqrt{x + y} - 1.$

31. $\dfrac{dM}{dx} = \cos^2{(M - x)} + 1.$

32. $\dfrac{dy}{dt} = 2t(y + 2t^2) - 4t.$

33. $\dfrac{dw}{ds} = \dfrac{w + s}{s} + \cos\left(\dfrac{w + s}{s}\right) - 1.$

2.4 EXACT DIFFERENTIAL EQUATIONS

Let $F(x, y) = x^2 + 2y^2$. If we think of $F(x, y) = x^2 + 2y^2 = c$ as defining y in terms of x, say $y = \varphi(x)$, then

$$\frac{d}{dx} F(x, \varphi(x)) = 2x + 4\varphi(x)\varphi'(x) = 2x + 4y\frac{dy}{dx} = 0.$$

Hence $y = \varphi(x)$ is a solution of the differential equation

$$2x + 4y\frac{dy}{dx} = 0$$

or

$$\frac{dy}{dx} = -\frac{x}{2y}.$$

Moreover, $F(x, y) = x^2 + 2y^2 = c$ is an implicitly given general solution of this differential equation.

This idea can be generalized. Given any function $F(x, y)$ and any constant c, consider the expression

(4.1) $$F(x, y) = c.$$

Suppose that this expression defines y implicitly in terms of x and the constant c, that is, $y = \varphi(x)$ and

(4.2) $$F(x, \varphi(x)) = c.$$

We differentiate (4.2) to obtain

$$F_x(x, \varphi(x)) + F_y(x, \varphi(x))\varphi'(x) = 0$$

or

(4.3) $$F_x(x, y) + F_y(x, y)\frac{dy}{dx} = 0.$$

Reversing this argument, we see that the differential equation (4.3) can be solved to obtain the (implicitly given) solution (4.1). The function $F(x, y)$ is called a **constant of the motion** determined by the differential equation (4.3). The term

integral of the motion is also used to describe F. For example, we have just seen that $x^2 + 2y^2$ is a constant of the motion determined by $y' = -x/(2y)$.

This discussion will now be applied to a differential equation of the form

(4.4) $$p(x, y) + q(x, y)\frac{dy}{dx} = 0.$$

For this equation we ask whether or not there is a function $F(x, y)$ such that

(4.5) $$F_x(x, y) = p(x, y), \qquad F_y(x, y) = q(x, y).$$

If there is such a function F and if F has continuous second partial derivatives, then we know from calculus that

$$\frac{\partial^2 F}{\partial x\,\partial y}(x, y) = \frac{\partial^2 F}{\partial y\,\partial x}(x, y).$$

Photo 7. In this conservative mechanical system energy is a constant of the motion. (Courtesy of the National Aeronautics and Space Administration.)

This equation together with (4.5) implies that

(4.6) $$\frac{\partial p}{\partial y}(x, y) = \frac{\partial q}{\partial x}(x, y).$$

Hence a necessary condition for the existence of the function F is (4.6). This condition is also sufficient in order that we can construct the function F in any rectangular region of the form $A_1 < x < A_2$, $B_1 < x < B_2$. Whenever there is an F such that (4.5) is true, we say that (4.4) is an **exact equation.**

EXAMPLE 4.1   Find a general solution of the differential equation

$$(2x + 2y^2) + (4xy + 3y^2)\frac{dy}{dx} = 0.$$

We write the equation in differential form,

$$(2x + 2y^2)\, dx + (4xy + 3y^2)\, dy = 0.$$

Thus $p(x, y) = 2x + 2y^2$, $q(x, y) = 4xy + 3y^2$ and condition (4.6) becomes

$$\frac{\partial}{\partial y}(2x + 2y^2) = 4y = \frac{\partial}{\partial x}(4xy + 3y^2).$$

Since (4.6) is true, there is a function F such that

(4.7) $$F_x(x, y) = 2x + 2y^2 \quad \text{and} \quad F_y(x, y) = 4xy + 3y^2.$$

We will need to make use of both equations in (4.7). We can start with either one. Suppose that we use the first. Since

$$F_x(x, y) = 2x + 2y^2,$$

then on integration with respect to x, it follows that

(4.8) $$F(x, y) = x^2 + 2xy^2 + \psi(y),$$

where ψ is an arbitrary function of y. To determine ψ, we take the partial derivative of (4.8) with respect to y and compare the result with the second equation in (4.7), that is,

$$4xy + \psi'(y) = F_y(x, y) = 4xy + 3y^2.$$

Thus $\psi'(y) = 3y^2$ and $\psi(y) = y^3 + c_1$, where c_1 is an arbitrary constant. We use this information in (4.8) to see that $F(x, y) = x^2 + 2xy^2 + y^3 + c_1$. A general solution is $x^2 + 2xy^2 + y^3 + c_1 = c_2$, where c_2 is an arbitrary constant. Since there is no need to keep two arbitrary constants, they can be combined to obtain $c = c_2 - c_1$. A general solution is

$$x^2 + 2xy^2 + y^3 = c. \quad \blacksquare$$

In general, if (4.6) is true, then $F(x, y)$ can be found as follows. Let $P(x, y)$ be any integral with respect to x of $p(x, y)$, that is,

$$P(x, y) = \int p(x, y) \, dx,$$

or equivalently, $\partial P/\partial x = p$. In Example 4.1 we used $P(x, y) = x^2 + 2xy^2$. Integrate the first equation in (4.5) with respect to x to obtain

(4.9) $$F(x, y) = P(x, y) + \psi(y),$$

where $\psi(y)$ is an arbitrary function of y. To determine ψ, differentiate (4.9) with respect to y and compare the result with the second equation in (4.5). This gives

$$\frac{\partial}{\partial y} P(x, y) + \psi'(y) = q(x, y)$$

or

(4.10) $$\psi'(y) = q(x, y) - \frac{\partial}{\partial y} P(x, y).$$

Since (4.6) is true, the right-hand side of (4.10) will not depend on x (i.e., it is a function of y only). To see this, compute

$$\frac{\partial}{\partial x} \left[q(x, y) - \frac{\partial}{\partial y} P(x, y) \right] = \frac{\partial}{\partial x} q(x, y) - \frac{\partial^2}{\partial x \, \partial y} P(x, y)$$

$$= q_x(x, y) - \frac{\partial^2}{\partial y \, \partial x} P(x, y) = q_x(x, y) - \frac{\partial}{\partial y} p(x, y)$$

$$= q_x(x, y) - p_y(x, y) = 0.$$

Thus (4.10) can be integrated with respect to y to determine ψ. When ψ is determined, then F is known and a general solution is $F(x, y) = c$. There is no need to put an arbitrary constant into the function ψ since an arbitrary constant c is supplied at the last step.

EXAMPLE 4.2   Find a general solution of the differential equation

$$(2xy + 1) + (x^2 + 4y)y' = 0.$$

Write the equation in the form

$$(2xy + 1) \, dx + (x^2 + 4y) \, dy = 0.$$

Condition (4.6) is true since

$$\frac{\partial}{\partial y} (2xy + 1) = 2x = \frac{\partial}{\partial x} (x^2 + 4y).$$

Thus there is a function F such that

(4.11) $$F_x(x, y) = 2xy + 1 \quad \text{and} \quad F_y(x, y) = x^2 + 4y.$$

Integrate the first equation in (4.11) with respect to x to obtain

(4.12) $F(x, y) = x^2y + x + \psi(y),$

where ψ is an arbitrary function of y. [We are taking $P(x, y) = x^2y + x$.] Differentiate (4.12) with respect to y and equate with the second expression in (4.11). This gives

$$x^2 + \psi'(y) = x^2 + 4y.$$

Thus $\psi'(y) = 4y$ and $\psi(y) = 2y^2$. The function $F(x, y) = x^2 + x + 2y^2$ is a constant of the motion. A common mistake is for students to say that "the general solution is $F(x, y) = x^2 + x + 2y^2$." This is incorrect. The general solution is

$$x^2y + x + 2y^2 = c. \quad \blacksquare$$

The roles of x and y can be reversed, as the following example shows.

EXAMPLE 4.3   Solve the initial value problem

$$(2x + 1 + 2y^2) + (4xy + 3y^2)y' = 0, \qquad y(0) = -1.$$

We first check that

$$\frac{\partial}{\partial y}(2x + 1 + 2y^2) = 4y = \frac{\partial}{\partial x}(4xy + 3y^2).$$

Thus there is a function F such that

(4.13) $F_x(x, y) = 2x + 1 + 2y^2 \quad \text{and} \quad F_y(x, y) = 4xy + 3y^2.$

Integrate the second expression in (4.13) to obtain

(4.14) $F(x, y) = 2xy^2 + y^3 + \psi(x),$

where ψ is an arbitrary function x. Differentiate (4.14) with respect to x and equate with the first expression in (4.13). This gives

$$2y^2 + \psi'(x) = 2x + 1 + 2y^2.$$

Thus $\psi'(x) = 2x + 1$ and $\psi(x) = x^2 + x$. A general solution of the equation is

$$2xy^2 + y^3 + x^2 + x = c.$$

Use $x = 0$ and $y = -1$ to compute $c = -1$. Thus the solution of the initial value problem is given implicitly by the expression

$$2xy^2 + y^3 + x^2 + x = -1. \quad \blacksquare$$

The procedure will fail if the equation is not exact. Indeed, (4.6) will not be true and one will be unable to proceed with the calculations.

EXAMPLE 4.4   Determine whether the following equation is exact:

$$2xy = (4y^2 + xy)y'.$$

Rewrite the equation as

$$2xy\,dx - (4y^2 + xy)\,dy = 0.$$

Since

$$\frac{\partial}{\partial y}(2xy) = 2x \neq \frac{\partial}{\partial x}(-4y^2 - xy) = -y,$$

the equation is not exact and cannot be solved by the methods in this section. ■

SUMMARY: EXACT DIFFERENTIAL EQUATIONS

Test for Exactness: For $p(x, y)\,dx + q(x, y)\,dy = 0$ to be exact one needs

$$(4.15) \qquad \frac{\partial p}{\partial y}(x, y) = \frac{\partial q}{\partial x}(x, y).$$

Solution Method: If (4.15) is true then integrate $p(x, y)$ with respect to x to obtain

$$(4.16) \qquad F(x, y) = \int p(x, y)\,dx + \psi(y).$$

To determine $\psi(y)$ take the partial derivative of (4.16) with respect to y and equate the result to $q(x, y)$. Simplify to find $\psi'(y)$. Integrate $\psi'(y)$ to get ψ and put the result in (4.16). Solutions have the form

$$F(x, y) = c,$$

for constant c.

When an exact equation is solved, the solution usually must be left in implicit form. This is not a very satisfying way to obtain the formula for a solution. However, in many applications the resulting constant of the motion can be used to obtain physically interesting information. We shall illustrate what can be done with such a constant of the motion when we discuss, in Section 2.7, a predator–prey population model.

PROBLEMS

In Problems 1–12, determine whether the equation is exact. Find a general solution of each equation that is exact.

1. $(e^x + x) + y\dfrac{dy}{dx} = 0.$

2. $(1 - xe^{xy})y' = (ye^{xy} + 1).$

3. $2xy + 1 = (x^2 + 4y)y'.$

4. $(3x + e^{x/y}) = e^{x/y}\dfrac{dy}{dx}.$

5. $(x^3 - 3y^2x)\dfrac{dy}{dx} = y^3 - 3x^2y - y\dfrac{dy}{dx}.$

6. $t\dfrac{dz}{dt} + z = 0.$

7. $t + z\dfrac{dz}{dt} = 0.$

8. $(y \cos xy + 1)\,dx + (x \cos xy + e^y)\,dy = 0.$

9. $(3t^2N - N^3) - (t^3 + 3N^2t)\dfrac{dN}{dt} = 0.$

10. $(2xy + x^2)y' + (1 + 2xy + y^2) = 0.$

11. $(e^t \sin y + 3y)\,dt - (3t - e^t \sin y)\,dy = 0.$

12. $(x + y^2)y' + (3x^2 + 2xy) = 0.$

In Problems 13–16, solve the initial value Problem.

13. $(x \cos xy)y' = -y \cos xy + 2x,\ y(1) = 2.$

14. $3x^2y^2y' + 2xy^3 = 0,\ y(1) = -1.$

15. $(\sin t + t^2e^y - 3)\dfrac{dy}{dt} + (y \cos t + 2te^y) = 0,\ y\!\left(\dfrac{\pi}{2}\right) = 0.$

16. $y' = -\dfrac{3x^2 + 2xy}{x^2 + y^2},\ y(1) = -1.$

17. For what values of a, b, c, and d is the following problem exact?

$$(ax + by)y' + (cx + dy) = 0, \qquad a^2 + b^2 \neq 0$$

18. Show that any separable equation is exact; that is, any equation of the form $P(x) + Q(y)y' = 0$ is exact.

MISCELLANEOUS PROBLEMS   In Problems 19–28, find a general solution.

19. $(2x - 1) + (3y + 4)y' = 0.$ **20.** $(x + 4y) = (2y - 4x)y'.$

21. $x^2y' = y^2 + x^2yy'.$

22. $18x + y \cos xy + (8y + x \cos xy)y' = 0.$

23. $xy' = y + xe^{y/x}.$ **24.** $\left(\dfrac{1}{x} + 1\right) + \left(\dfrac{1}{y} + 2\right)y' = 0.$

25. $4xy + x^{-1} = (e^y - 2x^2)y'.$ **26.** $\sin x = ye^{-y^2}y'.$

27. $(x^2 + xy + y^2) = x^2y'.$ **28.** $(2tN^2 + 2N) + (2t^2N + 2t)\dfrac{dN}{dt} = 0.$

29. In the region $|x| < 1$, $|y| < 1$, and $x^2 + y^2 \neq 0$ the problem

$$\frac{x}{x^2 + y^2} + \frac{y}{x^2 + y^2}\,y' = 0$$

cannot be treated by the methods of this section. Why? What hypothesis is not satisfied? Find a general solution in the region $0 < x < 1$, $-1 < y < 1$.

30. Given $p(x, y) + q(x, y)y' = 0$ in the rectangle $D = \{(x, y) : A_1 < x < A_2, B_1 < y < B_2\}$, suppose that $F(x, y)$ is an integral of the motion. Show that each statement is true.

(a) For any real number c, $cF(x, y)$ is also an integral of the motion.

(b) For any positive integer n, $F(x, y)^n$ is also an integral of the motion.

(c) If $F(x, y) \neq 0$ in D and if n is any positive integer, then $F(x, y)^{-n}$ is an integral of the motion.

(d) If $G(u)$ is any function such that G and G' are continuous for all u, $-\infty < u < \infty$, then $G(F(x, y))$ is an integral of the motion.

31. Consider the second-order equation

(4.15) $y'' = f(x, y, y')$,

where f, $\partial f/\partial y$, and $\partial f/\partial y'$ are defined and continuous on $D = \{(x, y, y') : A_1 < x < A_2, B_1 < y < B_2, C_1 < y' < C_2\}$. A function $F(x, y, y')$ is called an **integral** (or **constant**) **of the motion** determined by (4.15) if

$$\frac{\partial F}{\partial x} + \frac{\partial F}{\partial y}\frac{dy}{dx} + \frac{\partial F}{\partial y'} f = 0 \text{ in } D.$$

(a) Prove that if F is an integral of the motion and if $y = \varphi(x)$ is a solution of (4.15), then $F(x, \varphi(x), \varphi'(x))$ is constant.

(b) Show that $F(y, y') = ky^2 + (y')^2$ is an integral of the motion determined by

$$y'' + ky = 0.$$

32. Consider the system of differential equations

(4.16) $y_1' = f_1(x, y_1, y_2)$, $y_2' = f_2(x, y_1, y_2)$

in a rectangle $D = \{(x, y_1, y_2) : A_1 < x < A_2, B_1 < y < B_2, C_1 < y_2 < C_2\}$. A function $F(x, y_1, y_2)$ is called an **integral** (or **constant**) **of the motion** determined by (4.16) if

$$\frac{\partial F}{\partial x} + \frac{\partial F}{\partial y_1} f_1(x, y_1, y_2) + \frac{\partial F}{\partial y_2} f_2(x, y_1, y_2) = 0 \text{ in } D.$$

(a) Prove that if F is an integral of the motion and if $y_1 = \varphi_1(x)$ and $y_2 = \varphi_2(x)$ is a solution of (4.16), then $F(x, \varphi_1(x), \varphi_2(x))$ is constant.

(b) Show that $F(y_1, y_2) = (y_2^2/2m) + (1 - \cos y_1)$ is an integral of the motion determined by the equation

$$y_1' = \frac{1}{m} y_2, \qquad y_2' = -\sin y_1.$$

2.5 INTEGRATING FACTORS

As we saw in Section 2.4, any family of curves given in the form $F(x, y) = c$ determines a differential equation, namely $F_x(x, y) + F_y(x, y)y' = 0$. For example, given the family of curves

(5.1) $x^2 y^{-2} + y^{-1} = \dfrac{x^2 + y}{y^2} = c,$

the corresponding differential equation is

(5.2)
$$\frac{2x}{y^2} - \left(\frac{2x^2}{y^3} + \frac{1}{y^2}\right)y' = 0.$$

This equation can be significantly simplified if we multiply by y^3. The resulting equation is

(5.3)
$$2xy - (2x^2 + y)y' = 0.$$

The difficulty with simplifying is that (5.3) is no longer exact. We have no method to solve (5.3). On the other hand, if we multiply (5.3) by $\mu = y^{-3}$, we obtain back the exact equation (5.2). Hence, for $y \neq 0$, (5.1) is a general solution of (5.3). The term $\mu = y^{-3}$ is an *integrating factor* for (5.3). The purpose of this section is to discuss integrating factors for differential equations.

Suppose that the differential equation

(5.4)
$$p(x, y) + q(x, y)\frac{dy}{dx} = 0$$

is not exact. Suppose that

(5.5)
$$F(x, y) = c$$

is a general solution of (5.4) in implicit form. Differentiating (5.5) with respect to x, we obtain

(5.6)
$$F_x(x, y) + F_y(x, y)y' = 0.$$

We now eliminate y' from (5.4) and (5.6) and obtain

(5.7)
$$\frac{F_x(x, y)}{p(x, y)} = \frac{F_y(x, y)}{q(x, y)} = \mu(x, y)$$

where μ is the value of the common ratio. Thus (5.7) implies that

$$F_x(x, y) = \mu(x, y)p(x, y) \quad \text{and} \quad F_y(x, y) = \mu(x, y)q(x, y),$$

and hence that

(5.8)
$$\mu(x, y)(p(x, y) + q(x, y)y') = 0$$

is exact.

An **integrating factor** for (5.4) is a function $\mu(x, y)$ such that $\mu \neq 0$ and after multiplying (5.4) by μ the resulting equation [i.e., (5.8)] is exact. According to the discussion above, every equation has at least one integrating factor. Indeed, it will have an infinite number of them! (See the problem section.) Nevertheless, it is not usually an easy task to find one. However, if one has a candidate $\mu(x, y)$ in hand, it is simple to check whether or not it is an integrating factor.

EXAMPLE 5.1   Show that $\mu(x, y) = x^{-2}y^{-2}$ is an integrating factor for

(5.9)
$$(x^2y - y^4) + (2xy^3 - x^3)y' = 0.$$

It is clear that (5.9) is not exact since

$$\frac{\partial}{\partial y}(x^2y - y^4) = x^2 - 4y^3 \neq \frac{\partial}{\partial x}(2xy^3 - x^3) = 2y^3 - 3x^2.$$

Multiply (5.9) by $x^{-2}y^{-2}$ to obtain

$$\left(\frac{1}{y} - \frac{y^2}{x^2}\right) + \left(\frac{2y}{x} - \frac{x}{y^2}\right)y' = 0.$$

This equation is exact since

$$\frac{\partial}{\partial y}\left(\frac{1}{y} - \frac{y^2}{x^2}\right) = -\frac{1}{y^2} - \frac{2y}{x^2} = \frac{\partial}{\partial x}\left(\frac{2y}{x} - \frac{x}{y^2}\right).$$

A general solution can now be found by using the method of Section 2.4. ∎

In order that μ be an integrating factor, it is necessary that (5.8) be exact. This requires that $(\mu p)_y = (\mu q)_x$ or equivalently that

(5.10) $$\mu_y p - \mu_x q = \mu(q_x - p_y).$$

Notice that (5.10) is a first-order partial differential equation for μ. Normally, it will be as hard or harder to solve (5.10) for μ as it is to solve (5.4) for y. However, in certain interesting special cases (5.10) can be solved easily. The most important of these special cases occur when μ is a function of x only or of y only.

If $\mu = \mu(x)$ is a function of x only, then (5.10) reduces to

$$-\frac{d\mu}{dx}q = \mu(q_x - p_y)$$

or

(5.11) $$\frac{d\mu}{\mu} = \frac{p_y - q_x}{q}dx.$$

If $(p_y - q_x)/q$ is a function of x only, we can solve for μ using separation of variables.

By similar reasoning, if $\mu = \mu(y)$ is a function of y only, then we must have

(5.12) $$\frac{d\mu}{\mu} = \frac{q_x - p_y}{p}dy.$$

If $(q_x - p_y)/p$ depends only on y, we can solve this equation for μ.

EXAMPLE 5.2   Find a general solution of

(5.13) $$(x^2 - y^2) + 2xyy' = 0.$$

This equation is not exact, but

$$\frac{p_y - q_x}{q} = \frac{-2y - 2y}{2xy} = -\frac{2}{x}$$

is independent of y. Hence there is an integrating factor $\mu(x)$. This integrating factor is a solution of (5.11), that is, of the equation $\mu^{-1}\,d\mu = -2x^{-1}\,dx$. Hence $\log|\mu| = -2\log|x| + c$ and $\mu = K/x^2$, where $K = \pm e^c$. Since any integrating factor will do, we shall choose $K = 1$. Multiply (5.13) by μ to obtain

$$\left(1 - \frac{y^2}{x^2}\right) + \left(\frac{2y}{x}\right)y' = 0.$$

When the calculations leading to an integrating factor are done correctly, the resulting differential equation will always be exact. To make sure that no errors have been made, it is best to check that the differential equation obtained is indeed exact. For example, here we must check that

$$\frac{\partial}{\partial y}\left(1 - \frac{y^2}{x^2}\right) = \frac{-2y}{x^2} = \frac{\partial}{\partial x}\left(\frac{2y}{x}\right).$$

This equation is exact. The method of Section 2.4 gives

$$x + \frac{y^2}{x} = c. \quad \blacksquare$$

EXAMPLE 5.3   Find a general solution of

(5.14) $$y + (y^2 - x)y' = 0.$$

The equation is not exact. Since $(p_y - q_x)/q = 2/(y^2 - x)$, there is no integrating factor $\mu(x)$. To test for an integrating factor of the form $\mu(y)$, we compute

$$\frac{q_x - p_y}{p} = -\frac{2}{y}.$$

This expression is independent of x. Hence there is an integrating factor $\mu(y)$. This integrating factor is a solution of

$$\frac{d\mu}{\mu} = -\frac{2}{y}\,dy.$$

Thus $\mu(y) = y^{-2}$ will do. Multiply (5.14) by μ to obtain

$$y^{-1} + \left(1 - \frac{x}{y^2}\right)y' = 0.$$

This equation is exact since $(\partial/\partial y)(y^{-1}) = -y^{-2} = (\partial/\partial x)(1 - x/y^2)$. By the methods of Section 2.4 we find that a general solution is

$$y + \frac{x}{y} = c. \quad \blacksquare$$

SUMMARY: INTEGRATING FACTORS

1. A function $\mu(x, y)$ is an integrating factor for the differential equation $p + qy' = 0$ if the equation $(\mu p) + (\mu q)y' = 0$ is exact (and hence can be solved).
2. If $(p_y - q_x)/q$ is a function of x only, then there is an integrating factor $\mu(x)$. To find μ solve the equation

$$\frac{d\mu}{dx} = \frac{p_y - q_x}{q}\mu,$$

using separation of variables.
3. Similarly, if $(q_x - p_y)/p$ is a function of y only, then there is an integrating factor $\mu(y)$. To find this μ solve

$$\frac{d\mu}{dy} = \frac{q_x - p_y}{p}\mu,$$

using separation of variables.

PROBLEMS

In Problems 1–6, verify that the μ given is an integrating factor for the equation. Using this integrating factor, find a general solution.

1. $xy' - y = 0, \ \mu = \dfrac{2y}{x^3}.$

2. $xy' - y = 0, \ \mu = y^{-2}.$

3. $xy' - y = 0, \ \mu = (xy)^{-1}.$

4. $xy' - y = 0, \ \mu = x^{-2}.$

5. $x^2y^3 + x(1 + y^2)y' = 0, \ \mu = (xy^3)^{-1}.$

6. $N + (2t - Ne^N)\dfrac{dN}{dt} = 0, \ \mu = N.$

In Problems 7–14, solve by finding a suitable integrating factor.

7. $xy' + y = xyy'.$

8. $y - xy = yy'.$

9. $y' = x^2 + 2x - y.$

10. $t\dfrac{dN}{dt} = N - 1.$

11. $y'(xy - y) = 1.$

12. $(3t^2y + 2ty + y^3) + (t^2 + y^2)\dfrac{dy}{dt} = 0.$

13. $y = (ye^y - 2x)y'.$

14. $y' = \left(\sin x - \dfrac{y}{x}\right).$

15. Show that if $R = (q_x - p_y)/(xp - yq)$ is a function of xy only, then the differential equation (5.4) has an integrating factor of the form $\mu(xy)$, where μ solves the equation

$$\frac{d\mu}{ds} = R(s)\mu.$$

Then solve the differential equation $(xy^2 + y) + (x^2y - x)y' = 0$.

16. Show that if $R = (q_x - p_y)/(yp - xq)$ is a function of $(x^2 + y^2)$ only, then the differential equation (5.4) has an integrating factor of the form $\mu(x^2 + y^2)$. Find the formula for this integrating factor.

17. Show that if $S = (q_x - p_y)/(p - q)$ is a function of $(x + y)$ only, then the differential equation (5.4) has an integrating factor of the form $\mu(x + y)$. Find the formula for this integrating factor.

MISCELLANEOUS PROBLEMS

In Problems 18–21, find a general solution.

18. $t\,dz + z^2\,dt = 0$.

19. $x^2y' = 4y^2$.

20. $2t + \sin N + (t \cos N)\dfrac{dN}{dt} = 0$.

21. $\left(2 + \dfrac{\sin t}{N}\right)\dfrac{dN}{dt} + \cos t = 0$.

2.6 *LINEAR EQUATIONS*

An equation of the form

(6.1) $$y' + g(x)y = h(x)$$

is called a **first-order linear differential equation.** It is assumed that g and h are defined and continuous on some interval $J = (A_1, A_2)$. We seek a solution on this interval J. First consider the case where $h(x) = 0$, that is,

(6.2) $$y' + g(x)y = 0.$$

This equation is separable. Hence a general solution is

$$y(x) = ce^{-\int g(x)\,dx} = ce^{-G(x)},$$

where $G(x) = \int g(x)\,dx$ is any integral of $g(x)$ with respect to x.

EXAMPLE 6.1

Solve the initial value problem

$$xy' = (\log x)y, \qquad y(1) = 2.$$

Here we have $g(x) = -\log x/x$. The interval $J = (A_1, A_2)$ can be any interval that contains $x = 1$ and avoids $x = 0$. We shall use $J = (0, \infty)$ since this is the largest possible interval J. $G(x)$ is any integral of $g(x)$, that is,

$$G(x) = \int -\frac{\log x}{x} \, dx.$$

The integration can be done with the help of the substitution $u = \log x$. Then $du = dx/x$ and

$$G(x) = -\int \frac{\log x}{x} \, dx = -\int u \, du$$

$$= -\frac{u^2}{2} = -\frac{(\log x)^2}{2}.$$

Hence a general solution is

$$y = ce^{(\log x)^2/2}.$$

The initial condition $y(1) = 2$ implies that $c = 2$. ∎

When $h(x)$ is not identically zero, then (6.1) is no longer separable. However, it is not too difficult to verify that $e^{G(x)}$ is an integrating factor. This is accomplished as follows. Multiply (6.1) by $e^{G(x)}$ to obtain

(6.3) $$e^{G(x)}y' + e^{G(x)}g(x)y = e^{G(x)}h(x).$$

Since $y = \varphi(x)$, the left-hand side of (6.3) has the form

$$e^{G(x)}y' + e^{G(x)}g(x)y = e^{G(x)}\varphi'(x) + e^{G(x)}g(x)\varphi(x)$$
$$= e^{G(x)}\varphi'(x) + [e^{G(x)}]'\varphi(x)$$
$$= [e^{G(x)}\varphi(x)]'.$$

Hence (6.3) can be written as

(6.4) $$[e^{G(x)}\varphi(x)]' = e^{G(x)}h(x).$$

We integrate both sides of (6.4) to obtain

$$e^{G(x)}\varphi(x) = c + \int e^{G(x)}h(x) \, dx$$

or

(6.5) $$y = \varphi(x) = e^{-G(x)}\left[c + \int e^{G(x)}h(x) \, dx \right].$$

It is not necessary to memorize (6.5). Many students find it easier to remember the method used to derive (6.5) and to apply that method to each linear equation that is encountered.

SOLUTION METHOD: LINEAR EQUATIONS

---

1. Write the equation in the standard form $y' + g(x)y = h(x)$ and then identify $g(x)$.
2. Compute the integrating factor $\mu(x) = \exp\left(\int g(x)\, dx\right)$.
3. Multiply the equation by $\mu(x)$ and rearrange into the exact form

$$\frac{d}{dx}(\mu(x)y) = \mu(x)h(x).$$

Integrate this equation with respect to x and solve the resulting expression for y.

EXAMPLE 6.2   Solve

(6.6) $$y' = 2y + x, \qquad y(0) = 2.$$

First rewrite (6.6) as $y' - 2y = x$. Once the equation is in this form we see that $g(x) = -2$ and $h(x) = x$. The interval J may be chosen as $(-\infty, \infty)$ and $G(x) = -2x$. Multiply (6.6) by e^{-2x} and rearrange to obtain

$$e^{-2x}(y' - 2y) = (e^{-2x}y)' = xe^{-2x}.$$

Integration gives

$$e^{-2x}y = c + \int xe^{-2x}\, dx.$$

The integral on the right can be evaluated using integration by parts. Let $u = x$ and $dv = e^{-2x}\, dx$. Then $v = e^{-2x}/(-2)$ and

$$\int xe^{-2x}\, dx = \frac{xe^{-2x}}{-2} - \int \frac{e^{-2x}}{-2}\, dx$$

$$= -\frac{x}{2}e^{-2x} - \frac{1}{4}e^{-2x}.$$

Hence

$$e^{-2x}y = c - \left(\frac{1}{4} + \frac{x}{2}\right)e^{-2x}$$

and a general solution is

$$y = ce^{2x} - \frac{1}{4} - \frac{x}{2}.$$

Since $y(0) = 2$, then $2 = c - \frac{1}{4} - 0$ or $c = \frac{9}{4}$. The solution of (6.6) is

$$y = \frac{9}{4}e^{2x} - \frac{1}{4} - \frac{x}{2}, \qquad -\infty < x < \infty. \quad \blacksquare$$

A problem may become linear when the roles of x and y are reversed.

EXAMPLE 6 3   Find a general solution of

(6.7)
$$(x + 1)\frac{dy}{dx} = \frac{1}{y}.$$

This equation can be rewritten as

$$(x + 1)y = \frac{dx}{dy}.$$

This equation is linear in x. We see that $g(y) = -y$. Hence an integrating factor is $e^{-y^2/2}$. Multiply by this integrating factor and rearrange as follows:

$$\frac{d}{dy}(e^{-y^2/2}x) = e^{-y^2/2}\left(\frac{dx}{dy} - yx\right) = ye^{-y^2/2}$$

or

$$e^{-y^2/2}x = c + \int ye^{-y^2/2}\,dy.$$

The integral on the right can be evaluated with the help of the substitution $u = y^2/2$. Then $du = y\,dy$ and

$$\int ye^{-y^2/2}\,dy = \int e^{-u}\,du = -e^{-u} = -e^{-y^2/2}.$$

Hence the expression

$$e^{-y^2/2}(x + 1) = c$$

determines y implicitly in terms of x and c. $\blacksquare$

Let us now go back over our solution of (6.7) with a bit more care. We have replaced the differential equation

(6.8)
$$\frac{dy}{dx} = \frac{1}{(x + 1)y}$$

by the differential equation

(6.9)
$$\frac{dx}{dy} = (x + 1)y,$$

and then solved (6.9). We claim that solutions of (6.8) and (6.9) determine the same curves in the (x, y) plane as long as $(x + 1)y \neq 0$. More generally, we claim that solutions of

(6.10)
$$\frac{dy}{dx} = f(x, y)$$

and

(6.11)
$$\frac{dx}{dy} = \frac{1}{f(x, y)}$$

determine the same curves in the (x, y) plane as long as we stay in a rectangle in the (x, y) plane where $f(x, y)$ is *defined* and *continuous* and $1/f(x, y)$ is *defined*, that is, $f(x, y) \neq 0$. This can be seen as follows. Let $y = \varphi(x)$ solve (6.10) on $A_0 < x < A_1$ and suppose that $\varphi'(x) = f(x, \varphi(x))$ is never zero on $A_0 < x < A_1$. Then $\varphi(x)$ is either monotone increasing [if $f(x, \varphi(x)) > 0$] or it is monotone decreasing [if $f(x, \varphi(x)) < 0$]. In either case we know from calculus that the function $y = \varphi(x)$ has an inverse $x = \psi(y)$. Moreover, $dx/dy = 1/\varphi'(x)$, so that $x = \psi(y)$ solves

$$\frac{dx}{dy} = \frac{1}{dy/dx} = \frac{1}{f(x, y)}, \qquad A_0 < x < A_1.$$

Hence solutions of (6.10) and (6.11) determine the same curves.

The linear equation (6.1) has the special property that solutions will always exist over the *entire interval J* where $g(x)$ and $h(x)$ are defined and continuous. In Example 6.1 this interval was $J = (0, \infty)$. The solution

$$y = 2e^{(\log x)^2/2}$$

is indeed defined for all x in J but is not defined on any larger interval. Consider $x = 0$! Similarly, in (6.6) the interval is $J = (-\infty, \infty)$ and the solution that we found was defined for all x in $(-\infty, \infty)$. Because of this special property of linear equations it is usually worthwhile to determine an interval J and to take J as large as possible. For example, in the problem

(6.12)
$$xy' = (\log |x|)y, \qquad y(-2) = 3$$

we have $g(x) = -(\log |x|)/x$ and $h(x) \equiv 0$. We must choose J so that it contains $x = -2$ and avoids the trouble spot $x = 0$. The largest such J is $(-\infty, 0)$. *Without solving* (6.12) we can predict that the solution of (6.12) will exist over the entire interval $-\infty < x < 0$. Similarly, the solution of

$$y' + \frac{1}{1-x} y = \frac{1}{x+3}, \qquad y(0) = 0$$

will exist over the interval $-3 < x < 1$, the solution of

$$y' + \frac{1}{1-x} y = \frac{1}{x+3}, \qquad y(2) = 0$$

will exist over the interval $1 < x < \infty$, and the solution of

$$y' + \frac{1}{1-x} y = \frac{1}{x+3}, \qquad y(-5) = 0$$

will exist over the interval $-\infty < x < -3$.

Equations that are not linear are not as predictable. For example, the solution $y = 1/(1 - x)$ of

$$y' = y^2, \qquad y(0) = 1$$

exists on $-\infty < x < 1$ but is unbounded as $x \to 1^-$. No apparent reason for the problem at $x = 1$ can be found by examining the differential equation.

Linear equations are extremely important in applications. As an example consider heat flow. Heat flow is a complicated phenomenon which normally must be modeled by partial differential equations (see Chapter 11). In certain simple thermal systems a description using linear ordinary differential equations is possible. The crucial simplifying assumptions are that each element in the system is homogeneous and the temperature of each element can be considered constant throughout that element. For example, the temperature of a solid can be considered constant when the solid is small. The temperature of a liquid (or a gas) can be considered constant when the liquid (or the gas) is well stirred.

In such situations the differential equations which describe heat flow follow from the fact that heat added to a body equals heat stored plus heat carried away. Let T denote the temperature of a body, m denote its mass, and c denote its **specific heat.** The **heat energy** stored in the body when its temperature is raised from T_0 to T is

$$E = mc(T - T_0).$$

The constant mc measures the heat energy storage characteristics of the body. Large mass and high specific heat mean a large storage capacity, while small mass or small specific heat mean a smaller capacity. Heat energy flows from an area of high temperature to areas of lower temperature. The rate of heat energy flow from a body at temperature T to a second body at temperature T_1 is assumed to be proportional to the temperature difference of the bodies, that is,

$$\frac{dE}{dt} = \frac{T - T_1}{R}.$$

This assumption is realistic under the simplifying assumptions that we imposed earlier. The constant R is called the **thermal resistance.** High resistance impedes

TABLE 2.1   Thermal Symbols and Units

Symbol	Quantity	English Units	Metric Units
m	Mass	pounds	kilograms
c	Specific heat	Btu/(pound °F)	joules/(kilogram °C)
R	Thermal resistance	degrees/(Btu/minute)	degrees/(joule/second)
T	Temperature	°F	°C
E	Heat energy	Btu	joules
k	Thermal conductance	Btu/(minute °F)	joules/(second °C)

heat flow, while low resistance has the opposite effect. For thermal symbols and units, see Table 2.1.

EXAMPLE 6.4   A thin metal sheet initially at temperature T_0 is insulated on one side. Coolant at temperature T_1 is pumped by on the opposite side. What is the temperature T of the sheet for $t > 0$?

Let m be the mass of the sheet, c the specific heat of the metal, and R the thermal resistance between the coolant and the metal. The heat stored in the sheet between time zero and time t is $E = mc(T(t) - T_0)$, while heat flow between the coolant and the metal is $dE/dt = [T_1 - T(t)]/R$. Hence

$$mc \frac{dT}{dt} = \frac{T_1 - T}{R}, \qquad T(0) = T_0.$$

This is a linear equation of the form

$$\frac{dT}{dt} = -aT + b,$$

where $a = (mcR)^{-1}$ and $b = T_1/(mcR)$. The solution is found to be

$$T(t) = ce^{-t/(mcR)} + T_1.$$

From $T(0) = T_0$ we see that $c = T_0 - T_1$. Hence

$$T(t) = (T_0 - T_1)e^{-t/(mcR)} + T_1.$$

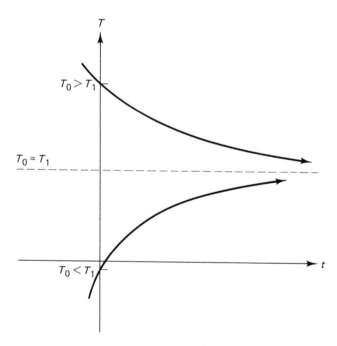

Figure 2.7. Typical solutions of a heat problem.

Some typical solutions are shown in Figure 2.7. Since the term $e^{-t/(mcR)}$ tends to zero monotonically as $t \to \infty$, then $T(t)$ tends monotonically to T_1 as $t \to \infty$. Moreover, $T(t)$ will tend more rapidly to T_1 when mc is small (i.e., the metal does not have a large heat storage capacity) or R is small (i.e., low resistance to heat transfer between the metal and the coolant). All of these mathematical predictions agree with intuition and experience. ∎

PROBLEMS

In Problems 1–10, find a general solution.

1. $y' = \pi y + 4$.

2. $xy' = y + \sqrt{x}, \; 0 < x < \infty$.

3. $y' + x = xy$.

4. $y' + 2xy = e^{-x^2}$.

5. $x(1 + x^2)y' = (1 - 2x^2 y)$.

6. $y = (y^2 - x)y'$.

7. $\dfrac{dx}{dt} + (\cos t)x = \cos^3 t$.

8. $(t^2 + 1)\dfrac{dN}{dt} + 2tN = t^2$.

9. $y' + (\log x)y = 0, \; 0 < x < \infty$.

10. $\cos t \dfrac{dR}{dt} = (\sin t)R + 1, \; -\dfrac{\pi}{2} < t < \dfrac{\pi}{2}$.

In Problems 11–20, solve the initial value problem.

11. $y' + y = 1 + x, \; y(0) = -2$.

12. $y' = 3y + xe^{2x}, \; y(1) = 1$.

13. $\dfrac{dN}{dt} + 3N = \sin t, \; N(0) = 0$.

14. $\dfrac{dy}{dx} + \dfrac{e^x}{1 + x^2} = y, \; y(1) = 0$.

15. $xy' + 3y = \dfrac{e^{-x^2}}{x}, \; y(1) = 0$.

16. $y^2 + 2xyy' = y' \sin y, \; y(1) = 1$.

17. $\dfrac{dz}{dt} + 3z = \cos 2t, \; z(0) = 1$.

18. $y' + \dfrac{y}{x} = \log x, \; y(1) = -1$.

19. $\dfrac{ds}{dx} = (\tan x)s + \sec x \tan x, \; s(0) = -1$.

20. $(\cos x)y' + y = \cos x, \; y(0) = 2$.

21. *Without solving*, find the largest possible interval on which you can be sure that the solution will exist.

   (a) $y' + e^{x^2}y = 1, \; y(0) = -1$.

   (b) $\sqrt{x + 1}\, y' + (\sin x)y = \sec x, \; y(1) = 1$.

   (c) $\sqrt{x + 1}\, y' + (\sin x)y = \sec x, \; y(5/3) = -1$.

   (d) $\sqrt{x + 1}\, y' + (\sin x)y = \sec x, \; y(\pi) = \dfrac{\pi}{2}$.

   (e) $e^{\sqrt{x}}y' + (\log |2 - x|)y = 4, \; y(1) = 2$.

   (f) $e^{\sqrt{x}}y' + (\log |2 - x|)y = 4, \; y(4) = -1$.

   (g) $x\dfrac{dR}{dx} + x^2 R = 1, \; R(-4) = -1$.

(h) $x\dfrac{dR}{dx} + x^2R = 1$, $R(5) = \pi$.

(i) $\log x\dfrac{dy}{dx} + \dfrac{x}{x-5}y = 0$, $y(2) = -1$.

(j) $\log x\dfrac{dy}{dx} + \dfrac{x}{x-5}y = 3$, $y(10) = -10$.

22. Verify that the solution of the initial value problem

$$y' = ay + h(x), \qquad y(\xi) = \eta$$

is

$$y(x) = \eta e^{a(x-\xi)} + \int_{\xi}^{x} e^{a(x-s)}h(s)\,ds.$$

23. Let $y = \varphi(x)$ be the solution of $y' = ay$, $y(0) = c$, where a and c are nonzero constants. Show that

(a) $\lim\limits_{x\to\infty} \varphi(x) = 0$ if $a < 0$.

(b) $\lim\limits_{x\to\infty} \varphi(x) = +\infty$ if $a > 0$ and $c > 0$.

(c) $\lim\limits_{x\to\infty} \varphi(x) = -\infty$ if $a > 0$ and $c < 0$.

24. Compute the limit as $x \to -\infty$ of any solution of $y' = 2y + 3$.

25. Show that there is one and only one number η such that the solution of

$$\frac{dy}{dt} = -y + \sin t, \qquad y(0) = \eta$$

is periodic of period 2π. Find this η.

26. Define

$$h(x) = \begin{cases} 1 & \text{on } 0 \le x < 2 \\ 0 & \text{on } 2 \le x < \infty. \end{cases}$$

Find a continuous function $y = \varphi(x)$ that satisfies the two conditions

$$y' + 3y = h(x) \quad \text{on } 0 < x < 2 \quad \text{and} \quad \text{on } 2 < x < \infty, \quad y(0) = -1.$$

27. (a) Solve the equation $y' = ay + bx$, $y(0) = c (a \neq 0)$.

(b) Compute $\partial y/\partial a$, $\partial y/\partial b$, and $\partial y/\partial c$.

28. In the problem $y' = ay + bx$, $y(0) = c$, suppose we determine experimentally that $a \cong 1.3$, $b \cong -2.1$, and $c \cong 3.4$. We are interested in the value of the solution $y(x)$ when $x = 2$. Is the value $y(2)$ most sensitive to errors in a, in b, or in c? *Hint:* Use Problem 27 and a calculator.

29. A metal rod at temperature 20°C is plunged into a coolant bath held at 90°C. Suppose that the metal has mass $m = 100$ grams and specific heat 394.5 joules per kilogram per °C.

(a) If, after 5 seconds, the temperature of the rod is 50°C, what is the thermal resistance R between the rod and the coolant?

(b) If the temperature of the rod after 5 seconds is $50 \pm 2°C$, how accurately can R be estimated?

30. A copper rod at temperature 150°F is plunged into a coolant bath at 80°F. The metal weighs 0.25 pound and has specific heat 0.094 Btu/(pound °F). If after 3 seconds the temperature of the rod is 95°F, what is the thermal resistance R between the rod and the coolant?

31. Repeat Problem 30 for a 0.25-pound rod of

(a) Iron with $c = 0.11$ Btu/(pound °F).

(b) Lead with $c = 0.031$ Btu/(pound °F).

(c) Aluminum with $c = 0.212$ Btu/(pound °F).

32. A metal rod of mass m_1 and specific heat c_1 is coated with a thin layer of a second material with specific heat c_2. The total mass of the coating is m_2. The rod, initially at temperature T_0, is plunged into a coolant bath held at temperature T_c. Let $T_1(t)$ and $T_2(t)$ be the temperatures of the two materials. Let R_1 be the thermal resistance between the two materials in the rod and R_2 the thermal resistance between the rod and the coolant.

(a) Write two differential equations that describe the heat transfer in this system.

(b) Assuming that m_2 is so small that it can safely be taken to be zero, show that the two differential equations derived in part (a) reduce to a single differential equation for T_1.

(c) Solve the differential equation obtained in part (b). Then compute the limit of $T_1(t)$ as $t \to \infty$.

33. A sheet of metal initially at temperature T_0 separates two coolant baths. The first bath is held at temperature T_1 and the second at T_2.

(a) Find a differential equation that describes this thermal system.

(b) Solve this equation assuming that $T_1 \le T_2$. Find the limit as $t \to \infty$ of the temperature of the metal.

34. The point kinetics model for a single-core nuclear reactor was discussed in Section 1.2. If a reactor that has been operating at a fixed power level $P_0 > 0$ experiences some difficulty (e.g., loss of coolant), then the reactor must be quickly shut down. This is accompliished by rapid insertion of the safety rods. Under such conditions delayed neutron effects can be ignored and the model reduces to the differential equation

$$\frac{l}{\beta} \frac{dP}{dt} = [k(t) - 1]P + \frac{l}{\beta} P_0,$$

where

$$k(t) = \begin{cases} -\gamma t & \text{on } 0 \le t \le T \\ -\gamma T & \text{on } t \ge T. \end{cases}$$

Here P is the reactor power, l and β are positive constants, γ is the speed of descent of the safety rods, and T is the time necessary for complete insertion of the safety rods.

(a) Solve for $P(t)$ on $0 \le t \le T$. What initial value do you use?

(b) Show that $\int_0^T P(t)\, dt$, the total power produced during the emergency shut down, is proportional to the preemergency power level P_0.

35. Let y solve $y' + ay = f(x)$, $y(0) = q_0$, where $a > 0$ and f is a continuous function that tends to zero as $x \to \infty$. Show that $y(x)$ tends to zero as $x \to \infty$. (Hard!)

MISCELLANEOUS PROBLEMS   In Problems 36–41, find a general solution.

36. $(e^y - x)y' = 1$.

37. $\dfrac{dz}{dt} = z + \sin t - 2 \cos t$.

38. $y' + xy = y$.

39. $xyy' = y^2 + x\sqrt{y^2 - x^2}$, $x > 0$.

40. $\dfrac{1}{1 + (x + y^2)^2} + \dfrac{2yy'}{1 + (x + y^2)^2} = 1$.

41. $\left(x + \cos\left(\dfrac{y}{x}\right)\right)xy' - y\cos\left(\dfrac{y}{x}\right) = 0$.

2.7 THE METHOD OF SUBSTITUTION

The method of *substitution*, also called the method of *changing variables*, can be used to change many ordinary differential equations into a form that can be solved. This method was introduced in Section 2.3. where homogeneous equations were studied. There we saw that the substitution $v = y/x$ will always reduce the given homogeneous equation to a new equation which is separable.

For a general nonlinear equation there is no way to predict what type of substitution may prove useful. Finding useful substitutions is an art that must be learned by doing. Hence we shall illustrate this technique by some examples.

The **Bernoulli equation** has the form

$$(7.1) \qquad\qquad y' = f(x)y + g(x)y^r,$$

where r is a real number. If $r = 0$ or $r = 1$, then this equation is linear in y and no substitution is needed. If $r \neq 0$ and $r \neq 1$, we set $w = y^{1-r}$, so that $y = w^{1/(1-r)}$. Hence (7.1), in terms of the new variable w, is

$$y' = \frac{1}{1 - r} w^{r/(1-r)} w' = f(x)w^{1/(1-r)} + g(x)w^{r/(1-r)}$$

or

$$(7.2) \qquad\qquad w' = (1 - r)f(x)w + (1 - r)g(x).$$

Note that (7.2) is linear in w. Hence it can be solved by the method of Section 2.6.

EXAMPLE 7.1   Solve

$$(7.3) \qquad\qquad xy' = y + e^x y^3, \qquad 0 < x < \infty.$$

This equation has the form of (7.1) with $r = 3$, $f(x) = x^{-1}$, and $g(x) = x^{-1}e^x$. Let $w = y^{-2}$ so that $y = w^{-1/2}$. Then $y' = (-1/2)w^{-3/2}w'$ and (7.3), written in terms of w, is

$$x(-\tfrac{1}{2}w^{-3/2}w') = w^{-1/2} + e^x w^{-3/2}$$

or

$$-\frac{x}{2}w' = w + e^x.$$

Thus we find that w must solve the linear equation

(7.4) $$w' + \frac{2}{x}w = -\frac{2}{x}e^x.$$

An integrating factor for this equation in $\mu(x) = x^2$. The solution of (7.4) is

$$w = cx^{-2} - 2x^{-2}\int xe^x \, dx,$$
$$= cx^{-2} - 2x^{-2}(xe^x - e^x),$$
$$= cx^{-2} - 2x^{-1}e^x + 2x^{-2}e^x.$$

Since $y = w^{-1/2}$, the solution of (7.3) is

$$y = (cx^{-2} - 2x^{-1}e^x + 2x^{-2}e^x)^{-1/2},$$

where c is an arbitrary constant. ∎

In this example notice that y and w are both functions of x, that is, $y(x)$ and $w(x)$. The notation y and w for $y(x)$ and $w(x)$ is simply a convenient shorthand. Hence when we differentiate $y = w^{-1/2}$ we get

$$y' = \frac{d}{dx}y(x) = -\frac{1}{2}w(x)^{-3/2}\frac{d}{dx}w(x) = -\frac{1}{2}w^{-3/2}w'.$$

This must always be kept in mind when a change of variables is used. Also notice that we need both the substitution $w = y^{-2}$ and its inverse $y = w^{-1/2}$. We derive (7.4) by first expressing the original equation (7.3) in terms of the new variable w and then simplifying. In problems that involve substitution we recommend that the student proceed systematically in order to avoid possible confusion. First write down the substitution. Next find the inverse substitution. Use these two formulas to express the given equation in terms of the new variables. Then simplify as much as possible to obtain the new differential equation. Next, solve the new equation. Finally, use the solution of the equation and the substitution to obtain the solution of the original differential equation.

In some equations it is necessary to change both the dependent variable y and the independent variable x. For example, any equation of the form

(7.5) $$\frac{dy}{dx} = f\left(\frac{ax + by + c}{dx + ey + g}\right),$$

with $ae \neq bd$, can be solved by means of the substitution $x = t - \alpha$, $y = w - \beta$. The constants α and β must be chosen so that the equation which results from this substitution is homogeneous. The inverse substitution is $t = x + \alpha$, $w = y + \beta$. Notice that

$$\frac{dy}{dx} = \frac{d}{dx}(w - \beta) = \frac{dw}{dx} = \frac{dw}{dt}\frac{dt}{dx} = \frac{dw}{dt}1 = \frac{dw}{dt}.$$

Moreover,

$$ax + by + c = a(t - \alpha) + b(w - \beta) + c,$$
$$= (at + bw) + (c - a\alpha - b\beta)$$

and

$$dx + ey + g = (dt + ew) + (g - d\alpha - e\beta).$$

We require that α and β be picked so that

(7.6) $c - a\alpha - b\beta = 0, \qquad g - d\alpha - e\beta = 0.$

Since (7.6) is a system of two linear equations for the two unknowns α and β and since $ae \neq bd$, then (7.6) has one and only one solution. If (7.6) is true, then (7.5), expressed in terms of the new variables w and t, is

$$\frac{dw}{dt} = f\left(\frac{at + bw}{dt + ew}\right).$$

This equation is homogeneous in w and t.

EXAMPLE 7.2   Solve the initial value problem

(7.7) $$\frac{dy}{dx} = \frac{4x - 3y + 13}{x - y + 3}, \qquad y(0) = 1.$$

The substitution is $x = t - \alpha$, $y = w - \beta$, where α and β are chosen to solve

$$4\alpha - 3\beta = 13, \qquad \alpha - \beta = 3.$$

This system of algebraic equations has solution $\alpha = 4$, $\beta = 1$. Hence we use $x = t - 4$, $y = w - 1$. The inverse substitution is $t = x + 4$, $w = y + 1$ and the new problem is seen to be

(7.8) $$\frac{dw}{dt} = \frac{4t - 3w}{t - w}, \qquad w(4) = 2.$$

Since (7.8) is homogeneous in t and w, we now use a second change of variables $v = w/t$ and proceed to solve (7.8). The solution is given implicitly by the equation

$$\frac{1}{v - 2} = \log |(v - 2)tc|.$$

Thus

$$\frac{t}{w - 2t} = \log |(w - 2t)c|$$

and

$$\frac{x + 4}{y - 2x - 7} = \log |c(y - 2x - 7)|.$$

At $x = 0$ we require that $y = 1$. Thus $c = \frac{1}{6}e^{-2/3} = 0.0855695\ldots$. ∎

Consider now an initial value problem for a *system* of two differential equations of the form

(7.9) $$\frac{dx}{dt} = h(x, y), \qquad \frac{dy}{dt} = g(x, y),$$

with $y(0) = y_0$ and $x(0) = x_0$. Since g and h do not depend on t, it is possible to write (7.9) as a single first-order differential equation. This is done as follows:

$$\frac{dy}{dx} = \frac{dy}{dt}\frac{dt}{dx} = \frac{dy}{dt}\bigg/\frac{dx}{dt} = \frac{g(x, y)}{h(x, y)}$$

or

(7.10) $$\frac{dy}{dx} = \frac{g(x, y)}{h(x, y)}, \qquad y(x_0) = y_0.$$

The process of going from (7.9) to (7.10) is really a change of variables. If $x = \varphi_1(t)$ and $y = \varphi_2(t)$ is the solution of (7.9) on $t_1 < t < t_2$ and if $h(\varphi_1(t), \varphi_2(t)) \neq 0$ on this interval, then $x = \varphi_1(t)$ is a monotone increasing function [if $h(\varphi_1(t), \varphi_2(t)) > 0$] or a monotone decreasing function [if $h(\varphi_1(t), \varphi_2(t)) < 0$]. The inverse function $t = \psi(x)$ exists and it has derivative

$$\frac{dt}{dx} = \psi'(x) = \frac{1}{d\varphi_1'(t)/dt} = \frac{1}{h(\varphi_1(t), \varphi_2(t))}.$$

Hence (7.9) and (7.10) have the same solution curves in any region of the (x, y) plane where $h(x, y) \neq 0$. If h may be 0 but $g(x, y) \neq 0$ in a given region, then instead of (7.10) one can use the equation

(7.11) $$\frac{dx}{dy} = \frac{h(x, y)}{g(x, y)}, \qquad x(y_0) = x_0.$$

If both $h(x, y) \neq 0$ and $g(x, y) \neq 0$, then (7.9)–(7.11) determine the same curves in the (x, y) plane. If there is a point (x_0, y_0) where both $h(x_0, y_0) = 0$ and $g(x_0, y_0) = 0$, then $\varphi_1(t) \equiv x_0$ and $\varphi_2(t) \equiv y_0$ is a **constant solution** or **equilibrium point** of (7.9). Constant solutions of (7.9) must be found separately since neither (7.10) or (7.11) can be used at such points.

EXAMPLE 7.3   We consider a model for population growth of two species, one of which is a predator and the second its prey. Assume uniformly distributed and homogeneous populations. Let x be the concentration of the prey and y be the concentration of the predator. Following Lotka and Volterra, x and y are assumed to satisfy the following system of differential equations:

$$(7.12) \qquad \frac{dx}{dt} = x(a - by), \qquad \frac{dy}{dt} = y(-c + fx).$$

Here a, b, c, and f are given positive constants. To find a particular solution we must specify two initial conditions, namely

$$(7.13) \qquad x(t_0) = x_0, \qquad y(t_0) = y_0.$$

System (7.12) is called the **Lotka–Volterra predator–prey model.**

The analysis of (7.12) must be accomplished in several steps. First assume that $y_0 = 0$. Then the constant solution $y(t) \equiv 0$ certainly satisfies the second equation, that is,

$$0 = \frac{dy}{dt} = y(t)[-c + fx(t)] = 0 \cdot [-c + fx(t)].$$

Since $y(t) \equiv 0$, the first equation in (7.12) reduces to $dx/dt = ax$, so that $x(t) = ke^{at}$ for some constant k. The first equation in (7.13) implies that

$$x(t_0) = x_0 = ke^{at_0}.$$

Thus $k = x_0 e^{-at_0}$ and

$$x(t) = ke^{at} = (x_0 e^{-at_0})e^{at} = x_0 e^{a(t - t_0)}.$$

We see that in the absence of the predator the prey population will increase indefinitely at the natural growth rate a.

On the other hand, if $x_0 = 0$ while $y_0 \geq 0$, then $x(t) \equiv 0$ satisfies the first equation in (7.12), while the second equation reduces to $dy/dt = -cy$. Hence $y(t) = y_0 e^{-c(t - t_0)}$. The model predicts that in the absence of prey, the predator will die out as time goes by.

Next we check for constant solutions, that is, solutions of the form $x(t) \equiv A$ and $y(t) \equiv B$. On substitution into (7.12) we find that

$$0 = A(a - bB), \qquad 0 = B(-c + fA).$$

There are two solutions, namely $A = B = 0$ or else $A = c/f$, $B = a/b$. The first solution point $0 = (0, 0)$ is the uninteresting case where both predator and prey populations start and remain at zero. The second solution represents positive equilibrium populations for both predator and prey which are represented by the point $E = (c/f, a/b)$ in the (x, y) plane.

The two constant solutions 0 and E and the solutions determined when $x_0 = 0$ or $y_0 = 0$ are graphed in Figure 2.8. Having disposed of the easy part of the analysis, we now consider (7.12) in general. We pick a point $P_0 = (x_0, y_0)$ with $x_0 \neq 0$, $y_0 \neq 0$, and $P_0 \neq E$. Since negative populations are not possible, we choose $x_0 > 0$ and $y_0 > 0$. In the first equation the term ax represents the

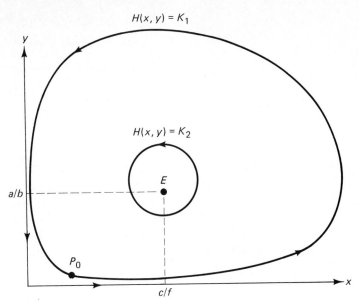

Figure 2.8. Preditor-prey model with $0 < K_1 < K_2$.

natural growth rate of species x, while the negative term $-bxy$ represents the decrease in population growth rate due to the actions of the predator. In the second equation $-cy$ represents the natural death rate of the predator, while the positive term fxy represents the beneficial effect of the prey on the predator population. We wish to reduce (7.12) to a single first-order differential equation by replacing the time variable t by x; that is, we consider

$$(7.14) \qquad \frac{dy}{dx} = \frac{y(-c + fx)}{x(a - by)}, \qquad y(x_0) = y_0,$$

or if we replace t by y, then

$$(7.15) \qquad \frac{dx}{dy} = \frac{x(a - by)}{y(-c + fx)}, \qquad x(y_0) = x_0.$$

Both (7.14) and (7.15) are separable. In either case we get

$$\frac{a - by}{y}\, dy = \frac{-c + fx}{x}\, dx,$$

$$\left(\frac{a}{y} - b \right) dy = \left(-\frac{c}{x} + f \right) dx,$$

and

$$(7.16) \qquad a \log |y| - by = -c \log |x| + fx + K,$$

where K is an arbitrary constant. Since x and y will be positive (negative populations are not of interest), then $|y| = y$ and $|x| = x$. Hence (7.16) can be simplified as follows:

$$a \log y - by = -c \log x + fx + K,$$

$$\log y^a - by = -\log x^c + fx + K,$$

$$\log y^a + \log x^c = by + fx + K,$$

$$\log (y^a x^c) = (by + fx) + K,$$

$$y^a x^c = e^{by + fx} e^K,$$

and finally

(7.17) $$y^a x^c e^{-(by + fx)} = K_1, \qquad K_1 = e^K > 0.$$

This is a solution when $x(a - by) \neq 0$ and also when $y(-c + fx) \neq 0$, that is, exactly the region where a solution was needed.

At first (7.17) does not seem to be a very satisfactory answer since it only determines solutions implicity. However, we shall see that (7.17) will yield some very interesting information about solutions of (7.12). Define

$$H(x, y) = y^a x^c e^{-(by + fx)} \qquad \text{for } x, y > 0.$$

According to (7.17), $H(x, y)$ is a constant of the motion (7.14) or (7.15) and hence is a constant of the motion (7.12). Clearly, H is a positive function in the region $D = \{(x, y): x > 0 \text{ and } y > 0\}$. Moreover, $H(x, y) = 0$ on the boundary of the region D. By this we mean that

$$h(x, 0) = 0, \qquad h(0, y) = 0,$$

$$\lim_{x \to \infty} h(x, y) = y^a e^{-by} \left[\lim_{x \to \infty} x^c e^{-fx} \right] = 0,$$

and

$$\lim_{y \to \infty} h(x, y) = x^c e^{-fx} \left[\lim_{y \to \infty} y^a e^{-by} \right] = 0,$$

for all $x > 0$ and for all $y > 0$. Hence $H(x, y)$ has a maximum value somewhere in the region D. To find this maximum, set $\partial H / \partial x = 0$ and $\partial H / \partial y = 0$, that is,

$$\frac{\partial H}{\partial x} (x, y) = cy^a x^{c-1} e^{-(by + fx)} + y^a x^c (-f) e^{-(by + fx)}$$

$$= \left(\frac{c}{x} - f \right) H(x, y) = 0$$

and

$$\frac{\partial H}{\partial y} (x, y) = ay^{a-1} x^c e^{-(by + fx)} + y^a x^c (-b) e^{-(by + fx)}$$

$$= \left(\frac{a}{y} - b \right) H(x, y) = 0.$$

This pair of equations is satisfied if and only if $x = c/f$ and $y = a/b$, that is, only at the equilibrium $E = (c/f, a/b)$. Since there are no other solutions to

$H_x = H_y = 0$, then H has no relative minima, no saddle points, and exactly one relative maximum (at E). The value of $H(x, y)$ is near zero when (x, y) is near the boundary of D and it grows to some maximum value K_m as (x, y) approaches the point E. If K_1 is a constant between zero and K_m, then (7.17) determines a simple closed curve containing the point E in its interior (see Figure 2.8). A solution $(x(t), y(t))$ of (7.12) which starts at a point $P_0 = (x_0, y_0)$ on the curve $H(x, y) = K_1$ will move around this curve in a counterclockwise direction. Indeed, from (7.12) we see that $x(t)$ will be increasing when $a - by(t) > 0$ and decreasing when $a - by(t) < 0$, while $y(t)$ will be increasing when $-c + fx(t) > 0$ and decreasing when $-c + fx(t) < 0$. The only way a solution can do this and remain on the curve $H(x, y) = K_1$, is a counterclockwise movement along the curve.

Consider the point $P_0 = (x_0, y_0)$ marked in Figure 2.8. This point is in the region $D_1 = \{(x, y):0 < x < c/f \text{ and } 0 < y < a/b\}$, where $x(t)$ is increasing and $y(t)$ decreasing. The prey population x is relatively small and the predator population y is also relatively small. With increasing time $x(t)$ will increase significantly while $y(t)$ will hardly change at all. As time goes by x and y will move along the curve until $y(t)$ finally begins to grow (in response to the plentiful prey). With further passage of time the predator population will become so plentiful that the prey population stops growing and begins to shrink. The predators eat themselves out of house and home as the prey population becomes small while the predator population is large. Then come hard times for the predator and the population shrinks until both x and y are small. At this point the prey population will begin to grow and we will be back at the starting point P_0, where the whole cycle will repeat.

When P_0 is close to E, then K_1 will be close to the maximum value K_m and the equation $H(x, y) = K_1$ determines a small curve encircling the point E. In this case the solution $x(t)$ will oscillate about the value c/f but will never stray too far away from c/f, while $y(t)$ will do small oscillations above and below a/b. When P_0 is farther away from E the oscillations in the two populations become more extreme. When P_0 is close to the x-axis, both populations will undergo extreme oscillations between nearly zero values and very large values. ■

Notice how much information has been obtained concerning solutions of (7.12) even though we never obtained explicit solutions to (7.12), (7.14), or (7.15)!

PROBLEMS

In Problems 1–6, find a general solution of the Bernoulli equation.

1. $y' + y = xy^3$.

2. $y^3 \dfrac{dy}{dx} + \dfrac{y^4}{x} = \dfrac{\cos x}{x^4}$.

3. $y' + xy = xy^3$.

4. $z^5 \dfrac{dz}{ds} = z^6 + e^s$.

5. $\dfrac{dR}{dt} - R = R^5$.

6. $xy' + 2y + (\sin x)y^{1/2} = 0$.

In Problems 7–10, reduce to a homogeneous equation and solve. Find a general solution in each case.

7. $y' = \dfrac{x - y + 5}{x + y - 1}.$

8. $y' = \dfrac{x + y + 3}{x - y + 3}.$

9. $\dfrac{dy}{dx} + \left(\dfrac{x + y + 3}{x + 1}\right)^2 = \dfrac{x + y + 3}{x + 1}.$

10. $\dfrac{dR}{dt} + \dfrac{4t + 3R + 11}{2t + R + 5} = 0.$

11. Solve $y' = \dfrac{3y + x + 5}{x - y - 1}, \; y(0) = 2.$

12. Solve $xy' = xy^2 \log x - y, \; y(1) = 1.$

13. Find a substitution under which the equation

$$y' = f(ax + by + c), \qquad b \neq 0$$

reduces to a separable equation.

Use Problem 13 to solve Problems 14 and 15.

14. $y' + \cos^2(x + y + 1) = 0.$

15. $y' = (x + 2y + 1)^2.$

16. Show that under the transformation $y = w'/(wg(x))$ the Riccati equation

$$\frac{dy}{dx} + f(x)y + g(x)y^2 = h(x)$$

reduces to the second-order linear equation

$$g(x)w'' - (g'(x) - f(x)g(x))w' - h(x)g(x)^2 w = 0.$$

17. Suppose that a population $P(t)$ lives in an environment with a seasonally varying ability to support life. Suppose the population varies according to the equation

$$\frac{dP}{dt} = +P\left(3 - \frac{\sin t}{2 + \cos t} - P\right), \qquad P(0) = P_0.$$

(a) Solve for $P(t)$.

(b) If a computer is available, compute and graph the solution $P(t)$ over $0 \le t \le 6$ when $P_0 = 3$, when $P_0 = 1$, and when $P_0 = 5$.

18. Suppose that two species, competing for the same resource, have populations x and y such that

$$(7.18) \qquad\qquad \frac{dx}{dt} = x(a - by), \qquad \frac{dy}{dt} = y(c - fx),$$

where a, b, c, and f are positive constants and suppose that

$$x(t_0) = x_0 \ge 0, \qquad y(t_0) = y_0 \ge 0.$$

(a) Solve when $x_0 = 0$ and $y_0 > 0$.

(b) Solve when $x_0 > 0$ and $y_0 = 0$.

(c) Find all constant solutions.

(d) Show that no solution determines a closed curve in the (x, y) plane. Hence no oscillations are possible. *Hint:* First find a constant of the motion.

(e) Let $D_1 = \{(x, y): 0 < x < c/f, \ 0 < y < a/b\}$. Show that as long as a solution $(x(t), y(t))$ remains in D_1, then both $x(t)$ and $y(t)$ must grow.

(f) Let $D_2 = \{(x, y): x > c/f \text{ and } y > a/b\}$. Show that as long as a solution remains in D_2, both $x(t)$ and $y(t)$ must decrease.

(g) What do $x(t)$ and $y(t)$ do in the regions $D_3 = \{(x, y): 0 < x < c/f \text{ and } y > a/b\}$ and $D_4 = \{(x, y): x > c/f \text{ and } 0 < y < a/b\}$?

(h) Draw a graph of several solutions (as in Figure 2.8).

19. (a) Show that if $x = \varphi_1(t)$ and $y = \varphi_2(t)$ is a solution of (7.12) and (7.13), then $x = \varphi_1(t + t_0)$, $y = \varphi_2(t + t_0)$ solve

$$(7.19) \quad \frac{dx}{dt} = x(a - by), \qquad \frac{dy}{dt} = y(-c + dx), \qquad x(0) = x_0, \qquad y(0) = y_0.$$

(b) Show that (7.12), (7.13), and (7.19) determine the same curve in the (x, y) plane.

(c) Show that two different solution curves of (7.12) in the (x, y) plane cannot intersect.

(d) Show that if $x_0 > 0$ and $y_0 > 0$, then the solutions of (7.12)–(7.13) satisfy $x(t) > 0$ and $y(t) > 0$ for all $t \geq t_0$.

20. (a) Use L′ Hospital's rule to prove that

$$\lim_{y \to \infty} y^a e^{-by} = 0$$

whenever $b > 0$ and a is a positive integer.

(b) Show that for any $a > 0$ and $b > 0$,

$$\lim_{y \to \infty} y^a e^{-by} = 0.$$

(c) Show that for any $c > 0$ and $f > 0$,

$$\lim_{x \to \infty} x^c e^{-fx} = 0.$$

21. Let $(x(t), y(t))$ be a solution of (7.18) on $t_0 \leq t \leq t_1$.

(a) Show that there is a continuous function $f(t)$ such that

$$(7.20) \qquad \qquad \frac{dx}{dt} = f(t)x.$$

(b) Using (7.20) show that if $x(t_0) = x_0 > 0$, then $x(t)$ is positive over the entire interval $t_0 \leq t \leq t_1$.

(c) Show that if $y(t_0) = y_0 > 0$, then $y(t)$ is positive over the entire interval $t_0 \leq t \leq t_1$.

22. Suppose that two insect populations x and y vary according to (7.12). Suppose the prey insect is an agricultural nuisance. Suppose one application of an insecticide will kill 99% of the nuisance insect but only 40% of the predator. What will happen to these populations after the application?

23. Suppose that two populations, when unhampered by man, vary according to (7.12). Now suppose that man continually harvests the prey species at the rate kx, where $0 < k < a$.

(a) Find all equilibrium solutions.

(b) Find a constant of the motion. Discuss the behavior of solutions. Tell how man's intervention has altered the behavior of the populations.

(c) If $k \geq a$, what will happen to the prey population?

2.8 SOME APPLICATIONS TO MECHANICS

The study of forces and the motions they produce is called **kinetics.** The fundamental laws of motion were formulated by Sir Isaac Newton. The most important of these laws is the following:

NEWTON'S SECOND LAW OF MOTION

If the sum of the forces acting on a body is not zero, the body will be accelerated in the direction of the net force. The magnitude of the net force is equal to the time rate of change of momentum.

We shall consider only rigid bodies of fixed mass. Since we shall consider only the translational motion of the center of mass of the bodies, we may assume that the bodies are point masses.

The **momentum** of a body with mass m and velocity v is mv. Since we assume that m is constant, then in our case $d(mv)/dt = m\, dv/dt$. The term $a = dv/dt$ is defined as the **acceleration** of the body. Under our assumptions Newton's second law states that

$$(8.1) \qquad\qquad ma = F,$$

where F is the component of the net applied force in the direction of the motion. Equation (8.1) must be expressed in a consistent set of units. In MKS units time is in seconds, distance is in meters, mass is in kilograms, and force is in newtons. In the English systems of units time is in seconds, distance is in feet, mass is in slugs, and force is in pounds. A table of symbols and units can be found in Section 3.12. (In English units one often encounters expressions such as a "2-pound mass." What is meant is a mass that weighs 2 pounds under the influence of standard gravity.)

Near the earth's surface the acceleration due to gravitation is nearly constant. Hence the gravitational force on a body of mass m near the earth's surface is directed downward and has a magnitude mg. The constant g, in MKS units, is approximately 9.8 meters per second^2 and in English units is approximately 32.2 feet per second^2. In particular, consider a body of mass m falling from a given height. If we neglect air resistance, the only force acting on the body is the gravitational force. In this case (8.1) takes the form

$$(8.2) \qquad\qquad ma = -mg.$$

If we take y to be the height of the body above the earth's surface, then $v = dy/dt$ is the body's velocity and $a = dv/dt = d^2y/dt^2$ is its acceleration.

EXAMPLE 8.1   A mass is dropped from rest from a height of 15 meters above ground level. Neglecting air friction, how soon will the mass hit the ground? What is its velocity on impact?

We assume that the mass is dropped at time $t = 0$. If y is its height above ground level, then $v = dy/dt$ is its velocity and according to (8.2) we have

$$m\frac{dv}{dt} = -gm, \qquad v(0) = 0, \qquad g = 9.8.$$

This equation can be solved for $v(t) = -gt$. Since $v = dy/dt$ and since $y(0) = 15$, then

$$y(t) = 15 - \frac{gt^2}{2}.$$

At impact $y = 0$. When $y = 0$ we see that t must equal $t^* = \sqrt{30/g} \cong 1.75$ seconds. Thus the impact time is t^* and the impact velocity is $v(t^*) = -g\sqrt{30/g} \cong 17.1$ meters per second.   ■

Air friction is a complex phenomena that can be accounted for in a variety of ways. The simplest way is to assume that air friction exerts a force on the mass proportional to the velocity of the mass. (This type of friction is called **viscous friction.**) Thus in (8.1) we have

(8.3) $$m\frac{dv}{dt} = -gm - kv,$$

where k is a positive constant called the **coefficient of air friction.**

EXAMPLE 8.2   A 2-slug mass is dropped from an airplane with initial downward velocity zero. Find $v(t)$ for $t \geq 0$ when the coefficient of air friction is $k = 0.1$ pound per (foot per second).

In (8.3) put $m = 2$, $g = 32.2$, and $k = 0.1$. The resulting equation for v is

$$\frac{dv}{dt} + \frac{k}{m}v = -g, \qquad v(0) = 0$$

or

(8.4) $$\frac{dv}{dt} + 0.05v = -32.2, \qquad v(0) = 0.$$

This equation is linear in v. (It is also separable.) The solution is

$$v(t) = -644 + ce^{-0.05t}.$$

Since $v(0) = -644 + c = 0$, then $c = 644$ and

$$v(t) = 644(e^{-0.05t} - 1).$$

Notice that $e^{-0.05t}$ is decreasing and goes to zero as $t \to \infty$. Hence, for large values of t, $v(t)$ is nearly equal to the constant -644. This constant is called the **terminal velocity** of the body. It can be shown that any falling body whose motion is described by (8.3) has a terminal velocity (see problem 10). ∎

Photo 8. Sky diving—terminal velocity. (Courtesy of Hashem H-Toroghi.)

Consider the mass–spring system depicted in Figure 2.9. Let y be the horizontal displacement of the mass M, as measured from its rest position, with positive y to the right. When the spring is compressed or extended it will exert a restoring force on the mass. We assume that the spring obeys **Hooke's law.** This means that the force exerted by the spring is proportional to the displacement y. Hence $F = -Ky$, where $K > 0$. The constant K is called the **stiffness coefficient** for the spring. If frictional forces are neglected, then according to Newton's second law the equation of motion for the mass–spring system is

(8.5) $$Ma = -Ky.$$

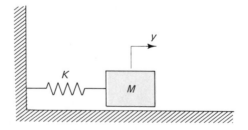

Figure 2.9. Mass-spring system.

Since $a = dv/dt$ and $v = dy/dt$, then (8.5) can be written as a system of two differential equations

(8.6)
$$\frac{dy}{dt} = v, \qquad M\frac{dv}{dt} = -Ky$$

or, equivalently, as a second-order differential equation

(8.7)
$$M\frac{d^2y}{dt^2} = -Ky.$$

To specify one and only one solution of (8.6) or of (8.7), the initial position x_0 and velocity v_0 must be given.

It is more convenient to solve (8.6) rather than (8.7). Following the methods of Section 2.7, we replace the independent variable t in (8.6) by y. Thus

$$M\frac{dv}{dy} = \left(M\frac{dv}{dt}\right)\frac{dt}{dy} = (-Ky)\frac{1}{v}$$

or

$$M\frac{dv}{dy} = -K\frac{y}{v}.$$

Since this equation is separable, we can solve it to obtain the constant of motion

(8.8)
$$M\frac{v^2}{2} + K\frac{y^2}{2} = c.$$

Clearly, $c \geq 0$. Notice that $Mv^2/2$ is the **kinetic energy** of the mass when its velocity is v. Moreover, $Ky^2/2$ is the **potential energy** stored in the spring when it is displaced the amount y from equilibrium. Hence (8.8) is the statement that along any solution of (8.6) or (8.7), *the total energy in the system remains constant.* If $c = 0$, then $y = v = 0$. In this case y remains at the rest position and v remains at zero. If $c > 0$, we can write (8.8) as

$$\frac{dy}{dt} = +\sqrt{\frac{2c}{M} - \frac{Ky^2}{M}} \quad \text{or} \quad \frac{dy}{dt} = -\sqrt{\frac{2c}{M} - \frac{Ky^2}{M}}.$$

To solve either equation we separate variables and obtain

$$\left(\frac{2c}{M} - \frac{K}{M}y^2\right)^{-1/2} dy = \pm\, dt$$

or

$$\left(\frac{2c}{K} - y^2\right)^{-1/2} dy = \pm\sqrt{\frac{K}{M}}\, dt.$$

Hence

$$\arcsin\left(\frac{y}{\sqrt{2c/K}}\right) = \pm\left(\sqrt{\frac{K}{M}}\, t + d\right)$$

or

(8.9)
$$y = \pm\sqrt{\frac{2c}{K}}\sin\left(\sqrt{\frac{K}{M}}t + d\right),$$

where $\pm\sqrt{c}$ and d are arbitrary constants. From (8.9) we see that solutions of (8.6) forever oscillate back and forth about the equilibrium position. Since the sine function is 2π-periodic, then $\sin(x + 2\pi) = \sin x$ for all x. Thus these oscillations are periodic with period T, where $\sqrt{K/M}\, T = 2\pi$, that is, $T = 2\pi\sqrt{M/K}$.

EXAMPLE 8.3   Suppose that in Figure 2.9 $M = 2$ kilograms and $K = 3$ newtons per meter. If the spring is stretched 20 centimeters to the right and then released (from rest), find the resulting motion.

The initial value problem that must be solved is

$$\frac{dy}{dt} = v, \qquad 2\frac{dv}{dt} = -3y, \qquad y(0) = 0.2, \qquad v(0) = 0.$$

From $2(dv/dy) = -3y/v$ we find that

$$v^2 + \tfrac{3}{2}y^2 = c.$$

Hence

$$\frac{dy}{dt} = \pm\sqrt{c - \frac{3}{2}y^2} = \pm\sqrt{\frac{3}{2}}\sqrt{\frac{2c}{3} - y^2}.$$

Applying separation of variables, it follows that

$$y = \pm\sqrt{\frac{2c}{3}}\sin\left(\sqrt{\frac{3}{2}}t + d\right) = c_1\sin\left(\sqrt{\frac{3}{2}}t + d\right),$$

where $c_1 = \pm\sqrt{2c/3}$ is an arbitrary constant. Since $y(0) = 0.2$ and $y'(0) = 0$, then

$$y(0) = c_1\sin d = 0.2, \qquad y'(0) = c_1\sqrt{\frac{3}{2}}\cos d = 0.$$

Hence we need $\cos d = 0$ or $d = \pi/2 + n\pi$ for any integer n. For simplicity we choose $n = 0$ so that $d = \pi/2$. We also need $c_1\sin d = c_1\sin(\pi/2) = 0.2$ or $c_1 = 0.2$. The solution is

$$y(t) = 0.2\sin\left(\sqrt{\frac{3}{2}}t + \frac{\pi}{2}\right).$$

We see that the solution y oscillates between $+0.2$ and -0.2 in a periodic manner. The period of this solution is $2\pi\sqrt{2/3} \cong 5.13$.   ∎

PROBLEMS

1. A lead block that weighs 3 pounds is set in motion in a straight line over smooth ice on a frozen lake. The initial velocity is 10 feet per second. The coefficient of viscous friction between the block and the ice is 0.02 pound per (foot per second). How far will the block travel? *Hint:* $m = 3/32.2$ slugs.

2. A $\frac{1}{4}$-kilogram steel ball is falling through oil. The oil exerts on the ball a frictional force $F_0 = -0.35v|v|$ newtons, where v is the velocity (in meters per second) of the ball. If the initial velocity of the ball is zero, compute v at $t = 5$ seconds. Show that $v(t)$ has a limit as $t \to \infty$ and compute this limit.

3. A ball is thrown vertically upward with initial velocity of 3 meters per second. Assuming no friction, find an expression for its velocity and one for its position at later times. Compute the time at which the ball will reach its maximal height.

4. A block of mass m slides down an inclined plane from a standing start. The inclined plane makes an angle α with the horizon so that the component of gravitational force in the direction of travel of the block is $mg \sin \alpha$, where g is the gravitational constant. Assuming no friction, find the velocity of the block as a function of time.

5. Repeat Problem 4 assuming viscous friction; that is, the frictional force exerted on the block is $-kv$.

6. Repeat Problem 4 assuming **dry friction;** that is, the frictional force exerted on the block is k.

7. A projectile is fired with muzzle velocity 5000 meters per second and at a positive angle α with the horizontal. Assume that the only force acting on the projectile is gravity. What angle α gives maximal range?

8. A ball weighing $\frac{1}{4}$ pound is thrown vertically downward from the top of a 300-foot building. The initial speed is 8 feet per second. Find the time t^* at which the ball will strike the ground and the velocity $v(t^*)$ (assuming no air resistance). If air resistance actually exerts a retarding force $-0.02v$ on the ball, what is the actual height and the actual velocity of the ball at time t^*?

9. Suppose that the muzzle velocity of a howitzer firing an HE-type shell is 850 feet per second. When the barrel is elevated to $20°$ the range of the shell is 4000 yards. Find the reduction in range caused by air resistance.

10. If m and k in (8.3) are positive, show that for any initial condition $v(t_0) = v_0$ the solution $v(t)$ has a limit as $t \to \infty$. This limit is called the **terminal velocity** of the body. Compute this terminal velocity.

11. If a falling body obeys (8.3), show that when the mass of the body and its terminal velocity are known, then k, the coefficient of air friction, can be determined.

12. If a body weighing $\frac{1}{4}$ pound has coefficient of air friction $k = 0.002$ (in English units), determine its terminal velocity. If this body is dropped from 10,000 feet with initial velocity zero, at what height will it reach 99% of its terminal velocity?

13. If a 3-kilogram body has a terminal velocity of 50 meters per second, determine its coefficient of air friction. If this body is dropped from 3000 meters with initial downward velocity zero, how long will it take for the body to reach a velocity of 49 meters per second?

14. If a 1-kilogram body has coefficient of air friction $k = 0.18$ newton per (meter per second), find its terminal velocity. How long will it take for it to reach 99% of its terminal velocity when dropped with initial velocity zero?

15. A 2-pound body has terminal velocity 165 feet per second. If this body is dropped, with initial downward velocity zero, from a plane at an altitude of 5000 feet, compute the altitude and vertical velocity of the body after 3 seconds and after 5 seconds.

16. A mass of 1 kilogram ± 1 gram has terminal velocity 50 ± 2 meters per second. Assume that g is exactly 9.80665 meters per second^2. How accurately can one estimate k, the coefficient of air friction?

17. A two-stage fireworks rocket works as follows. The initial charge sends a 1-pound package upward at an initial velocity of 97 feet per second. After 3 seconds a second explosion sends out a huge shower of red and propels a $\frac{1}{3}$-pound package upward at the rate of 40 feet per second (with respect to the ground). After one more second the $\frac{1}{3}$-pound package explodes in a shower of green. Assuming no air resistance, at what height does the green explosion occur?

18. A rocket is propelled upward from a howitzer with initial velocity of 500 feet per second. After 1 second of flight the rocket engine ignites and propels the rocket upward with 40 pounds of thrust. The rocket initially weighs 20 pounds. The engine consumes $\frac{1}{4}$ pound of fuel per second and burns for 60 seconds. What velocity is attained by the rocket in 61 seconds (assuming no air resistance)? *Hint:* This is not a fixed-mass problem.

19. For this problem you will need a programmable calculator or computer and a root-finding program.

    (a) In Problem 12, how long will it take the body, dropped from 10,000 feet, to reach an altitude of 5000 feet? What is its velocity at that time?

    (b) In Problem 13, how long will it take the body, dropped from 3000 meters, to reach an altitude of 1000 meters? What is its velocity at that time?

20. (a) Show that $\sin (Z + \pi) = -\sin Z$ for any real number Z.

    (b) Show that $y = A \sin (\sqrt{K/M}\, t + B)$ is a general solution of (8.7).

21. Show that all solutions of (8.6) are periodic. Compute the period. Does the period depend on the initial conditions?

22. For the system depicted in Figure 2.9, show that the system oscillates faster as the mass is made smaller or the spring stiffer.

23. For the mass–spring system of Figure 2.9, suppose that the mass is a 1-pound weight and $K = 48$ pounds per foot. Find the solutions $y(t)$ that satisfy each initial condition.

    (a) The mass is pulled out to stretch the spring 6 inches. Then the mass is released (from rest).

    (b) The mass is pushed in to compress the spring by 6 inches. Then the mass is released (from rest).

    (c) The mass, resting at equilibrium, is hit by a hammer in such a way that the mass moves toward the spring with an initial speed of 3 feet per second.

24. Repeat Problem 23 but with a 5-pound mass.

25. Repeat Problem 23 but with $K = 32$ pounds per foot.

26. For the system depicted in Figure 2.9, suppose that M is 2 kilograms and $K = 32$ newtons per meter. If $y(0) = 0$ and $y'(0) = 2$ meters per second, find the period of the resulting oscillation. What is the maximum compression of the spring?

27. Show that if $y = \varphi(t)$ solves (8.7), then so does

$$y = -\varphi(t).$$

28. Show that if $y = \varphi(t)$ solves (8.7), then so does

$$y = \varphi(-t).$$

29. For the mass–spring system depicted in Figure 2.10, write the equation of motion. (Both springs satisfy Hooke's law.) Find a general solution.

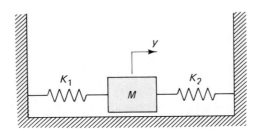

Figure 2.10. Mass-double spring system.

30. In Problem 29, suppose that $M = 250$ grams, $K_1 = 1$ newton per meter, and $K_2 = 3$ newtons per meter. Find the solutions that satisfy the following initial conditions.

(a) $y(0) = 3,\ v(0) = 0$.   (b) $y(0) = 0,\ v(0) = -3$.

(c) $y(0) = 0,\ v(0) = 0$.

31. In Problem 30, show that if $y = \varphi(t)$ and $v = \varphi'(t)$ is a solution, then so is $y = \varphi(t + t_0),\ v = \varphi'(t + t_0)$. Find the solutions that satisfy the following initial conditions.

(a) $y(2) = 3,\ v(2) = 0$.   (b) $y(-4) = 3,\ v(-4) = 0$.

(c) $y(5) = 0,\ v(5) = -3$.   (d) $y(4) = 0,\ v(4) = 0$.

(e) $y(-\pi) = 0,\ y'(-\pi) = -3$.

32. In the system depicted in Figure 2.9, suppose that we add a frictional force $-Bv$ on the mass.

(a) Show that the equations of motion are

$$y' = v, \quad Mv' = -Ky - Bv.$$

(b) Find all constant solutions.

(c) Show that the total energy in the system is nonincreasing with time t.

(d) Find a constant of the motion, that is, a function $H(y, v)$ which is constant along solutions. Assume that $B = 2$ and $K = 1$.

33. Show that the solution $y = A \sin(\sqrt{K/M}\,t + B)$ of (8.7) can be written in the form

$$y = c_1 \sin(\sqrt{K/M}\,t) + c_2 \cos(\sqrt{K/M}\,t)$$

for some constants c_1 and c_2. If A and B are restricted to $A \geq 0$ and $0 \leq B \leq 2\pi$, what restrictions are placed on c_1 and c_2?

2.9 APPLICATIONS TO CHEMICAL KINETICS

Problems involving chemical reactions often lead to interesting differential equations. We shall consider only reactions during which the temperature and pressure are held constant and the reacting chemicals, called **substrates,** are well stirred. For such reactions the law of mass action will apply. (These assumptions are crucial assumptions. In particular, temperature change will usually have a very marked effect on a reaction.) We shall consider only **closed systems,** that is, systems where we neither add nor withdraw any substrate or product during the course of the reaction.

The **molecularity** of a chemical reaction is the number of molecules that are altered in the reaction. For example, if one molecule of S_1 is changed into one molecule of P, that is,

$$S_1 \to P,$$

the reaction is **unimolecular.** If one molecule of S_1 plus one molecule of S_2 combine to give one molecule of P, that is,

$$S_1 + S_2 \to P,$$

the reaction is **bimolecular.** Similarly, $S_1 + S_2 + S_3 \to P$ and $2S_1 + S_2 \to P$ are **trimolecular,** and so on. The **order of a reaction** is a description of the kinetics of the reaction. It defines how many concentration terms must be multiplied together to get an expression for the **rate,** or **velocity,** of the reaction. For a **first-order reaction** the velocity of the reaction is proportional to one concentration. For example, in

$$S_1 \xrightarrow{k} P,$$

if s_i is the concentration in moles per liter of S_i and p is the concentration in moles per liter of P, then

$$\frac{dp}{dt} = ks_1.$$

Similarly, the bimolecular reaction $S_1 + S_2 \xrightarrow{k} P$ is **second order** and

$$\frac{dp}{dt} = ks_1s_2.$$

A typical trimolecular reaction is

$$S_1 + S_2 \xrightarrow{k_1} X, \qquad X + S_3 \xrightarrow{k_2} P.$$

It consists of two second-order reactions whose velocities are described by

$$\frac{dx}{dt} = k_1 s_1 s_2 - k_2 x s_3, \qquad \frac{dp}{dt} = k_2 x s_3.$$

Consider the bimolecular reaction $S_1 + S_2 \xrightarrow{k} P$; that is, one molecule of S_1 plus one molecule of S_2 are changed into one molecule of P. Since concentrations are always expressed in moles per liter and since the system is closed, the concentrations $s_1 + p$ and $s_2 + p$ will remain constant over the course of the reaction; that is, $s_1 + p \equiv q_1$ and $s_2 + p \equiv q_2$. Hence

$$\frac{dp}{dt} = k s_1 s_2 = k(q_1 - p)(q_2 - p);$$

that is, the velocity equation can be reduced to a first-order differential equation for p. If $p(0)$ is known, then $p(t)$ can be computed for all $t \geq 0$.

EXAMPLE 9.1   Consider the second-order bimolecular reaction

$$S_1 + S_2 \xrightarrow{k} P,$$

where $k = 2$. Suppose that the initial concentration of S_1 is 3 moles per liter, and the initial concentration of S_2 is 1 mole per liter while no product P is initially present. Solve for $p(t)$.

The initial value problem that must be solved is

(9.1) $$\frac{dp}{dt} = 2s_1 s_2 = 2(3 - p)(1 - p), \qquad p(0) = 0.$$

This equation is separable. Before using separation of variables we shall check for constant solutions and also do a sign analysis of the function

$$f(p) = 2(3 - p)(1 - p)$$

in order to see what general information can be obtained about the behavior of solutions. Now f is zero at $p = 1$ and 3. Hence there are two constant (or equilibrium) solutions, namely $p \equiv 1$ and $p \equiv 3$. Since $f(p) > 0$ when $p < 1$ and when $p > 3$, then solutions of $p' = f(p)$ will be increasing on the intervals $(-\infty, 1)$ and $(3, \infty)$. Since $f(p) < 0$ on $1 < p < 3$, the solutions are decreasing when p is in that interval. Since in our problem $p(0) = 0$, then $p(t)$ will be increasing and will remain less than the constant solution $p = 1$.

To solve (9.1) we use separation of variables, that is,

$$2dt = \frac{1}{(3 - p)(1 - p)} \, dp = \frac{1}{(p - 3)(p - 1)} \, dp.$$

Partial fractions can be used to decompose the right-hand side, that is,

$$\frac{1}{(p - 1)(p - 3)} = \frac{A}{p - 1} + \frac{B}{p - 3},$$

for some A and B. On multiplying by $(p-1)(p-3)$, we obtain

$$1 = A(p-3) + B(p-1).$$

Set $p = 1$ to find $A = -\frac{1}{2}$ and set $p = 3$ to find $B = \frac{1}{2}$. Hence we integrate

$$\left[-\frac{1}{2} \frac{1}{p-1} + \frac{1}{2} \frac{1}{p-3} \right] = 2dt,$$

to obtain

$$-\frac{1}{2} \log |p-1| + \frac{1}{2} \log |p-3| = \log \left(\left| \frac{p-3}{p-1} \right| \right)^{1/2} = 2t + c$$

or

$$\frac{p-3}{p-1} = (\pm e^{2c})e^{4t} = c_1 e^{4t},$$

where $c_1 = \pm e^{2c}$. Since $p(0) = 0$, then $c_1 = 3$. Hence

$$\frac{p-3}{p-1} = 3e^{4t}$$

or

$$p(t) = \frac{3e^{4t} - 3}{3e^{4t} - 1} = 1 - \frac{2}{3e^{4t} - 1}.$$

Once the solution is in hand, the predictions that were made using a sign analysis of $f(p)$ can be verified. Clearly, $p(0) = 0$, $p(t) < 1$ and $p(t) \to 1$ as $t \to \infty$. Also, p is increasing, since

$$p'(t) = (3e^{4t} - 1)^{-2}(24e^{4t}) > 0. \quad \blacksquare$$

EXAMPLE 9.2   Find $p(t)$ in Example 9.1 if the initial concentration of the product P is 2 moles per liter.

In this case $s_1 + p = 3 + 2 = 5$ and $s_2 + p = 1 + 2 = 3$. The initial value problem that must be solved is

$$\frac{dp}{dt} = 2s_1 s_2 = 2(5-p)(3-p), \qquad p(0) = 2.$$

The constant solutions are $p \equiv 3$ and $p \equiv 5$. When $-\infty < p < 3$, then $2(5-p)(3-p) > 0$, so that solutions are increasing on this interval. Since $p(0) = 2$, we expect that $2 \le p(t) < 3$ and we expect $p(t)$ to be increasing. On separating variables we obtain

$$2dt = \frac{1}{(5-p)(3-p)} dp = \left(\frac{1}{2} \frac{1}{p-5} - \frac{1}{2} \frac{1}{p-3} \right) dp,$$

$$2t + c = \frac{1}{2} \log |p-5| - \frac{1}{2} \log |p-3| = \log \left(\left| \frac{p-5}{p-3} \right| \right)^{1/2},$$

and

$$\frac{p-5}{p-3} = (\pm e^{2c})e^{4t} = c_1 e^{4t}.$$

Since $p(0) = 2$, then $c_1 = 3$. Hence

$$\frac{p-5}{p-3} = 3e^{4t}$$

or

$$p(t) = \frac{9e^{4t} - 5}{3e^{4t} - 1} = 3 - \frac{2}{3e^{4t} - 1}.$$

Clearly, $p(0) = 2$, $p'(t) > 0$, and $p(t) \to 3$ when $t \to \infty$. This information is consistent with our predictions. ∎

Many reactions are **reversible.** A reversible unimolecular reaction is written as

(9.2) $$S_1 \underset{k_{-1}}{\overset{k_1}{\rightleftharpoons}} P,$$

or in terms of velocities,

$$\frac{dp}{dt} = k_1 s_1 - k_{-1}p, \qquad \frac{ds_1}{dt} = -k_1 s_1 + k_{-1}p = -\frac{dp}{dt}.$$

EXAMPLE 9.3 For the reversible reaction (9.2), suppose that $k_1 = 3$ and $k_{-1} = 1$. If $s_1(0) = 5$ moles per liter and $p(0) = 0$, solve for $p(t)$.

Under the given conditions

$$\frac{dp}{dt} = 3s_1 - p, \qquad s_1 + p = 5, \qquad p(0) = 0.$$

Hence

$$\frac{dp}{dt} = 3(5 - p) - p = 15 - 4p, \qquad p(0) = 0.$$

The equation is linear. It has the general solution

$$p = \tfrac{15}{4} + ce^{-4t}.$$

Since $p(0) = 0$, then $c = -\tfrac{15}{4}$ and

$$p(t) = \tfrac{15}{4}(1 - e^{-4t}). \qquad ∎$$

In a similar manner a reversible second-order bimolecular reaction is written as

$$S_1 + S_2 \underset{k_{-1}}{\overset{k_1}{\rightleftharpoons}} P$$

or

$$\frac{dp}{dt} = k_1 s_1 s_2 - k_{-1} p.$$

Since the system is closed, then $s_1 + p = q_1$ and $s_2 + p = q_2$ are constant. Hence

$$\frac{dp}{dt} = k_1(q_1 - p)(q_2 - p) - k_{-1} p.$$

Reversible reactions of other orders are treated in the same manner. In case k_{-1} is small, it is often possible to set $k_{-1} = 0$ and treat the reaction as an irreversible one.

EXAMPLE 9.4   Write a set of differential equations that describe the kinetics of the reaction

$$S_1 + S_2 + S_3 \underset{k_{-1}}{\overset{k_1}{\rightleftharpoons}} X, \qquad X \underset{k_{-2}}{\overset{k_2}{\rightleftharpoons}} P.$$

The appropriate differential equations are

$$\frac{dx}{dt} = (k_1 s_1 s_2 s_3 - k_{-1} x) + (-k_2 x + k_{-2} p), \qquad \frac{dp}{dt} = k_2 x - k_{-2} p.$$

Since the system is closed, then $s_i + x + p = q_i$ is constant for $i = 1, 2, 3$. Hence $s_i = q_i - x - p$ and

$$\frac{dx}{dt} = k_1(q_1 - x - p)(q_2 - x - p)(q_3 - x - p) - (k_{-1} + k_2)x + k_{-2} p,$$

(9.3)

$$\frac{dp}{dt} = k_2 x - k_{-2} p.$$

This is a system of two equations. Hence two initial conditions $p(0) = p_0$ and $x(0) = x_0$ are needed in order to specify a solution. There is no general technique for solving such systems except for numerical approximation using a computer. ■

A **catalyst** is a substance that either accelerates a chemical reaction or is necessary for the reaction to occur at all. **Enzymes** are interesting examples. They are organic catalysts, usually proteins. They are extremely important and effective catalysts since they are extremely specific (i.e., they catalyze only one or only a small group of reactions), they work at low temperatures and pressures (e.g., body temperature and one atmosphere pressure), and they work in the presence of low concentrations of substrates. They are truly remarkable proteins!

In a typical enzyme reaction the enzyme E combines with a substrate S to form an intermediate product X which then produces a product P and releases the enzyme, that is,

(9.4)
$$E + S \xrightarrow[k_{-1}]{k_1} X \xrightarrow{k_2} E + P.$$

We wish to find dp/dt in terms of the concentration s. The equation presented here was first developed by the biologists L. Michaelis and M. Menten in 1913 when they studied the enzyme invertase. They noticed that the first reaction in (9.4) will take place very fast compared with the second reaction. Hence a simplifying approximation can be made via a technique called **singular perturbation theory**. The resulting mathematical model for the reaction has the form

(9.5)
$$\frac{dp}{dt} = \frac{Vs}{s + K_m}.$$

The constant V is the maximum possible velocity of the reaction, the constant K_m is called the **Michaelis constant** for the reaction, and (9.5) is known as the **Michaelis–Menten equation**.

EXAMPLE 9.5   Suppose that the reaction $S \to P$ has the kinetic equation

(9.6)
$$\frac{dp}{dt} = \frac{Vs}{s + K_m}.$$

If initially there are s_0 moles per liter of S and there is no P, find $p(t)$.

The reaction $S \to P$ is considered to be an enzyme-catalyzed reaction of the form (9.4). Rather then attempting to identify the appropriate enzyme and then measure k_1, k_{-1}, and k_2 we have gone directly to (9.6). The constants V and K_m must be estimated from data about the reaction. Since the system is closed, $s + p = s_0$ and

(9.7)
$$\frac{dp}{dt} = \frac{V(s_0 - p)}{s_0 - p + K_m} = f(p), \qquad p(0) = 0.$$

Since $f(p) = 0$ only if $p = s_0$ while $f(p) > 0$ for $p < s_0$, the only constant solution of (9.7) is $p(t) \equiv s_0$. In the region $-\infty < p < s_0$ solutions are increasing. Hence we expect the solution $p(t)$ of (9.7) to be increasing and to remain less than s_0.

We now separate variables in (9.7), that is,

$$V \, dt = \frac{s_0 - p + K_m}{s_0 - p} \, dp = \left(1 + \frac{K_m}{s_0 - p}\right) dp$$

or

$$Vt + c = p - K_m \log(s_0 - p).$$

Since $p(0) = 0$, then $c = -K_m \log s_0$ and

(9.8)
$$Vt = p - K_m \log\left(1 - \frac{p}{s_0}\right).$$

This expression determines p implicitly in terms of t. ∎

The velocity equation (9.6) seems to be a good approximation in a wide variety of reactions, some of which are much more complex than (9.4). For such reactions V and K_m must be determined for the given reaction.

PROBLEMS

1. Use the law of mass action to write a kinetic equation for each reaction. (All reactions are closed.) List as many conserved quantities as possible.

(a) $S_1 \xrightarrow{k} P.$

(b) $S_1 \xrightarrow{k_1} X \underset{k_{-2}}{\overset{k_2}{\rightleftharpoons}} P.$

(c) $S_1 \xrightarrow{k_1} X_1 \xrightarrow{k_2} X_2 \xrightarrow{k_3} P.$

(d) $S_1 \xrightarrow{k_1} X_1 \xrightarrow{k_2} X_2 \underset{k_{-3}}{\overset{k_3}{\rightleftharpoons}} P.$

(e) $2S_1 \xrightarrow{k} P.$

(f) $2S_1 \underset{k_{-1}}{\overset{k}{\rightleftharpoons}} P.$

(g) $S_1 + S_2 + S_3 \xrightarrow{k} P.$

(h) $S_1 + S_2 \xrightarrow{k} X, X + S_3 \xrightarrow{k_2} P.$

2. For each reaction in Problem 1, parts (a)–(f), find all constant solutions of the corresponding kinetic equation.

In Problems 3–13, find $p(t)$. Use the law of mass action.

3. $S_1 \xrightarrow{k} P, k = 3, s_1(0) = 4, p(0) = 0.$

4. $S_1 \xrightarrow{k} P, k > 0, s_1(0) = q > 0, p(0) = 0.$

5. $S_1 \xrightarrow{k} P, s_1(0) = c, p(0) = q, q > 0, k > 0, c > 0.$

6. $S_1 \xrightarrow{k} P, s_1(t_0) = c, p(t_0) = q, q > 0, k > 0, c > 0.$

7. $S_1 \xrightarrow{k} P, s_1(t_0) = 0, p(t_0) = q, q > 0, k > 0.$

8. $S_1 \overset{k_1}{} X \underset{k_{-2}}{\overset{k_2}{\rightleftharpoons}} P, s_1(0) = q > 0, x(0) = p(0) = 0, k_1 = k_2 = k_{-2} = 1.$

   Hint: First determine $s_1(t)$.

9. $S_1 \overset{k_1}{} X \underset{k_{-2}}{\overset{k_2}{\rightleftharpoons}} P, s_1(0) = 0, x(0) = x_0 > 0, p(0) = p_0 > 0, \text{ all } k_j = 1.$

10. $S_1 \xrightarrow{k_1} X_1 \xrightarrow{k_2} X_2 \xrightarrow{k_3} P, s_1(0) = s_0 > 0, x_1(0) = x_2(0) = p(0) = 0, \text{ where } k_j \neq k_i$ for $i \neq j.$

11. $2S_1 \xrightarrow{k} P, s_1(0) = s_0 > 0, p(0) = 0, k > 0.$

12. $2S_1 \underset{k_{-1}}{\overset{k_1}{\rightleftharpoons}} P, s_1(0) = 1, p(0) = 0, k_1 = 4, k_{-1} = 1.$

13. $3S_1 \xrightarrow{k} P$, $s_1(0) = s_0 > 0$, $p(0) = 0$, $k > 0$.

14. In $S_1 + S_2 + S_3 \xrightarrow{k} P$ suppose that $s_1(0) = 2$, $s_2(0) = 1$, $s_3(0) = \frac{3}{2}$, and $p(0) = 0$. Write a kinetic equation

$$\frac{dp}{dt} = f(p)$$

which describes this reaction. Determine all constant solutions of this equation. Use a sign analysis of $f(p)$ in order to give a description of the general behavior of the solution of this differential equation.

15. For $S_1 + S_2 \xrightarrow{k} P$ find $p(t)$ given that $k = 1$, $s_1(0) = 2$, $s_2(0) = 1$, $p(0) = 1$.

16. For $S_1 + S_2 \underset{k_{-1}}{\overset{k_1}{\rightleftarrows}} P$ find $p(t)$ given that $k_1 = 2$, $k_{-1} = 4$, $s_1(0) = s_2(0) = 1$, $p(0) = 0$.

17. For $S_1 \underset{k_{-1}}{\overset{k_1}{\rightleftarrows}} P$ let $s_1(0) = a > 0$ and $p(0) = 0$. The solution p depends on t, k_1, k_{-1}, and a. Compute

(a) $\partial p / \partial k_1$.   (b) $\partial p / \partial k_{-1}$.   (c) $\partial p / \partial a$.

18. In Problem 17, let $k_1 \cong 2$, $k_{-1} \cong 1$, and $a \cong 3$. When $t = 2$ is p more sensitive to small errors in the measurement of k_1, k_{-1}, or a? (You will need a calculator for this problem.)

19. It is known that the rate constants in the velocity equations are very sensitive to variations in temperature. For the reaction $S_1 \xrightarrow{k} P$ suppose that $s_1(0) = a > 0$ and $p(0) = b > 0$. Suppose a cyclic variation in temperature causes the rate constants to vary in such a way that

$$k = 2 + \cos\left(\frac{\pi t}{12}\right).$$

Find $p(t)$.

20. In (9.8) show that $p(t)$ has a limit $p(\infty)$ as $t \to \infty$. Compute $p(\infty)$.

21. Suppose that in a mixture of S_1 and S_2 the two reactions

$$S_1 \xrightarrow{k_1} P_1, \qquad S_1 + S_2 \xrightarrow{k_2} P_2$$

occur where $k_1 = k_2 = 1$. Let $s_1(0) = 2$, $s_2(0) = 1$, $p_1(0) = 0$, and $p_2(0) = 0$.

(a) Assuming that the law of mass action applies, write four velocity equations for these reactions.

(b) Find all conserved quantities. (The system is closed!)

(c) Show that $p_2 = 1 - e^{-(k_2/k_1)p_1}$.

(d) Given part (c), use sign analysis and the equation

$$\frac{dp_1}{dt} = k_1 s_1 = k_1(2 - p_1 - p_2)$$

to describe the general behavior of the solution $p_1(t)$.

CHAPTER REVIEW

Given the initial value problem

(E) $$y' = f(x, y), \qquad y(x_0) = a_0,$$

suppose that f and $\partial f / \partial y$ are defined and continuous for all (x, y) in a rectangle $D = \{(x, y): A_1 < x < A_2, B_1 < y < B_2\}$. If the initial conditions x_0 and a_0 are chosen so that (x_0, a_0) is in D, then (E) has a unique solution.

A **linear** (first-order) **equation** is an equation of the form

(L) $$y' = g(x)y + h(x),$$

where g and h are defined and continuous on an open interval J. The linear equation (L) is **homogeneous** if $h(x) \equiv 0$ on J. Otherwise it is a **nonhomogeneous** linear equation. For any real number a_0 and any x_0 in J, problem (L) has a unique solution satisfying $y(x_0) = a_0$. This solution is defined for all x in J.

The methods of solution of first-order equations which were presented in this chapter are the following:

1. *Separation of Variables.* The equation can be written in the form

$$p(x) + q(y)\frac{dy}{dx} = 0.$$

The solution is

$$\int^x p(x)\, dx + \int^y q(y)\, dy = c.$$

Constant solutions should be found separately. Sign analysis can often be used to obtain properties of solutions.

2. *Homogeneous Equations.* The equation can be written in the form

$$y' = F\left(\frac{y}{x}\right).$$

Use the substitution $y = xv$ and reduce the equation to a separable one.

3. *Exact Equations.* The equation can be written in the form

$$p(x, y) + q(x, y)\frac{dy}{dx} = 0$$

and $\partial p / \partial y = \partial q / \partial x$ in the rectangle D. There is a function $F(x, y)$ such that $\partial F / \partial x = p$ and $\partial F / \partial y = q$. Solutions have the form $F(x, y) = c$.

4. *Integrating Factors.* Here (E) is written in the form

$$p(x, y) + q(x, y)\frac{dy}{dx} = 0.$$

A function $\mu(x, y)$ is found such that $(\mu p) + (\mu q)y' = 0$ is exact. The most important cases are when μ is a function of x only or of y only.

5. *Linear Equations.* The equation has the form (L). The function $\mu(x) = e^{-\int g(x)\, dx}$ is an integrating factor, indeed

$$e^{-\int g(x)dx}(y' - g(x)y) = (e^{-\int g(x)dx}y)' = h(x)e^{-\int g(x)dx}.$$

Integrate each side with respect to x to obtain a solution.

6. *Method of Substitution.* Various substitutions, often suggested by the form of the equation, reduce (E) to a new equation which is solvable. Also systems of two equations of the form $y'_1 = f_1(y_1, y_2), y'_2 = f_2(y_1, y_2)$ can be reduced to one first-order equation.

Some differential equations can be solved by more than one method. When this is true, then the solutions obtained by different methods, correctly applied, will be equivalent.

CHAPTER REVIEW PROBLEMS

In Problems 1–40, solve the equation. Find the general solution if no initial condition is given.

1. $3\dfrac{dy}{dx} + y \sin x = 0$.

2. $\dfrac{dK}{dt} = 4K + t,\ K(0) = 4$.

3. $\dfrac{dy}{dx} = (x + y - 2)^2,\ y(1) = 2$.

4. $2\dfrac{dA}{dt} = \dfrac{t^2 + A^2}{t^2}$.

5. $x\dfrac{dy}{dx} + y = 2\dfrac{dy}{dx} + 3x - 8$.

6. $\cos v\ du - u\ dv = 0$.

7. $\dfrac{y^2 - 3x}{y}\dfrac{dy}{dx} = 1$.

8. $\dfrac{dR}{ds} = \dfrac{R^2 - s^2}{2Rs + 2s^2}$.

9. $x\ dy + xy\ dx = (1 - y)\ dx$.

10. $\dfrac{dD}{dt} - D = \dfrac{1}{1 + e^{-t}},\ D(0) = 4$.

11. $(3x^2 + y)\ dx + (x + e^{-y})\ dy = 0,\ y(1) = 0$.

12. $(2B + 3t)\ dt + t\ dB = 0$.

13. $(2x + ye^{xy}) + (y + xe^{xy})y' = 0$.

14. $\dfrac{dB}{dt} + B \sin t = 3B^2 \sin t$.

15. $\dfrac{dy}{dx} = y^{1/3},\ y(0) = 3$.

16. $\dfrac{dS}{dt} = S^2,\ S(0) = 1$.

17. $(t + e^y)\dfrac{dy}{dt} - 1 = 0$.

18. $y' + 4y = 1 + e^{-4t},\ y(0) = 2$.

19. $\tan x\ dy + \tan y\ dx = 0$.

20. $\dfrac{dR}{dt} = -\dfrac{12t^2R + 3R^2}{4t^3 + 6tR}$.

21. $(2 + 2y^3)\ dx + 3xy^2\ dy = 0$.

22. $xy' - y = \sqrt{x^2 - y^2}$.

23. $y' = e^{x+y},\ y(1) = 0$.

24. $(2x + ye^{y/x})\ dx - xe^{y/x}\ dy = 0$.

25. $y' = xy + 2x - y - 2$.

26. $x\dfrac{dy}{dx} + 3y = \dfrac{\sin x}{x},\ y\left(\dfrac{\pi}{2}\right) = 2$.

27. $(t^2 + y^2)\dfrac{dy}{dt} + 2t(y + 2t) = 0$.

28. $(3x^2 - 8xy + 6y^2) = (4x^2 + 6y^2 - 12xy)\dfrac{dy}{dx}$.

29. $2\dfrac{dS}{dt} = St(S - 2), \ S(0) = \pi.$

30. $y' = (6x + 3y + 5)^2.$

31. $y \, dx - (x + y^3) \, dy = 0.$

32. $\sin 2y \, dx + 2x \cos 2y \, dy = 0.$

33. $\dfrac{dB}{dx} = \dfrac{2x^2 + B^2}{3B^2 - 2Bx}.$

34. $\dfrac{dy}{dt} - (\tan t)y = 1.$

35. $(t^2 - N^2) \, dt + 2tN \, dN = 0.$

36. $y' + \dfrac{y}{x} = \dfrac{3 \sin x}{y}.$

37. $y = 2(y^2 + x)\dfrac{dy}{dx}.$

38. $x\dfrac{dy}{dx} - y - y^2 e^{2x} = 0.$

39. $y^2 + (y')^2 = 1, \ y(0) = \dfrac{1}{\sqrt{2}}.$

40. $\dfrac{dy}{dx} = \dfrac{3x + y + 6}{3x + y + 7}.$ *Hint:* Substitute $w = 3x + y + 7.$

41. Show that both $\varphi_1(x) = 1 - x$ and $\varphi_2(x) = -x^2/4$ solve

$$\frac{dy}{dx} = \frac{-x + \sqrt{x^2 + 4y}}{2}, \qquad y(2) = -1 \qquad \text{for } x \geq 2.$$

Why does this not contradict the existence and uniqueness theorem?

42. Show that the equation $y' = F(y/x)$ has the integrating factor

$$\mu = \left(y - xF\left(\frac{y}{x}\right) \right)^{-1}.$$

43. Show that $\mu = (xy(p(xy) - q(xy)))^{-1}$ is an integrating factor for the equation $yp(xy) + xq(xy)y' = 0.$

44. Develop a method of solving the **Riccati equation**

$$y' + f(x)y + g(x)y^2 = h(x),$$

in the special case where $h(x) \equiv 0$. Use your method to solve the following initial value problems:

(a) $y' - \dfrac{2}{x}y + \dfrac{\sin x^2}{x}y^2 = 0, \qquad y(1) = 1.$

(b) $y' + 2y + y^2 = 0, \qquad y(2) = 1.$

45. Find a general solution of each equation.

(a) $\dfrac{dw}{dx} = \dfrac{x - w - 2}{x + w + 1}.$

(b) $\dfrac{dy}{dt} + 2 = \sqrt{2t + y + 1}.$

(c) $y' = \sqrt{y - 3x} + 3.$

(d) $\dfrac{d\mu}{dx} = \dfrac{\mu}{x} + x \sec x.$

(e) $\dfrac{dT}{ds} = (s + T)^2.$

46. A constant torque T is applied to a rotating shaft. The shaft has moment of inertia J. There is viscous damping Bw, where w is the shaft speed. Hence by Newton's law of motion

$$J\frac{dw}{dt} + Bw = T \qquad (J > 0, B > 0, T \neq 0).$$

(a) Given $w(0) = w_0$, solve this equation.

(b) Show that $w(t)$ has a limit as $t \to \infty$ and compute this limit.

47. Let $y(t)$ be the concentration of a yeast growing in an anaerobic medium. Let a be the natural growth rate of this yeast. Since yeasts make alcohol and alcohol inhibits growth, it is found that

$$\frac{dy}{dt} = y(a - by) \qquad (a > 0, b > 0)$$

is a good growth model. Suppose that the initial concentration $y(0) = y_0$ and the concentration $y(t_1) = y_1$ at time t_1 are known. Determine b in terms of a, y_0, y_1, and t_1.

48. Suppose that a closed system contains chemicals S_1, S_2, and S_3 and that the reaction $S_1 + S_2 + S_3 \xrightarrow{k} P$ is governed by the law of mass action. Suppose the initial concentration of these chemicals are $s_1(0) = q_1 > 0$, $s_2(0) = q_2 > 0$, $s_3(0) = q_3 > 0$, and $p(0) = p_0 \geq 0$.

(a) Write a differential equation that p satisfies.

(b) Solve this equation assuming that $k = 1$, $q_1 = 1$, $q_2 = 2$, $q_3 = 3$, and $p_0 = 0$.

(c) Solve this equation assuming that $k = 1$, $q_1 = q_2 = 1$, $q_3 = 2$, and $p_0 = 0$.

(d) Solve this equation assuming that $k = 1$, $q_1 = q_2 = q_3 = 1$, and $p_0 = 0$.

49. A thin sheet of metal is insulated on one face. Gas at 50°C is blown by the opposite face. The initial temperature of the sheet is 100°C. After 5 minutes the temperature is 70°C.

(a) How long will it take to cool the sheet to 60°C?

(b) Show that $T(t)$ has a limit as $t \to \infty$. Compute this limit.

(c) If things were arranged so that the initial temperature were 20°C, find the temperature $T(t)$ of the sheet for $t \geq 0$.

50. A ball weighing 10 pounds is dropped from a 600-foot building. Air resistance is assumed to exert a retarding force $-kv$ on the ball. After 2 seconds the ball's speed is 36 feet per second.

(a) Find the speed of the ball when $t = 3$.

(b) What is the kinetic energy of the ball at the instant of impact with the ground? (You will need a programmable calculator or a computer plus a root-finding program to do this problem.)

51. Given the equation $y' = yg(x, y)$ suppose that g and $\partial g / \partial y$ are defined and continuous for all (x, y).

(a) Show that $y \equiv 0$ is a solution.

(b) Show that if $y = \varphi(x)$ is a solution on an interval (A_1, A_2) and if $\varphi(x_0) > 0$ at some point x_0 in (A_1, A_2), then $\varphi(x) > 0$ at all points in (A_1, A_2).

(c) Show that if $y = \varphi(x)$ is a solution on an interval (A_1, A_2) and if $\varphi(x_0) < 0$ at some x_0 in (A_1, A_2), then $\varphi(x) < 0$ for all x in (A_1, A_2).

52. A population P in a seasonally varying environment satisfies the equation $dP/dt = P(a(t) - b(t)P)$, where $a(t)$ and $b(t)$ are continuous, periodic functions. Show that if $P(0) = P_0 > 0$, then $P(t) > 0$ for as long as the solution is defined.

53. Suppose that $y(x)$ solves the differential inequality

$$y'(x) \leq ky(x) + f(x), \qquad 0 \leq x \leq A,$$

where k is a constant and $f(x)$ is a continuous function. Show that

$$y(x) \leq y(0)e^{kx} + \int_0^x e^{k(x-s)}f(s) \, ds, \qquad 0 \leq x \leq A.$$

Hint: There is a continuous and nonnegative function $g(x)$ such that

$$y' + g(x) = ky + f(x).$$

54. Suppose that $y = \varphi(x)$ solves $y' = yg(x, y)$, $y(0) = 1$ on $0 \leq x \leq A$, where $g(x, y)$ is a bounded and continuous function in the (x, y) plane. Show that there is a constant B such that $\varphi(x) \leq e^{Bx}$ for all x in $[0, A]$.

55. Given that $y(x)$ solves the equation

$$y'(x) = -y(x) + 2y(x - 1), \qquad x > 0$$

let $y(x) = 1$ on $-1 \leq x \leq 0$.

(a) Find $y(x)$ on $0 < x \leq 1$.   (b) Find $y(x)$ on $1 < x \leq 2$.

(c) Explain how to solve for $y(x)$ on any interval $n < x \leq n + 1$, where $n = 2, 3, 4, \ldots$?

56. Given the problem

$$y'(x) = 2y(x) - y(x - 1), \qquad x > 0$$

let $y(x) = x + 2$, $-1 \leq x \leq 0$.

(a) Find $y(x)$ on $0 < x \leq 1$.   (b) Find $y(x)$ on $1 < x \leq 2$.

(c) Explain how to solve for $y(x)$ on any interval $n < x \leq n + 1$, where $n = 2, 3, 4, \ldots$.

57. A home water heater is schematically depicted in Figure 2.11. Water at temperature $T_i \degree F$ flows into the heater tank at the rate f pounds per second. Water at the tank temperature $T \degree F$ flows out at the same rate. The tank is surrounded by insulation with thermal resistance R degrees per (Btu per second). The room temperature in the room where the heater is located is $T_r \degree F$. The heating element of the water heater will add heat energy to the water at the rate H Btu per second. The tank contains W pounds of water. [The specific heat of water is 1 Btu per (pound $\degree F$).] We make the following simplifying assumptions.

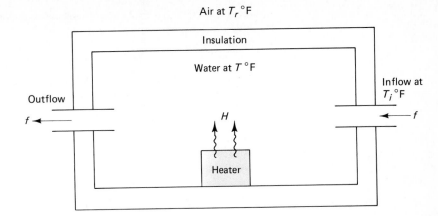

Figure 2.11. Home water heater.

(i) No heat is stored in the insulation.

(ii) There is small constant water use; that is, f is a small nonnegative constant.

(iii) The tank is designed in such a way that the water temperature inside the tank is uniform (i.e., perfect mixing.)

(a) Write a differential equation for $T(t)$ that describes the heat flow balance.

(b) Solve this equation assuming that $T(0) = T_0$ is known.

(c) Show that the solution obtained in part (b) has a limit as $t \to \infty$.

58. In Problem 57, assume that the inflowing water is at 40°F, the temperature of the surrounding air is 70°F, the tank holds 334 pounds of water (approximately 40 gallons), and $H = 12.5$ Btu per second (i.e., the heater is rated at 45,000 Btu per hour).

(a) Suppose that $R = 15$, $T(0) = 105°F$, and $f = 0.25$ pound per second (about 1.8 gallons per minute). Compute the limit as $t \to \infty$ of $T(\infty)$. How long will it take before $T(t)$ is within 1°F of $T(\infty)$?

(b) Suppose that $R = 10$, $T(0) = 105°F$, and $f = 0.5$ pound per second. Find the limit as $t \to \infty$ of $T(t)$. Suppose that after 1 hour you get home. You are very hot and sweaty. Would you like to use the shower under these conditions?

(c) Suppose that $R = 15$, $T(0) = 145°F$, and $f = 0.08$ pound per second (about 0.6 gallon per minute). The dishwasher needs water at approximately 140°F for satisfactory operation. Can this condition be met throughout the day?

(d) Suppose that $R = 15$, $T(0) = 48°F$, and $f = 0$ (no water use). How long will it take the water in the tank to reach 150°?

(e) Suppose that $R = 30$, $T(0) = 48°F$, and $f = 0$. How long will it take for the water in the tank to reach 150°F? [Compare parts (c) and (d). It can pay to insulate!]

(f) Suppose that the heater is automatically turned on when the water temperature falls below 148°F and is turned off when the temperature rises to 152°F. Suppose this device fails in such a way that the heater remains on. Under the conditions of part (d), will the temperature rise to 212°F? Under the conditions of part (e), will the temperature rise to 212°F? What will happen to a home water heater if the temperature reaches 212°F and remains there?

(g) Suppose that a family of four uses 1000 cubic feet of water per month and 5% of this is hot water. Suppose hot water is used to a steady rate for 16 hours each day and no water is used for 8 hours each night. If $R = 15$ and if the water in the heater is at 150°F at the start of each day, will the heater deliver an adequate supply of hot water (at 140°F or more) during each day? What would your answer be if 10% of the water used is hot water? (*Note:* One gallon = 0.13368 cubic foot. One cubic foot of water weighs approximately 62.43 pounds.)

CHAPTER THREE

Second-Order Equations

We now study second-order ordinary differential equations which have the form

(E) $$y'' = f(x, y, y').$$

Here $f(x, y, z)$ is a function of three variables which is defined in a region D of (x, y, z) space. We assume that f, $\partial f/\partial y$, and $\partial f/\partial z$ are defined and continuous in the region D and $D = \{(x, y, z): A_1 < x < A_2, B_1 < y < B_2, C_1 < z < C_2\}$.

We shall either find a general solution of (E) or else shall seek to solve (E) subject to two initial conditions of the form

(0.1) $$y(x_0) = a_0 \quad \text{and} \quad y'(x_0) = a_1,$$

where (x_0, a_0, a_1) is some specified point in the region D. There is one and only one solution of (E) that satisfies the initial conditions (0.1). A general solution of (E) must contain two arbitrary constants. These two constants can be determined by giving initial conditions of the form (0.1).

3.1 SECOND-ORDER NONLINEAR EQUATIONS

Little is known about how to solve the nonlinear problem (E) except in certain special cases. Two interesting and useful special cases occur when the nonlinear equations has one of the following forms:

(1.1) $$F(x, y', y'') = 0$$

or

(1.2) $$F(y, y', y'') = 0.$$

99

> ### EQUATIONS WITH DEPENDENT VARIABLE MISSING
>
> ---
>
> In (1.1) the variable y does not occur in the equation. In this case define $y' = v$ so that $y'' = v'$. Hence (1.1) takes the form
>
> $$F(x, v, v') = 0.$$
>
> This is a first-order equation in v which can often be solved by the methods of Chapter 2. Once (1.1) is solved for $v = y'$, then v can be integrated to obtain y.

EXAMPLE 1.1   Solve $xy'' + 2y' + x = 1$, $y(1) = 2$, and $y'(1) = 1$.

This equation does not contain y. Hence we set $v = y'$. In terms of v the equation given is

$$xv' + 2v + x = 1.$$

This equation is linear in v. Thus v is found to be

$$v = c_1 x^{-2} + \frac{1}{2} - \frac{x}{3}.$$

Since $v = 1$ when $x = 1$, then $c_1 = \frac{5}{6}$. On integrating the expression for $v = y'$, we get

$$y = c_2 - \frac{5}{6x} + \frac{x}{2} - \frac{x^2}{6}.$$

Since $y(1) = 2$, then $c_2 = \frac{5}{2}$. The solution is defined for $0 < x < \infty$. ∎

Equations of the form (1.1) often occur with different names used for the variables. Consider the following example.

EXAMPLE 1.2   In Section 2.8 we studied the motion of a body of mass M which is in free fall near the earth's surface. Let g be the gravitational constant. If we assume that air friction exerts a retarding force on the body that is proportional to the velocity of the body and if y is the height of the body above the earth's surface, then from Newton's second law of motion it follows that

$$M\frac{d^2 y}{dt^2} = -Mg - B\frac{dy}{dt}, \qquad B > 0.$$

The velocity is $v = dy/dt$. Hence the equation of motion is

$$M\frac{dv}{dt} = -Mg - Bv.$$

This linear equation can be solved to obtain

$$v(t) = -\frac{Mg}{B} + c_1 e^{-Bt/M}$$

and then

$$y(t) = c_2 - \frac{Mg}{B} t - \frac{Mc_1}{B} e^{-Bt/M}. \quad \blacksquare$$

EQUATIONS WITH INDEPENDENT VARIABLE MISSING

Equations of the form (1.2) can be reduced to first-order equations by substituting $v = y'$. Equation (1.2) is now replaced by an equivalent system of two equations, namely

$$y' = v, \qquad F(y, v, v') = 0.$$

We now use y as the independent variable. Under this substitution

$$y'' = \frac{dv}{dx} = \frac{dv}{dy}\frac{dy}{dx} = \frac{dv}{dy}v,$$

so that (1.2) is reduced to the first-order equation

$$F\!\left(y, v, v\frac{dv}{dy}\right) = 0.$$

EXAMPLE 1.3   Solve $y'' + (y')^3 y = 0$, $y(0) = 1$, and $y'(0) = -1$.

Since the equation is free of x, we put $v = y'$ and let y be the independent variable. The given equation goes over to the new equation

$$v\frac{dv}{dy} + v^3 y = 0.$$

Since this equation separates, we find that $v = 2(y^2 - 2c_1)^{-1}$. Since $v = -1$ when $y = 1$, then $c_1 = \frac{3}{2}$. Thus

$$v = \frac{dy}{dx} = \frac{2}{y^2 - 3}.$$

This equation separates. We easily compute

$$\frac{y^3}{3} - 3y = 2x + c_2$$

and $c_2 = -\frac{8}{3}$. $\blacksquare$

When this method of solution is used, it is necessary to assume that dy/dx is not zero. Hence no constant solutions can be obtained in this way. One must separately check to see if $y \equiv A$ is a solution for any real number A.

EXAMPLE 1.4   Find all constant solutions of $y'' + (y')^3 y = 0$, then find the solution that satisfies $y(0) = 3$, $y'(0) = 0$.

We substitute $y = A$ in the equation. This gives

$$y'' + (y')^3 y = 0 + (0)^3 A = 0.$$

Hence any constant A will do. If $y(0) = 3$ and $y'(0) = 0$, then $y \equiv 3$ is the required solution. ∎

An **integral of the motion** for the second-order equation (1.2) is a function $G(y, y')$ such that along any solution of (1.2), G remains constant. Our proposed method of solution of (1.2) will always produce an integral of the motion. This integral can often be used to deduce useful properties of solutions. (For example, see Problem 20.)

EXAMPLE 1.5   Find an integral of the motion for

(1.3) $$y'' + y + y^3 = 0.$$

Let $v = dy/dx$, so that

$$\frac{dv}{dy} = \frac{dv}{dx}\frac{dx}{dy} = (-y - y^3)\frac{1}{v}.$$

Since this equation is separable, we obtain

$$v\, dv = -(y + y^3)\, dy$$

or

$$\frac{v^2}{2} = -\left(\frac{y^2}{2} + \frac{y^4}{4}\right) + c.$$

Hence an integral of the motion (1.3) is

(1.4) $$G(y, v) = \frac{v^2}{2} + \left(\frac{y^2}{2} + \frac{y^4}{4}\right) = c.$$

To make sure that there are no integration errors, it is advisable to check that (1.4) does indeed define an integral of the motion. To do this we let $y = \varphi(x)$ be a solution of (1.3) and check that

$$\frac{d}{dx} G(\varphi(x), \varphi'(x)) \equiv 0.$$

Since $\varphi''(x) = -\varphi(x) - \varphi(x)^3$, then $dG(\varphi(x), \varphi'(x))/dx$ is computed as

$$\frac{d}{dx}\left[\frac{\varphi'(x)^2}{2} + \frac{\varphi(x)^2}{2} + \frac{\varphi(x)^4}{4}\right] = \varphi'(x)\varphi''(x) + \varphi(x)\varphi'(x) + \varphi(x)^3\varphi'(x)$$

$$= \varphi'(x)[-\varphi(x) - \varphi(x)^3] + \varphi(x)\varphi'(x) + \varphi(x)^3\varphi'(x)$$

$$\equiv 0.$$

Hence (1.4) is indeed an integral of the motion.

When $c = 0$ in (1.4), then $y = v = 0$. This point in the (v, y) plane corresponds to a constant solution of (1.3). For $c > 0$ a typical curve defined by (1.4) is graphed in Figure 3.1. For any point (y_0, v_0) on this curve, if $y = \varphi(x)$ is a solution of (1.3) such that $\varphi(x_0) = y_0$, $\varphi'(x_0) = v_0$, then $(\varphi(x), \varphi'(x))$ must remain on the curve as x varies. Indeed, the point $(\varphi(x), \varphi'(x))$ must move along the curve in a clockwise direction, must eventually return to the starting point (v_0, y_0), and then must traverse the curve again. For more details, see the problem section. ■

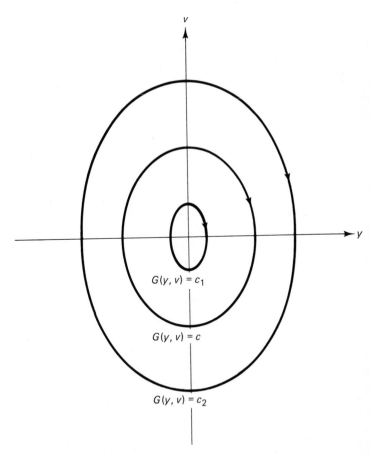

Figure 3.1. Typical solution curves for $y'' + y + y^3 = 0$ with $0 < c_1 < c < c_2$.

PROBLEMS

In Problems 1–15, solve the equation. If no initial conditions are given, find a general solution.

1. $x^2y'' + 2xy' = 1, 0 < x < \infty$.

2. $x^2y'' = 1 - x, 0 < x < \infty$.

3. $yy'' = (y')^2$.

4. $(1 - x^2)y'' = xy', -1 < x < 1$.

5. $u^2 \dfrac{d^2A}{du^2} = (1 - 2u)\dfrac{dA}{du}, u > 0$.

6. $t\dfrac{d^2y}{dt^2} = 4t - 2\dfrac{dy}{dt}, t > 0$.

7. $y'' + y = 0, y(0) = 0, y'(0) = 1$.

8. $y'' - y = 0, y(0) = 0, y'(0) = 1$.

9. $y'' = yy', y(0) = 0, y'(0) = \frac{1}{2}$.

10. $y'' = yy', y(0) = y'(0) = 0$.

11. $yy'' - 2(y')^2 + 4y^2 = 0, y(1) = 1, y'(1) = 2$.

12. $yy'' - 2(y')^2 + y^2 = 0, y(1) = 1, y'(1) = 1$.

13. $(\sin y')y'' = \sin x, y(1) = 2, y'(1) = 1$.

14. $2t^2\dfrac{d^2B}{dt^2} + \left(\dfrac{dB}{dt}\right)^3 = 2t\dfrac{dB}{dt}, 0 < t < \infty, B(2) = -1, B'(2) = 1$.

15. $x(y'' + (y')^2) = y', y(1) = 2, y'(1) = -1$.

16. Solve $y'' = 1 + (y')^2$. Which method is easier?

17. Let $f(y, z)$, $\partial f(y, z)/\partial y$, and $\partial f(y, z)/\partial z$ be continuous in the region $R = \{(y, z): B_1 < y < B_2 \text{ and } C_1 < z < C_2\}$. If $y = \varphi(x)$ solves

$$y'' = f(y, y'), \qquad y(x_0) = q_0, \qquad y'(x_0) = q_1,$$

where $(q_0, q_1) \in R$ and if there is a number $T > 0$ such that $\varphi(x_0 + T) = q_0$, $\varphi'(x_0 + T) = q_1$, show that $\varphi(x)$ is periodic in x, that is, $\varphi(x + T) = \varphi(x)$ for all x.

18. Let (y_0, v_0) be any point on the curve

$$G(y, v) = \dfrac{v^2}{2} + \dfrac{y^2}{2} + \dfrac{y^4}{4} = c > 0.$$

Let $\theta = \arctan v/y$, where y solves $y'' + y + y^3 = 0$, $v = y'$, $y(x_0) = y_0$, and $y'(x_0) = v_0$.

(a) Show that for as long as $y > 0$, one has $d\theta/dx \le -1$.

(b) Show that for as long as $y < 0$, one has $d\theta/dx \le -1$.

(c) Show that if $y = \varphi(x)$ solves (1.3), $(\varphi(x), \varphi'(x))$ must traverse the curve $G(y, v) = c$ at least once in the clockwise direction by the time that x reaches 2π.

19. Show that each nonconstant solution of (1.3) is periodic of some period T. Show that $T \le 2\pi$. Use Problems 17 and 18.

20. (a) Show that $G_1(y, v) = mv^2/2 + ky^2/2$ is an integral of the motion $my'' + ky = 0$ ($m > 0$ and $k > 0$).

(b) Show that the curve $G_1(y, v) = c > 0$ is an ellipse in the (y, v) plane.

(c) Show that all solutions of $my'' + ky = 0$ are periodic.

(d) What can you say about the periods of solutions?

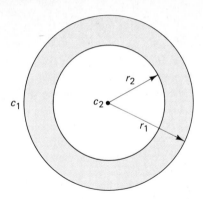

Figure 3.2. Cylindrical membrane problem.

21. Diffusion is a complicated phenomenon that must usually be modeled by partial differential equations (see Chapter 11). However, in certain simple situations ordinary differential equations will suffice. Let c be the concentration, in moles per liter, of a chemical in solution. A cylindrical membrane is introduced into a salt bath with constant concentration c_1 (see Figure 3.2). If the concentration inside the membrane is held at a different concentration c_2, diffusion will occur across the membrane according to the equation

$$\frac{d^2c}{dr^2} + \frac{1}{r}\frac{dc}{dr} = 0, \qquad c(r_1) = c_1, \qquad c(r_2) = c_2$$

where r is distance as measured from the center of the cylindrical membrane. Find the concentration inside the membrane; that is, find $c(r)$ when $r_2 < r < r_1$.

3.2 SECOND-ORDER LINEAR EQUATIONS

The general second-order linear equation has the form

(2.1)
$$a_2(x)\frac{d^2y}{dx^2} + a_1(x)\frac{dy}{dx} + a_0(x)y = h(x),$$

where $a_0(x)$, $a_1(x)$, $a_2(x)$, and $h(x)$ are defined and continuous on some open interval $J = \{x : A_1 < x < A_2\}$. Throughout this chapter it will be assumed that $a_2(x) \neq 0$ for all x in J. The study of (2.1) in case $a_2(x)$ is zero at some point x_0 of J is interesting but complicated. The study of (2.1) in such cases will be postponed until Chapter 5.

Since we assume that $a_2(x)$ is never zero, we can divide (2.1) by $a_2(x)$. The resulting equation has the form

(N)
$$\frac{d^2y}{dx^2} + b_1(x)\frac{dy}{dx} + b_0(x)y = g(x),$$

where $b_0(x)$, $b_1(x)$, and $g(x)$ are continuous functions on the interval J. This is the type of equation that we shall study in the remainder of this chapter. When $g(x)$ is identically zero over the interval J, the equation takes the form

(H)
$$\frac{d^2y}{dx^2} + b_1(x)\frac{dy}{dx} + b_0(x)y = 0.$$

The linear equation (H) is called **homogeneous.** In contrast, (N) is called **non-homogeneous** to signify that $g(x)$ is not necessarily zero. The function $g(x)$ is called the **nonhomogeneous term** or the **forcing function,** while the functions $b_0(x)$ and $b_1(x)$ are called the **coefficients** of the linear equation.

A linear differential equation is said to have **constant coefficients** when $b_0(x) \equiv c$ and $b_1(x) \equiv b$ are constants. A linear differential equation with constant coefficients may be either homogeneous, that is,

$$y'' + by' + cy = 0,$$

or nonhomogeneous,

$$y'' + by' + cy = g(x).$$

LINEAR DIFFERENTIAL OPERATORS

We define a **differential operator** L by the relation

$$L = \frac{d^2}{dx^2} + b_1(x)\frac{d}{dx} + b_0(x).$$

Hence if $\varphi(x)$ is any twice-continuously-differentiable function defined for x in J, then

$$L\varphi = \varphi'' + b_1\varphi' + b_0\varphi.$$

The differential operator L is **linear.** By this we mean that it satisfies the two relations

(a) $L(c\varphi) = cL\varphi$, and

(b) $L(\varphi_1 + \varphi_2) = L\varphi_1 + L\varphi_2$,

for all twice-differentiable functions φ, φ_1, and φ_2 and for all constants c.

The student should check that (a) and (b) are indeed true. With this notation (N) can be written in the form $Ly = g$, and (H) can be written as $Ly = 0$.

EXAMPLE 2.1   If $b_1(x) = x + 1$ and $b_0(x) = \sin x$, then

$$L\varphi(x) = \varphi''(x) + (x + 1)\varphi'(x) + (\sin x)\varphi(x).$$

In particular, if $\varphi(x) = x^2$, then

$$L(x^2) = (x^2)'' + (x + 1) \cdot (x^2)' + (\sin x) \cdot x^2$$
$$= 2 + (x + 1)(2x) + (\sin x)x^2$$
$$= 2x^2 + 2x + 2 + x^2 \sin x.$$

If $\varphi(x) = \cos 2x$, then

$$L(\cos 2x) = (\cos 2x)'' + (x + 1) \cdot (\cos 2x)' + \sin x \, (\cos 2x)$$
$$= -4\cos 2x + (x + 1)(-2 \sin 2x) + \sin x \, (\cos 2x)$$
$$= -4\cos 2x - (2x + 2) \sin 2x + \sin x \cos 2x.$$

If $\varphi(x) = e^{\lambda x}$ for some real number λ, then

$$L(e^{\lambda x}) = (e^{\lambda x})'' + (x + 1) \cdot (e^{\lambda x})' + \sin x(e^{\lambda x})$$
$$= \lambda^2 e^{\lambda x} + (x + 1)\lambda e^{\lambda x} + \sin x(e^{\lambda x})$$
$$= e^{\lambda x}[\lambda^2 + \lambda(x + 1) + \sin x].$$

In this case the coefficients $b_0(x) = \sin x$ and $b_1(x) = x + 1$ are defined and continuous over the interval $-\infty < x < \infty$. ∎

EXAMPLE 2.2   The equation

$$x^2 y'' + 2xy' + 3y = 0$$

can be put in the form (H) by dividing by x^2. The resulting equation is

$$y'' + \frac{2}{x} y' + \frac{3}{x^2} y = 0.$$

Hence

$$L = \frac{d^2}{dx^2} + \frac{2}{x}\frac{d}{dx} + \frac{3}{x^2}.$$

The interval J can be taken as $(-\infty, 0)$ or as $(0, \infty)$. The point $x = 0$ must be avoided since $a_2(x) = x^2$ is zero there. This equation is homogeneous. ∎

EXAMPLE 2.3   The equation $2y'' + 3y' - y = \sin x$ can be put in the form (N). The resulting equation has the form $Ly = g$, where $L\varphi = \varphi'' + \frac{3}{2}\varphi' - \frac{1}{2}\varphi$. Moreover, $g(x) = (\sin x)/2$ is the forcing function. The interval J is $-\infty < x < \infty$. This equation is nonhomogeneous and has constant coefficients. ∎

Notice that (N) can be written in the form

$$y'' = f(x, y, y'),$$

where f is the function defined by the relation

$$f(x, y, z) = -b_1(x)z - b_0(x)y + g(x),$$

for all x in J, for all y and for all z. Since the partial derivatives

$$\frac{\partial f}{\partial y}(x, y, z) = -b_0(x), \qquad \frac{\partial f}{\partial z}(x, y, z) = -b_1(x)$$

are continuous functions, the basic existence and uniqueness theorem of Chapter 1 applies. That theorem tells us that we can specify one and only one solution by giving two initial conditions of the form

$$(2.2) \qquad\qquad y(x_0) = a_0 \quad \text{and} \quad y'(x_0) = a_1,$$

where x_0 is any point in J and a_0 and a_1 are any real numbers. A special property of linear equations is that the solution determined by (N) and (2.2) will be defined over the entire interval J.

EXAMPLE 2.4   Consider the equation

$$(2.3) \qquad\qquad x^2 y'' - xy' - 8y = 0, \qquad 0 < x < \infty.$$

This homogeneous equation has coefficients $b_1(x) = -1/x$ and $b_0(x) = -8/x^2$. These coefficients are defined and are continuous on the interval $J = (0, \infty)$. Hence any solution of (2.3) will be defined over the interval $0 < x < \infty$ but will not necessarily be defined over a larger interval.

The function $y = \varphi(x) = x^{-2}$ is a solution of (2.3). This can be verified by putting x^{-2} into (2.3), since $y' = -2x^{-3}$ and $y'' = 6x^{-4}$; then

$$x^2(6x^{-4}) - x(-2x^{-3}) - 8x^{-2} = 0,$$

as required. This solution is defined over the interval $J = (0, \infty)$ but not on any larger interval. ∎

PROBLEMS   In Problems 1–6, determine the associated operator L and a suitable interval J. State whether the equation is homogeneous. State whether the equation has constant coefficients.

1. $y'' + 3y' + 2y = 0.$ 2. $y'' + 3xy' + 2y = 0.$

3. $xy'' + 3y' + y = x.$ 4. $xy'' + xy = 4.$

5. $(1 - x^2)y'' + xy' + y = 0.$ 6. $x^2 y'' + xy' - 4y = \sin x.$

7. The conditions $(x^2 - 4)y'' + y = 0$, $y(0) = 1$, $y'(0) = 0$ determine one and only one solution $y = \varphi(x)$. On what interval J can you be sure that this solution is defined?

8. Verify that $y = 1/x^2$ is a solution of

$$x^2 y'' + 2xy' - 2y = 0, \qquad y(1) = 1, \qquad y'(1) = -2.$$

On what interval J is this solution defined?

9. Define $Ly = y'' - xy$ and $My = 3y'$. Compute

   (a) $Ly + My$.

   (b) $3Ly - My$.

   (c) MLy.

   (d) LMy.

   Show that there is a three-times-continuously-differentiable function $\varphi(x)$ such that $LM\varphi \neq ML\varphi$.

10. Define two operators L and M by the relations

$$Ly = y'' + by' + cy \quad \text{and} \quad My = y'' + dy' + ey,$$

   where b, c, d, and e are constants. Show that $LMy = MLy$ for all four-times-continuously-differentiable functions y.

11. Let $Ly = y'' + 3y' + 2y$. Compute

   (a) $L(e^x)$.

   (b) $L(e^{-x})$.

   (c) $L(x^2)$.

   (d) $L(e^{rx})$, where r is a real constant.

   (e) $L(x^r)$, where r is a real constant.

   (f) $L(\log x)$.

   (g) $L(\sin x + 1)$.

   (h) $L(x^2 + e^{-x})$.

   (i) $L(3e^x)$.

   (j) $L(-e^{-x})$.

   (k) $L(3e^{rx})$.

   (l) $L(ae^{rx})$.

3.3 *LINEAR HOMOGENEOUS EQUATIONS*

We will now study the second-order linear homogeneous equation

(H) $$Ly = y'' + b_1(x)y' + b_0(x)y = 0,$$

where b_0 and b_1 are continuous over some fixed open interval J. The following result will prove to be extremely important.

THEOREM 3.1: LINEAR COMBINATIONS

If $y_1(x)$ and $y_2(x)$ are solutions of the differential equation (H) on J and if c_1 and c_2 are any constants, then $y = c_1y_1 + c_2y_2$ is also a solution of (H) on J.

To see that this is correct, first notice that since y_1 and y_2 are solutions, then $Ly_1 = y_1'' + b_1y_1' + b_0y_1 = 0$ and $Ly_2 = y_2'' + b_1y_2' + b_0y_2 = 0$. Thus

$$Ly = L(c_1 y_1 + c_2 y_2)$$
$$= (c_1 y_1 + c_2 y_2)'' + b_1(c_1 y_1 + c_2 y_2)' + b_0(c_1 y_1 + c_2 y_2)$$
$$= c_1(y_1'' + b_1 y_1' + b_0 y_1) + c_2(y_2'' + b_1 y_2' + b_0 y_2)$$
$$= c_1 L y_1 + c_2 L y_2 = c_1 \cdot 0 + c_2 \cdot 0 = 0.$$

Hence $y = c_1 y_1 + c_2 y_2$ solves (H).

In Theorem 3.1 two special cases are of particular interest. If $c_2 = 0$. then $y = c_1 y_1$. Thus we see that a constant multiple of any solution of (H) is again a solution of (H). If $c_1 = 1$ and $c_2 \pm 1$, then $y = y_1' \pm y_2$. Thus we see that the sum and the difference of any two solutions of (H) is again a solution.

EXAMPLE 3.2   It is easy to verify that $y_1 = \cos x$ and $y_2 = \sin x$ are both solutions of

$$y'' + y = 0.$$

Indeed, let $Ly = y'' + y$. Then

$$L(\cos x) = (\cos x)'' + \cos x = (-\cos x) + \cos x = 0,$$

and

$$L(\sin x) = (\sin x)'' + \sin x = (-\sin x) + \sin x = 0.$$

Hence $y = c_1 \cos x + c_2 \sin x$ is also a solution for any constants c_1 and c_2.   ∎

EXAMPLE 3.3   Both $y_1 = x$ and $y_2 = x^{-2}$ solve

$$x^2 y'' + 2xy' - 2y = 0, \qquad 0 < x < \infty.$$

Hence $y = c_1 x + c_2 x^{-2}$ is also a solution where c_1 and c_2 are arbitrary constants.   ∎

Given two solutions y_1 and y_2 of (H), the combination

(3.1) $$y = c_1 y_1 + c_2 y_2$$

is a solution of (H) that contains two arbitrary constants. Hence it is a candidate for a general solution of (H). This expression will be a general solution of (H) provided that for any initial conditions

(3.2) $$y(x_0) = a_0 \quad \text{and} \quad y'(x_0) = a_1 \qquad \text{with } x_0 \text{ in } J$$

the solution (3.1) will satisfy (3.2) when c_1 and c_2 are suitably chosen. To see whether c_1 and c_2 can be suitably chosen, we fix x_0 and choose a_0 and a_1. We insert (3.1) into (3.2) and obtain the following two linear algebraic equations:

$$c_1 y_1(x_0) + c_2 y_2(x_0) = a_0$$
$$c_1 y_1'(x_0) + c_2 y_2'(x_0) = a_1.$$

This system of algebraic equations can always be solved for c_1 and c_2 no matter how x_0, a_0, and a_1 are chosen if and only if the determinant

$$(3.3) \qquad W(y_1, y_2)(x) = \begin{vmatrix} y_1(x) & y_2(x) \\ y_1'(x) & y_2'(x) \end{vmatrix} = y_1(x)y_2'(x) - y_1'(x)y_2(x) \neq 0$$

for every $x = x_0$ in the interval J.

The determinant $W(y_1, y_2)$ defined in (3.3) is called the **Wronskian** of y_1 and y_2 after the Polish mathematician H. Wronski. Furthermore, a set $\{y_1, y_2\}$ of solutions of (H) is called a **fundamental set** of solutions if every solution of (H) can be expressed as a linear combination of y_1 and y_2, that is, every solution of (H) can be put in the form (3.1) for some choice of the constants c_1 and c_2. The argument in the preceding paragraphs proves the following result.

THEOREM 3.4

Suppose that the coefficients of (H) are continuous over the interval J and that y_1 and y_2 are solutions of (H). Then $\{y_1, y_2\}$ is a fundamental set of solutions of (H) if and only if the Wronskian $W(y_1, y_2)(x) \neq 0$ for all x in J.

It is convenient to express (3.3) in another, equivalent way. We say that two functions y_1 and y_2 defined over J are **linearly independent** over J if the identity

$$(3.4) \qquad c_1 y_1(x) + c_2 y_2(x) = 0 \qquad \text{for all } x \text{ in } J,$$

is true only when $c_1 = c_2 = 0$. If constants c_1 and c_2, not both zero, can be found so that (3.4) is true, then y_1 and y_2 are said to be **linearly dependent** over J. Hence y_1 and y_2 are linearly dependent if and only if one of the functions is a constant multiple of the other.

EXAMPLE 3.5 The functions $y_1(x) = 1$ and $y_2(x) = x$ are linearly independent over the interval $-\infty < x < \infty$. To see this, suppose that

$$(3.5) \qquad c_1 \cdot 1 + c_2 x = 0 \qquad \text{for all } x.$$

Since this is true for all x, it is true for $x = 0$. However, if $x = 0$, then (3.5) becomes $c_1 = 0$. Once we know that c_1 is zero, we choose $x = 1$ in (3.5) to see that $c_2 = 0$. Hence $c_1 = c_2 = 0$. Thus y_1 and y_2 are linearly independent over $(-\infty, \infty)$. ∎

EXAMPLE 3.6   The functions $y_1(x) = \sin x$ and $y_2(x) = \cos(x + \pi/2)$ are linearly dependent. To see this, note that $y_2(x) = \cos(x + \pi/2) = -\sin x$. Hence $y_1(x) + y_2(x) = 0$ for all x. Thus (3.4) is true with $c_1 = c_2 = 1$. ∎

We are particularly interested in linear independence or dependence in the case where y_1 and y_2 are solutions of (H) over the interval J.

THEOREM 3.7

Let y_1 and y_2 be solutions of (H) over the interval J. Then y_1 and y_2 are linearly independent if and only if the Wronskian $W(y_1, y_2)(x) \neq 0$ for all x in the interval J.

To see that the theorem is true, note that if (3.4) is true for all x in J, one can differentiate (3.4) and see that both

(3.6) $c_1 y_1(x) + c_2 y_2(x) = 0$ and $c_1 y_1'(x) + c_2 y_2'(x) = 0$

for all x in J. But (3.6) can be true for some c_1 and c_2, not both zero, if and only if $W(y_1, y_2)(x) = 0$ for all x in J. Next notice that if one defines $z = W(y_1, y_2)$ then,

$$z' = y_1'y_2' + y_1 y_2'' - y_1'' y_2 - y_1' y_2'$$

$$= y_1 y_2'' - y_1'' y_2$$

$$= y_1(-b_1 y_2' - b_0 y_2) - (-b_1 y_1' - b_0 y_1)y_2,$$

since y_1 and y_2 both satisfy (H). Thus z satisfies the differential equation

$$z' = -b_1(y_1 y_2' - y_1' y_2) = -b_1 z.$$

The solution of this equation is

(3.6) $z = W(y_1, y_2)(x) = W(y_1, y_2)(x_0)e^{-\int_{x_0}^{x} b_1(s)\, ds}.$

In particular, this argument shows that $W(y_1, y_2)(x)$ is nonzero at one point x_0 in J if and only if it is nonzero at all x in J. This proves Theorem 3.7. It also proves the next result. ∎

THEOREM 3.8

Let y_1 and y_2 be solutions of (H). Then either $W(y_1, y_2)(x)$ is identically zero on J or else it is never zero there.

EXAMPLE 3.9   We have seen that $y_1(x) = \cos x$ and $y_2(x) = \sin x$ solve $y'' + y = 0$ on $J = (-\infty, \infty)$. The Wronskian is

$$W(y_1, y_2)(x) = \det \begin{vmatrix} \cos x & \sin x \\ -\sin x & \cos x \end{vmatrix}$$

$$= \cos^2 x + \sin^2 x = 1 \neq 0. \quad \blacksquare$$

EXAMPLE 3.10   The pair of functions $y_3(x) = \sin x$, $y_4(x) = \cos(x + \pi/2)$ both solve the equation $y'' + y = 0$. The Wronskian is

$$W(y_3, y_4)(x) = \det \begin{vmatrix} \sin x & \cos\left(x + \dfrac{\pi}{2}\right) \\ \cos x & -\sin\left(x + \dfrac{\pi}{2}\right) \end{vmatrix}$$

$$= \det \begin{vmatrix} \sin x & -\sin x \\ \cos x & -\cos x \end{vmatrix} = 0,$$

for all x in $(-\infty, \infty)$. $\quad \blacksquare$

We now combine the preceding results into one theorem.

THEOREM 3.11: FUNDAMENTAL SETS

Let the coefficients of (H) be continuous on the interval J. Let y_1 and y_2 be two given solutions of (H) on J. If any one of the following statements is true, then all of the others are also true.

    (a) $W(y_1, y_2)(x) \neq 0$ for all x in J.
    (b) $W(y_1, y_2)(x_0) \neq 0$ for at least one x_0 in J.
    (c) $\{y_1, y_2\}$ is a fundamental set of solutions of (H).
    (d) y_1 and y_2 are linearly independent solutions of (H) on J.

Thus we see that when dealing with (H), finding a fundamental set $\{y_1, y_2\}$ of solutions is equivalent to finding two linearly independent solutions y_1 and y_2. A systematic way to check that two solutions y_1 and y_2 are linearly independent is to show that their Wronskian is not zero at some convenient point x_0. If this can be done, we will know that a general solution of (H) is $y = c_1 y_1 + c_2 y_2$, where c_1 and c_2 are arbitrary constants.

EXAMPLE 3.12   Consider $y'' + y = 0$. Two solutions are $y_1(x) = \cos x$ and $y_2(x) = \sin x$. In Example 3.9 we showed that $W(y_1, y_2)(x) = 1 \neq 0$ for all x on the real line. Hence a general solution of the given equation is $y = c_1 \cos x + c_2 \sin x$. $\quad \blacksquare$

EXAMPLE 3.13   Consider the equation $x^2 y'' + 2xy' - 2y = 0$ over the interval $J = (0, \infty)$. Two solutions are $y_1(x) = x$ and $y_2(x) = x^{-2}$. At $x = 1$ we compute

$$W(y_1, y_2)(1) = \begin{vmatrix} x & x^{-2} \\ 1 & -2x^{-3} \end{vmatrix}_{x=1} = \begin{vmatrix} 1 & 1 \\ 1 & -2 \end{vmatrix} = -3 \neq 0.$$

Hence we know that a general solution of this equation on $(0, \infty)$ is

(3.7) $y = c_1 x + c_2 x^{-2}$

The same type of calculation can be used to show that (3.7) defines a general solution over the interval $(-\infty, 0)$. ∎

PROBLEMS   In Problems 1–8, verify that the functions given solve the equation. Decide whether or not the set of solutions is linearly dependent or independent.

1. $y'' - y = 0$, $y_1 = e^x$ and $y_2 = e^{-x}$ over $-\infty < x < \infty$.

2. $y'' - 4y = 0$, $y_1 = \sinh 2x$ and $y_2 = \cosh 2x$ over $-\infty < x < \infty$.

3. $y'' + 3y' + 2y = 0$, $y_1 = e^{-2x}$ and $y_2 = e^{-2x} + e^{-x}$ over $-\infty < x < \infty$.

4. $x^2 y'' - xy' - 3y = 0$, $y_1 = 2x^3$ and $y_2 = x^{-1}$ over $0 < x < \infty$.

5. $y'' + 9y = 0$, $y_1 = \cos 3x$ and $y_2 = \cos(3x + \pi)$ over $-\infty < x < \infty$.

6. $y'' + 9y = 0$, $y_1 = \cos 3x$ and $y_2 = \cos(3x + \pi/3)$ over $-\infty < x < \infty$.

7. $y'' - 2y' + y = 0$, $y_1 = e^x$ and $y_2 = xe^x$ over $-\infty < x < \infty$.

8. $y'' + y = 0$, $y_1 = \sin x$ and $y_2 = 0$ over $-\infty < x < \infty$.

9. Show that $y = c_1 e^{-2x} + c_2 e^x$ is a general solution of $y'' + y' - 2y = 0$. Find the solutions of this equation that satisfy the following initial conditions.

(a) $y(0) = 1$, $y'(0) = 0$.   (b) $y(0) = -1$, $y'(0) = 1$.

(c) $y(1) = 0$, $y'(1) = 0$.   (d) $y(\log 2) = 0$, $y'(\log 2) = 1$.

10. Show that $y = c_1 x + c_2 x \log x$ is a general solution of

$$x^2 y'' - xy' + y = 0, \qquad 0 < x < \infty.$$

Find the solution of this equation that satisfies the following initial conditions.

(a) $y(1) = 1$, $y'(1) = 0$.   (b) $y(2) = 0$, $y'(2) = 0$.

(c) $y(1) = 1$, $y'(1) = -1$.

11. Show that the homogeneous equation (H) always has at least one fundamental set of solutions. (In fact, it has infinitely many.) *Hint:* For any x_0 in J the existence and uniqueness theorem implies that there is a solution y_1 of (H) which satisfies $y_1(x_0) = 1$, $y(x_0) = 0$. Find a y_2 to go with this y_1.

12. Let y_1 and y_2 be solutions of $y'' + y' - 4y = 0$ such that $y_1(0) = 1$, $y_1'(0) = 0$, and $y_2(0) = 2$, $y_2'(0) = 1$. Compute $W(y_1, y_2)(x)$ for $x = 0, 1$ and 2. *Hint:* Use (3.6).

13. Let y_1 and y_2 be two solutions of $y'' - 3y' + y = 0$ such that

$$y_1(0) = 1, \qquad y_1'(0) = 2 \quad \text{and} \quad y_2(0) = -1, \qquad y_2'(0) = 3.$$

Compute $W(y_1, y_2)(x)$ for $x = 1$, $x = -1$, and $x = 3$. *Hint:* Use (3.6).

14. (a) Locate an algebra textbook and review Cramer's rule.

(b) Show that if

$$\det \begin{vmatrix} b_{11} & b_{12} \\ b_{21} & b_{22} \end{vmatrix} = b_{11}b_{22} - b_{12}b_{21} \neq 0,$$

and if x_1 and x_2 solve

$$b_{11}x_1 + b_{12}x_2 = a_0$$

$$b_{21}x_1 + b_{22}x_2 = a_1,$$

then

$$x_1 = \det \begin{vmatrix} a_0 & b_{12} \\ a_1 & b_{22} \end{vmatrix} \Big/ \det \begin{vmatrix} b_{11} & b_{12} \\ b_{21} & b_{22} \end{vmatrix}.$$

(c) Find a similar formula for x_2.

(d) Let y_1 and y_2 be a fundamental set of solutions of (H) over J so that $y = c_1y_1 + c_2y_2$ is a general solution. In order that y satisfy the initial conditions.

$$y(x_0) = a_0,\ y'(x_0) = a_1 \qquad \text{for some } x_0 \text{ in } J$$

show that

$$c_1 = \det \begin{vmatrix} a_0 & y_2(x_0) \\ a_1 & y_2'(x_0) \end{vmatrix} \Big/ W(y_1,\ y_2)(x_0).$$

(e) Find a similar formula for c_2.

Solve the **boundary value problems** 15–20 by first finding a general solution in the form $y = c_1\varphi_1(x) + c_2\varphi_2(x)$. Then use the two boundary conditions to determine c_1 and c_2. Each problem may have no solution, one solution, or infinitely many solutions.

15. $y'' + y = 0$, $y(0) = y(2\pi) = 0$. *Hint:* See Example 3.9.

16. $y'' + y = 0$, $y(0) = 0$, $y(\pi) = 1$.

17. $y'' + y = 0$, $y'(0) = 0$, $y(1) = 2$.

18. $y'' + y = 0$, $y(0) = y'(0)$, $y(1) = 1$.

19. $x^2y'' + 2xy' - 2y = 0$, $y(1) = 0$, $y(2) = 1$. *Hint:* See Example 3.13.

20. $x^2y'' + 2xy' - 2y = 0$, $y'(1) = 1$, $y(2) = 2$.

3.4   HOMOGENEOUS EQUATIONS WITH CONSTANT COEFFICIENTS

We will now consider methods of finding solutions of second-order linear equations that are homogeneous and have constant coefficients. These equations have the form

(4.1) $Ly = ay'' + by' + cy = 0,$

where a, b, and c are given constants and $a \neq 0$. Equations that have constant coefficients are somewhat special but are also extremely important in applications. In this section and in Section 3.5 we develop methods for finding a general solution of (4.1). Nonhomogeneous equations with constant coefficients will be studied later in this chapter.

We introduce some new notation for derivatives and for the operator L in (4.1). Define $D = d/dx$ and in general $D^n = d^n/dx^n$. Thus

$$D(\cos x) = \frac{d}{dx}(\cos x) = -\sin x,$$

$$D^2(\cos x) = \frac{d^2}{dx^2}(\cos x) = -\cos x,$$

and so on. With this notation one can rewrite (4.1) as follows:

$$Ly = (a\frac{d^2}{dx^2} + \frac{d}{dx} + c)y = (aD^2 + bD + c)y = 0.$$

Recall that for a first-order linear equation with constant coefficients, that is,

$$y' - ky = (D - k)y = 0,$$

the function $y = e^{kx}$ is a solution. Reasoning by analogy we shall try to find a solution of (4.1) of the form $y = e^{\lambda x}$, where λ is an undetermined constant. Substitute $y = e^{\lambda x}$ in (4.1). Since $De^{\lambda x} = \lambda e^{\lambda x}$ and $D^2 e^{\lambda x} = \lambda^2 e^{\lambda x}$, then

$$L(e^{\lambda x}) = a\lambda^2 e^{\lambda x} + b\lambda e^{\lambda x} + ce^{\lambda x}$$
$$= (a\lambda^2 + b\lambda + c)e^{\lambda x} = 0.$$

Since $e^{\lambda x}$ is never zero, we must have $a\lambda^2 + b\lambda + c = 0$.

The polynomial

$$p(\lambda) = a\lambda^2 + b\lambda + c$$

is called the **characteristic polynomial** for (4.1) and the equation $p(\lambda) = 0$ is called the **characteristic equation** for (4.1). The roots of $p(\lambda)$ are called the **characteristic roots** of (4.1). Notice that $p(\lambda)$ can be written down immediately if L is first written in the D notation, that is,

$$L = aD^2 + bD + c.$$

We shall now proceed to solve (4.1) in those cases where $p(\lambda)$ has real roots.

Case 1. The Roots of $p(\lambda)$ Are Real and Not Equal.

We are assuming that the characteristic equation has two real roots λ_1 and λ_2 and that $\lambda_1 \neq \lambda_2$. In this case two solutions of (4.1) are

$$y_1 = e^{\lambda_1 x} \quad \text{and} \quad y_2 = e^{\lambda_2 x}.$$

The Wronskian of this pair of solutions is

$$W(y_1, y_2)(x) = \begin{vmatrix} e^{\lambda_1 x} & e^{\lambda_2 x} \\ \lambda_1 e^{\lambda_1 x} & \lambda_2 e^{\lambda_2 x} \end{vmatrix} = (\lambda_2 - \lambda_1)e^{(\lambda_1 + \lambda_2)x}.$$

Since $\lambda_2 - \lambda_1 \neq 0$, this Wronskian is not zero for all real numbers x. Hence a general solution is

$$y = c_1 e^{\lambda_1 x} + c_2 e^{\lambda_2 x}.$$

EXAMPLE 4.1   Find a general solution of $y'' - 2y' - 8y = 0$.
   The characteristic polynomial is $\lambda^2 - 2\lambda - 8 = (\lambda - 4)(\lambda + 2)$. The characteristic roots are $\lambda_1 = 4$ and $\lambda_2 = -2$. A general solution is

$$y = c_1 e^{4x} + c_2 e^{-2x}. \quad \blacksquare$$

EXAMPLE 4.2   Solve $y'' + y' = 0$, $y(0) = 1$, $y'(0) = -\frac{1}{2}$.
   The characteristic equation is $p(\lambda) = \lambda^2 + \lambda = \lambda(\lambda + 1) = 0$. The characteristic roots are $\lambda_1 = 0$ and $\lambda_2 = -1$. Recall that $e^{0 \cdot x} = 1$ for all real numbers x. Hence two linearly independent solutions are $y_1 = e^{0 \cdot x} = 1$ and $y_2 = e^{-x}$. The general solution is

$$y = c_1 + c_2 e^{-x}.$$

The two initial conditions imply that c_1 and c_2 satisfy the equations

$$1 = c_1 + c_2 \quad \text{and} \quad -\tfrac{1}{2} = -c_2.$$

Hence $c_1 = c_2 = \frac{1}{2}$ and the solution is $y = (1 + e^{-x})/2$. $\quad \blacksquare$

If the characteristic polynomial is not readily factorable, the characteristic roots can be found by applying the quadratic formula to $p(\lambda) = a\lambda^2 + b\lambda + c = 0$. This gives

$$\lambda_1 = \frac{-b + \sqrt{b^2 - 4ac}}{2a}, \qquad \lambda_2 = \frac{-b - \sqrt{b^2 - 4ac}}{2a}.$$

If λ_1 and λ_2 are real and unequal, the preceding method of solution applies.

EXAMPLE 4.3   Find a general solution of $y'' + y' - y = 0$.
   The characteristic equation is $\lambda^2 + \lambda - 1 = 0$. It has roots

$$\lambda_1 = \frac{-1 + \sqrt{5}}{2} \quad \text{and} \quad \lambda_2 = \frac{-1 - \sqrt{5}}{2}.$$

A general solution is

$$y = c_1 \exp\left[\left(\frac{-1 + \sqrt{5}}{2}\right)x\right] + c_2 \exp\left[\left(\frac{-1 - \sqrt{5}}{2}\right)x\right]. \quad \blacksquare$$

Case 2. The Two Roots of $p(\lambda)$ Are Real and Equal.
   In this case $\lambda_1 = \lambda_2$ and $p(\lambda) = a\lambda^2 + b\lambda + c = a(\lambda - \lambda_1)^2$. One solution is $y_1 = e^{\lambda_1 x}$. Since $e^{\lambda_2 x} = e^{\lambda_1 x}$, then y_2, a second solution such that $\{y_1, y_2\}$ is

linearly independent, is not yet known. To find a suitable y_2 we notice that (4.1) can be written as

$$(aD^2 + bD + c)y = a(D - \lambda_1)^2 y = 0$$

or

(4.2) $$(D - \lambda_1)[(D - \lambda_1)y] = 0.$$

Define $w = (D - \lambda_1)y$, where y is a solution of (4.1). Then from (4.2) it follows that

$$(D - \lambda_1)w = (D - \lambda_1)[(D - \lambda_1)y] = 0.$$

Hence w satisfies the first-order linear equation

$$(D - \lambda_1)w = 0.$$

This first-order equation can be solved for w; indeed, $w = c_1 e^{\lambda_1 x}$. Once w is known, we can solve

(4.3) $$(D - \lambda_1)y = w$$

for y. Rewrite (4.3) in the form

(4.4) $$y' - \lambda_1 y = c_1 e^{\lambda_1 x}.$$

This is a first-order linear equation. A suitable integration factor is $e^{-\lambda_1 x}$. On multiplying (4.4) by $e^{-\lambda_1 x}$, we find that

$$e^{-\lambda_1 x}(y' - \lambda_1 y) = (e^{-\lambda_1 x}y)' = c_1.$$

Hence

$$e^{-\lambda_1 x}y = c_1 x + c_2$$

and

$$y = (c_1 x + c_2)e^{\lambda_1 x}.$$

Since $y_1 = e^{\lambda_1 x}$, the result of our calculation is that $y_2 = xe^{\lambda_1 x}$. The pair $y_1 = e^{\lambda_1 x}$ and $y_2 = xe^{\lambda_1 x}$ form a fundamental set of solutions since

$$W(y_1, y_2)(x) = \begin{vmatrix} e^{\lambda_1 x} & xe^{\lambda_1 x} \\ \lambda_1 e^{\lambda_1 x} & e^{\lambda_1 x} + \lambda_1 xe^{\lambda_1 x} \end{vmatrix}$$

$$= e^{2\lambda_1 x} \neq 0.$$

EXAMPLE 4.4   Find a general solution of $y'' - 4y' + 4y = 0$.
    Since $p(\lambda) = \lambda^2 - 4\lambda + 4 = (\lambda - 2)^2$, then $\lambda_1 = 2$ is a characteristic root of multiplicity 2. Hence a general solution is

$$y = c_1 e^{2x} + c_2 xe^{2x}. \quad \blacksquare$$

EXAMPLE 4.5   Solve $(D^2 + 2D + 1)y = 0$, $y(0) = 1$, $y'(0) = -2$.

Since $p(\lambda) = \lambda^2 + 2\lambda + 1 = (\lambda + 1)^2$, then $\lambda_1 = -1$ is a characteristic root of multiplicity 2. A general solution is

$$y = c_1 e^{-x} + c_2 x e^{-x}.$$

The derivative of y is

$$y' = -c_1 e^{-x} + c_2 e^{-x} - c_2 x e^{-x}.$$

To satisfy the initial conditions, we require that c_1 and c_2 satisfy

$$c_1 = 1 \quad \text{and} \quad -c_1 + c_2 = -2.$$

Thus $c_1 = 1$, $c_2 = -1$ and the required solution is

$$y = e^{-x} - x e^{-x} = (1 - x)e^{-x}. \quad \blacksquare$$

METHOD OF SOLUTION: REAL ROOTS

---

1. If $p(\lambda) = 0$ has two real and distinct roots λ_1 and λ_2, then a general solution is

$$y = c_1 e^{\lambda_1 x} + c_2 e^{\lambda_2 x}.$$

2. If $\lambda_1 = \lambda_2$ is a real double root of the characteristic equation, then a general solution is

$$y = (c_1 + c_2 x)e^{\lambda_1 x}.$$

PROBLEMS   In Problems 1–16, solve the equation. Find a general solution if no initial conditions are given.

1. $y'' - 2y' - 3y = 0$.

2. $(2D^2 - D - 1)y = 0$.

3. $y'' - 4y = 0$.

4. $(D^2 - 2D)y = 0$.

5. $\dfrac{d^2 y}{dt^2} - 2\dfrac{dy}{dt} - 2y = 0$.

6. $(D^2 - 6D + 9)y = 0$.

7. $4y'' + 4y' + y = 0$.

8. $(4D^2 - 2D + \frac{1}{4})y = 0$.

9. $y'' - y = 0$, $y(0) = 1$, $y'(0) = 0$.

10. $y'' - 5y' + 6y = 0$, $y(0) = 0$, $y'(0) = 1$.

11. $y'' - 2y' = 0$, $y(1) = 0$, $y'(1) = 2$.

12. $y'' - y' + \dfrac{y}{4} = 0$, $y(0) = -1$, $y'(0) = 2$.

13. $(D^2 - 8D + 16)y = 0$, $y(0) = 0$, $y'(0) = 1$.

14. $(D^2 - 3\pi D + 2\pi^2)y = 0.$

15. $(D^2 - D - 6)y = 0,$ $y(0) = 0,$ $y'(0) = -1.$

16. $\dfrac{d^2B}{dx^2} - 10\dfrac{dB}{dx} + 25B = 0.$

17. (a) There are many fundamental sets of solutions. Show that for $\alpha > 0$, $y_1(x) = \sinh \alpha x$ and $y_2(x) = \cosh \alpha x$ is a fundamental set of solutions of

$$y'' - \alpha^2 y = 0.$$

   (b) Find the solution that satisfies $y(0) = 1,$ $y'(0) = 0.$

   (c) Find the solution that satisfies $y(0) = 0,$ $y'(0) = 1.$

18. If $\{y_1, y_2\}$ is a fundamental set of solutions of (4.1) and if

$$w_1 = \frac{y_1 + y_2}{2}, \qquad w_2 = \frac{y_1 - y_2}{2},$$

show that $\{w_1, w_2\}$ is a fundamental set of solutions.

19. If $\{y_1, y_2\}$ is a fundamental set of solutions of (H) and if the determinant

$$\begin{vmatrix} a & b \\ c & d \end{vmatrix} \neq 0,$$

show that $\{w_1, w_2\}$, where

$$w_1 = ay_1 + by_2 \quad \text{and} \quad w_2 = cy_1 + dy_2,$$

is also a fundamental set of solutions of (4.1).

20. Let $Ly = ay''' + by'' + cy' + dy$ and let $p(\lambda) = a\lambda^3 + b\lambda^2 + c\lambda + d.$ Prove each statement.

   (a) If λ_1 is a root of $p(\lambda) = 0$, then $y = e^{\lambda_1 x}$ is a solution of $Ly = 0.$

   (b) If λ_1 is a root of $p(\lambda)$ of multiplicity 2, then $y = xe^{\lambda_1 x}$ is a solution of $Ly = 0.$

   (c) If λ_1 is a root of $p(\lambda)$ of multiplicity 3, then $y_2 = xe^{\lambda_1 x}$ and $y_3 = x^2 e^{\lambda_1 x}$ are solutions of $Ly = 0.$

21. Solve

   (a) $(D - 1)(D + 1)(D - 2)y = 0,$ $y(0) = 1,$ $y'(0) = 0,$ $y''(0) = 0.$

   (b) $(D - 1)^2(D + 1)y = 0,$ $y(0) = 0,$ $y'(0) = 1,$ $y''(0) = 1.$

   (c) $(D - 1)^3 y = 0,$ $y(0) = y'(0) = 0,$ $y''(0) = 2.$

   Hint: Use Problem 20.

22. (a) Show that all solutions of

$$(aD^2 + bD + c)y = Ae^{\lambda x}$$

   are solutions of

$$(D - \lambda)(aD^2 + bD + c)y = 0.$$

   (b) Show that all solutions of

$$(aD^2 + bD + c)y = Axe^{\lambda x}$$

are solutions of

$$(D - \lambda)^2(aD^2 + bD + c)y = 0.$$

23. (a) Show that if $y = \varphi(x)$ is the solution of

$$ay'' + by' + cy = 0, \qquad y(0) = a_0, \qquad y'(0) = a_1,$$

then $y = \varphi(x - x_0)$ is the solution of

$$ay'' + by' + cy = 0, \qquad y(x_0) = a_0, \qquad y'(x_0) = a_1.$$

(b) Solve $y'' - 16y = 0$, $y(2) = 1$, $y'(2) = 0$. *Hint:* See Problem 17.

(c) Solve $y'' - 9y = 0$, $y(-1) = 0$, $y'(-1) = 1$.

(d) Solve $y'' - 2y = 0$, $y(\pi) = 1$, $y'(\pi) = 0$.

24. (a) Show that under the transformation $y = w'/(rw)$, the nonlinear equation $y' + qy + ry^2 = g(x)$ becomes

$$w'' + qw' - rg(x)w = 0.$$

(b) Using part (a), solve $y' + 3y^2 = 7$, $y(0) = 0$. Then show that

$$\lim_{t \to \infty} y(t) = y_\infty$$

exists. Compute y_∞.

(c) Apply sign analysis to $y' + 3y^2 = 7$. What general properties of the solution can you predict? Is the value y_∞ surprising?

3.5 COMPLEX CHARACTERISTIC ROOTS

The purpose of this section is to develop a method to solve the linear homogeneous constant coefficient equation

(5.1) $$Ly = (aD^2 + bD + c)y = 0$$

in the case where the characteristic equation $p(\lambda) = a\lambda^2 + b\lambda + c = 0$ has complex roots. We have already encountered some situations of this type. For example, we know that $y = c_1 \cos x + c_2 \sin x$ is a general solution of

$$y'' + y = 0.$$

The corresponding characteristic equation $\lambda^2 + 1 = 0$ has the complex roots $\lambda_1 = i$ and $\lambda_2 = -i$, where $i^2 = -1$. In Section 2.8 it was shown that

$$M\frac{d^2y}{dt^2} + Ky = 0 \qquad (M > 0, K > 0),$$

has a general solution of the form

(5.2) $$y = A \sin\left(\sqrt{\frac{K}{M}}\,t + B\right),$$

where A and B are arbitrary constants. The corresponding characteristic equation $M\lambda^2 + K = 0$ has complex roots $\lambda_1 = \sqrt{K/M}\,i$ and $\lambda_2 = -\sqrt{K/M}\,i$. The method of solution that will be developed here will cover both of these equations and more.

Consider the homogeneous equation (5.1). Assume that a, b, and c are real numbers such that $b^2 - 4ac < 0$. Then the two roots of the characteristic equation $p(\lambda) = a\lambda^2 + b\lambda + c = 0$ are complex and are conjugates, that is,

$$\lambda_1 = \frac{-b + i\sqrt{4ac - b^2}}{2a}, \qquad \lambda_2 = \frac{-b - i\sqrt{4ac - b^2}}{2a}.$$

For example, in $y'' + 2y' + 10y = 0$ the characteristic polynomial is $p(\lambda) = \lambda^2 + 2\lambda + 10$ and the characteristic roots are $\lambda_1 = -1 + 3i$ and $\lambda_2 = -1 - 3i$. For the equation $y'' - 2y' + 3y = 0$ one has $p(\lambda) = \lambda^2 - 2\lambda + 3$ while $\lambda_1 = 1 + \sqrt{2}\,i$ and $\lambda_2 = 1 - \sqrt{2}\,i$.

In those cases where λ_1 and λ_2 are complex numbers we ask whether there is some reasonable way to define $e^{\lambda_1 x}$ and $e^{\lambda_2 x}$. If there is, then we ask whether $y_1 = e^{\lambda_1 x}$ and $y_2 = e^{\lambda_2 x}$ are solutions of (5.1) over $-\infty < x < \infty$. Since most applications require real-valued solutions, we also wish to know whether real-valued solutions of (5.1) can be readily found.

Before we deal with these questions we need to review some ideas about complex numbers. Complex numbers have the form $z = u + iv$, where u and v are real numbers and $i^2 = -1$. Since u or v or both can be zero, complex numbers include as special cases all real numbers (i.e., $u + i0$, u any real number) and also all purely imaginary numbers (i.e., $0 + iv$, v any real number). Given $z = u + iv$, the **real part** of z is u, written

$$\operatorname{Re} z = u,$$

and the **imaginary part** of z is v, written

$$\operatorname{Im} z = v.$$

The **conjugate** of z is defined by the relation

$$\bar{z} = u - iv.$$

Given two complex numbers $z_1 = u_1 + iv_1$ and $z_2 = u_2 + iv_2$, then

$$z_1 + z_2 = (u_1 + u_2) + i(v_1 + v_2)$$

and

$$z_1 z_2 = (u_1 u_2 - v_1 v_2) + i(u_1 v_2 + u_2 v_1).$$

With these definitions, addition and multiplication satisfy the usual rules of arithmetic. Moreover, if $z = u + iv$, the absolute value of z is defined by

$$|z| = \sqrt{z\bar{z}} = (u^2 + v^2)^{1/2}$$

and

$$\frac{1}{z} = \frac{\bar{z}}{z\bar{z}} = \frac{1}{|z|^2}\,\bar{z}, \qquad z \neq 0.$$

We also note that

$$\text{Re } z = \frac{z + \bar{z}}{2} \quad \text{and} \quad \text{Im } z = \frac{z - \bar{z}}{2i}.$$

From calculus we know that e^x has a Taylor's series about $x = 0$ of the form

$$e^x = 1 + x + \frac{x^2}{2!} + \frac{x^3}{3!} + \dots = \sum_{n=0}^{\infty} \frac{x^n}{n!}$$

for any real number x. Now we shall replace x by ix in this series and use the resulting series as the definition of e^{ix}. Hence

$$e^{ix} = \sum_{n=0}^{\infty} \frac{(ix)^n}{n!} = 1 + ix - \frac{x^2}{2!} - i\frac{x^3}{3!} + \frac{x^4}{4!} + i\frac{x^5}{5!} - \dots$$

$$= \left(1 - \frac{x^2}{2!} + \frac{x^4}{4!} - \frac{x^6}{6!} + \dots\right) + i\left(x - \frac{x^3}{3!} + \frac{x^5}{5!} - \dots\right)$$

$$= \cos x + i \sin x.$$

In other words, we define e^{ix} by the **Euler formula**

$$(5.3) \qquad\qquad e^{ix} = \cos x + i \sin x$$

for all real numbers x. For complex numbers $z = u + iv$ define

$$e^{u+iv} = e^u e^{iv} = e^u(\cos v + i \sin v)$$

or

$$(5.4) \qquad\qquad e^z = e^{\text{Re } z}[\cos (\text{Im } z) + i \sin (\text{Im } z)].$$

Note that

$$(5.5) \qquad\qquad e^{\bar{z}} = e^{\text{Re } z}[\cos (\text{Im } z) - i \sin (\text{Im } z) = \overline{e^z}$$

We now return to the differential equation (5.1). Assume that the characteristic polynomial $p(\lambda) = a\lambda^2 + b\lambda + c$ has a pair of complex conjugate roots, namely

$$\lambda_1 = u + iv \quad \text{and} \quad \lambda_2 = u - iv = \bar{\lambda}_1.$$

Since we define y_1 by the formula

$$y_1 = e^{\lambda_1 x} = e^{ux}(\cos vx + i \sin vx),$$

then

$$\frac{dy_1}{dx} = \frac{d}{dx}(e^{\lambda_1 x})$$

$$= ue^{ux}(\cos vx + i \sin vx) + e^{ux}(-v \sin vx + iv \cos vx)$$

$$= ue^{ux}(\cos vx + i \sin vx) + ive^{ux}(\cos vx + i \sin vx)$$

$$= (u + iv)y_1 = \lambda_1 y_1$$

and

$$\frac{d^2 y_1}{dx^2} = \frac{d}{dx}\left(\frac{dy_1}{dx}\right) = \frac{d}{dx}(\lambda_1 y_1) = \lambda_1 \frac{dy_1}{dx} = \lambda_1^2 y_1.$$

Hence

$$a\frac{d^2 y_1}{dx^2} + b\frac{dy_1}{dx} + cy_1 = (a\lambda_1^2 + b\lambda_1 + c)y_1 = 0.$$

By a similar calculation we see that $y_2 = e^{\lambda_2 x} = \bar{y}_1$ is also a solution. Hence

$$y = c_1 e^{\lambda_1 x} + c_2 e^{\lambda_2 x}$$

is a general solution. Unfortunately, the solutions y_1 and y_2 are complex valued. However, we can obtain real-valued solutions as follows. Define

$$y_3 = \frac{y_1 + y_2}{2} \quad \text{and} \quad y_4 = \frac{y_1 - y_2}{2i}.$$

Since y_3 and y_4 are linear combinations of the solutions y_1 and y_2, then they are also solutions. Moreover, since $y_2 = \bar{y}_1$, then

$$y_3 = \frac{y_1 + \bar{y}_1}{2} = \text{Re } y_1, \qquad y_4 = \frac{y_1 - \bar{y}_1}{2i} = \text{Im } y_1,$$

or

$$y_3 = e^{ux} \cos vx \quad \text{and} \quad y_4 = e^{ux} \sin vx.$$

These two solutions are linearly independent since

$$W(y_3, y_4)(x) = ve^{2ux} \neq 0.$$

METHOD OF SOLUTION: COMPLEX ROOTS

If $p(\lambda) = 0$ has a pair of complex roots $\lambda = u \pm iv$, then a general solution is

$$y = e^{ux}(c_1 \cos vx + c_2 \sin vx).$$

EXAMPLE 5.1   Find a general solution of $y'' + 2y' + 10y = 0$.
   The roots of $\lambda^2 + 2\lambda + 10$ are $\lambda_1 = -1 + 3i$ and $\lambda_2 = -1 - 3i$. Two complex-valued solutions are

$$e^{(-1 \pm 3i)} = e^{-x}(\cos 3x \pm i \sin 3x).$$

Hence $\{e^{-x} \cos 3x, e^{-x} \sin 3x\}$ is a real-valued fundamental set of solutions. A general solution is

$$y = c_1 e^{-x} \cos 3x + c_2 e^{-x} \sin 3x. \quad \blacksquare$$

EXAMPLE 5.2   Solve $y'' + 4y = 0$, $y(0) = 2$, $y'(0) = -1$.
    The roots of $\lambda^2 + 4 = 0$ are $\lambda = \pm 2i$. Since

$$e^{2ix} = \cos 2x + i \sin 2x,$$

a real-valued general solution is

$$y = c_1 \cos 2x + c_2 \sin 2x.$$

Since $y' = -2c_1 \sin 2x + 2c_2 \cos 2x$, the initial conditions are satisfied when $c_1 = 2$ and $c_2 = -\frac{1}{2}$. ∎

EXAMPLE 5.3   Find a general solution of $(2D^2 - 2D + 1)y = 0$.
    The roots of $2\lambda^2 - 2\lambda + 1 = 0$ are $\lambda = (1 \pm i)/2$. Since

$$e^{(1 \pm i)x/2} = e^{x/2}\left[\cos\left(\frac{x}{2}\right) \pm i \sin\left(\frac{x}{2}\right)\right],$$

a real-valued general solution is

$$y = c_1 e^{x/2} \cos\left(\frac{x}{2}\right) + c_2 e^{x/2} \sin\left(\frac{x}{2}\right). \quad ■$$

The equations mentioned at the beginning of this section can be solved by the given method. For example, $y'' + y = 0$ has characteristic roots $\lambda_1 = i$ and $\lambda_2 = -i$. Since

$$e^{ix} = \cos x + i \sin x,$$

then $\{y_1 = \cos x,\ y_2 = \sin x\}$ is a real-valued fundamental set of solutions. The mass–spring problem

$$(5.6) \qquad M\frac{d^2 y}{dt^2} + Ky = 0$$

was solved in Section 2.8 by a long and complicated calculation. Finding a general solution is now comparatively easy. The characteristic equation $M\lambda^2 + K = 0$ has roots $\pm i\sqrt{K/M}$. Since

$$e^{i\sqrt{K/M}\,t} = \cos\left(\sqrt{\frac{K}{M}}\,t\right) + i \sin\left(\sqrt{\frac{K}{M}}\,t\right),$$

then $\{y_1 = \sin \sqrt{K/M}\,t,\ y_2 = \cos \sqrt{K/M}\,t\}$ is a real-valued fundamental set of solutions over $-\infty < t < \infty$. A general solution is

$$(5.7) \qquad y = c_1 \sin \sqrt{\frac{K}{M}}\,t + c_2 \cos \sqrt{\frac{K}{M}}\,t.$$

The mass–spring problem (5.6) and its solution will be discussed in more detail in Section 3.12.

PROBLEMS

In Problems 1–7, solve the equation. If no initial conditions are given, find a general solution.

1. $y'' + 9y = 0$.

2. $y'' - y' + 2y = 0$.

3. $2y'' + y' + y = 0$.

4. $(2D^2 + 2D + 1)y = 0$.

5. $y'' + 2y = 0$, $y(0) = 1$, $y'(0) = 2$.

6. $y'' + 2y' + 3y = 0$, $y(0) = 0$, $y'(0) = 3$.

7. $y'' - 2y' + 17y = 0$, $y(0) = 1$, $y'(0) = 0$.

Problems 8–14 are review problems.

8. $\dfrac{d^2y}{dt^2} + 4y = 0$, $y(0) = 1$, $y'(0) = 0$.

9. $\dfrac{d^2y}{dt^2} - 4y = 0$, $y(0) = 1$, $y'(0) = 0$.

10. $4y'' + 4y' + y = 0$, $y(0) = 0$, $y'(0) = 1$.

11. $\dfrac{d^2P}{dt^2} - 4\dfrac{dP}{dt} + 5P = 0$.

12. $\dfrac{d^2N}{ds^2} + \pi N = 0$.

13. $\dfrac{d^2N}{dx^2} - 4\dfrac{dN}{dx} + 13N = 0$.

14. $Q'' + 2Q' + Q = 0$.

15. Show that if $y = \varphi(x)$ is a solution of $(aD^2 + bD + c)y = 0$, $y(0) = a_0$, $y'(0) = a_1$, then $y = \varphi(x - x_0)$ solves the initial value problem
$$(aD^2 + bD + c)y = 0, \qquad y(x_0) = a_0, \qquad y'(x_0) = a_1.$$
Then solve each initial value problem.

(a) $y'' + 3y = 0$, $y(0) = 1$, $y'(0) = -1$.

(b) $y'' + 3y = 0$, $y(3) = 1$, $y'(3) = -1$.

(c) $y'' + 3y = 0$, $y(-2) = 1$, $y'(-2) = -1$.

(d) $y'' + 2y' + 17y = 0$, $y(0) = 0$, $y'(0) = -2$.

(e) $y'' + 2y' + 17y = 0$, $y(1) = 0$, $y'(1) = -2$.

(f) $y'' + 2y' + 17y = 0$, $y(\pi) = 0$, $y'(\pi) = -2$.

(g) $y'' + 2y = 0$, $y(0) = 0$, $y'(0) = \sqrt{2}$.

(h) $y'' + 2y = 0$, $y(5) = 0$, $y'(5) = \sqrt{2}$.

(i) $y'' + 2y = 0$, $y(-\sqrt{\pi}) = 0$, $y'(-\sqrt{\pi}) = \sqrt{2}$.

16. For $Ly = (b_0D^3 + b_1D^2 + b_2D + b_3)y = 0$ suppose that λ_1 is a complex root of $p(\lambda) = b_0\lambda^3 + b_1\lambda^2 + b_2\lambda + b_3 = 0$. Show that

(a) $y = e^{\lambda_1 x}$ is a solution of $Ly = 0$.

(b) $y = \operatorname{Re}(e^{\lambda_1 x})$ is a solution of $Ly = 0$.

(c) $y = \operatorname{Im}(e^{\lambda_1 x})$ is a solution of $Ly = 0$.

17. Solve $(D^2 + 1)(D - 1)y = 0$, $y(0) = 1$, $y'(0) = 0$, $y''(0) = 0$.

18. Solve $(D^2 + D + 2)(D + 1)y = 0$, $y(0) = 1$, $y'(0) = 0$, $y''(0) = 0$.

19. (a) Let w be a general solution of $(aD^2 + bD + c)w = Ae^{\lambda x}$. Show that w solves $(D - \lambda)(aD^2 + bD + c)w = 0$.

(b) Let $\{y_1, y_2\}$ be a fundamental set of solutions of $(aD^2 + bD + c)y = 0$. Show that $w = c_1 y_1 + c_2 y_2 + Be^{\lambda x}$, where B is a fixed constant and c_1 and c_2 are arbitrary constants provided that $a\lambda^2 + b\lambda + c \neq 0$.

(c) Solve $(D^2 + 2D + 6)w = e^{-x}$, $w(0) = -1$, $w'(0) = 0$.

20. (a) Show that if w solves $(aD^2 + bD + c)w = \sin vx$, then w solves $(D^2 + v^2)(aD^2 + bD + c)w = 0$.

(b) Let $\{y_1, y_2\}$ be a fundamental set of solutions of $(aD^2 + bD + c)y = 0$. Show that w can be written in the form $w = c_1 y_1 + c_2 y_2 + A \cos vx + B \sin v$, where A and B are certain fixed constants while c_1 and c_2 are arbitrary constants provided that $a(iv)^2 + b(iv) + c \neq 0$.

(c) Solve $(D^2 + 1)w = \sin \sqrt{3}x$, $w(0) = 0$, $w'(0) = 0$.

Solve the **boundary value problems** 21–25 by first finding a general solution in the form $y = c_1 \varphi_1(x) + c_2 \varphi_2(x)$. Then use the two boundary conditions to determine c_1 and c_2. Each problem may have no solution, one solution, or infinitely many solutions.

21. $y'' + 4y = 0$, $y(0) = 0$, $y(1) = \pi/2$.

22. $y'' + 4y = 0$, $y(0) = 0$, $y(\pi/2) = 1$.

23. $y'' + 9y = 0$, $y(0) = 0$, $y(\pi/2) = 1$.

24. $y'' - 2y' + 17y = 0$, $y(0) = 0$, $y(1) = 0$.

25. $y'' - 2y' + 17y = 0$, $y(0) = 0$, $y(2) = 1$.

26. Find all real numbers λ such that the boundary value problem $y'' + \lambda y = 0$, $y'(0) = y'(1) = 0$ has at least one solution $y(x)$ with $y(x) \neq 0$.

3.6 NONHOMOGENEOUS LINEAR EQUATIONS

A general solution of

(6.1) $$y'' - 5y' + 6y = 4$$

is $y = c_1 e^{3x} + c_2 e^{2x} + \frac{2}{3}$. This can be checked by computing

$$y' = 3c_1 e^{3x} + 2c_2 e^{2x} \quad \text{and} \quad y'' = 9c_1 e^{3x} + 4c_2 e^{2x},$$

and then

$$\begin{aligned}
y'' - 5y' + 6y &= (9c_1 e^{3x} + 4c_2 e^{2x}) - 5(3c_1 e^{3x} + 2c_2 e^{2x}) \\
&\quad + 6(c_1 e^{3x} + c_2 e^{2x} + \tfrac{2}{3}) \\
&= (9 - 15 + 6)c_1 e^{3x} + (4 - 10 + 6)c_2 e^{2x} + 4 \\
&= 4.
\end{aligned}$$

The term $y_p = \frac{2}{3}$ is a solution of (6.1), while $y_c = c_1 e^{3x} + c_2 e^{2x}$ is a general solution of the homogeneous equation

$$y'' - 5y' + 6y = 0.$$

The solution of (6.1) is the sum $y = y_c + y_p$. The general solution of (6.1) turns out to be the sum of a particular solution y_p of the nonhomogeneous equation plus a general solution y_c of the corresponding homogeneous equation. It will turn out that any solution of any second-order nonhomogeneous linear equation can be decomposed in this way.

Consider now a second-order, linear, nonhomogeneous equation

$$(6.2) \qquad Ly = g, \qquad Ly = y'' + b_1(x)y' + b_0(x)y,$$

where b_0, b_1, and g are defined and continuous over an interval $J = \{x : A_1 < x < A_2\}$. Recall that L is a linear operator, that is,

$$L(d_1 y_1 + d_2 y_2) = d_1 L y_1 + d_2 L y_2$$

for all constants d_i and for all functions y_i that have two continuous derivatives. A general solution of (6.2) can be put together as follows.

THEOREM 6.1: PRINCIPLE OF SUPERPOSITION

Let y_p be any fixed (or particular) solution of $Ly = g$, and let y_1 and y_2 be two linearly independent solutions of the homogeneous problem $Ly = 0$. Then a general solution of (6.2) can be written in the form

$$(6.3) \qquad\qquad y = c_1 y_1 + c_2 y_2 + y_p,$$

where c_1 and c_2 are arbitrary constants.

To see that (6.3) is a solution of (6.2) we use the linearity of L to compute

$$Ly = L(c_1 y_1 + c_2 y_2 + y_p) = c_1 L y_1 + c_2 L y_2 + L y_p$$
$$= c_1 \cdot 0 + c_2 \cdot 0 + g = g.$$

Thus y is a solution of $Ly = g$ that contains two arbitrary constants c_1 and c_2. These constants can be used to satisfy any given initial conditions $y(x_0) = a_0$ and $y'(x_0) = a_1$. Indeed, it is only necessary to pick c_1 and c_2 so that

$$c_1 y_1(x_0) + c_2 y_2(x_0) + y_p(x_0) = a_0$$

and

$$c_1 y_1'(x_0) + c_2 y_2'(x_0) + y_p'(x_0) = a_1.$$

Hence we must solve the simultaneous system

$$y_1(x_0)c_1 + y_2(x_0)c_2 = (a_0 - y_p(x_0))$$
$$y_1'(x_0)c_1 + y_2'(x_0)c_2 = (a_1 - y_p'(x_0))$$

for c_1 and c_2. Since y_1 and y_2 are linearly independent, the determinant

$$\det \begin{vmatrix} y_1(x_0) & y_2(x_0) \\ y_1'(x_0) & y_2'(x_0) \end{vmatrix} = y_1(x_0)y_2'(x_0) - y_1'(x_0)y_2(x_0) = W(y_1, y_2)(x_0) \neq 0.$$

Thus c_1 and c_2 can be found in one and only one way.

EXAMPLE 6.2   Solve $y'' + 5y' + 4y = 3e^{2x}$, $y(0) = 1$, $y'(0) = 0$ given the particular solution $y_p = e^{2x}/6$.

It is easy to check that y_p solves the equation but not the initial conditions. To find a solution that satisfies the initial conditions, it is first necessary to find two linearly independent solutions of $y'' + 5y' + 4y = 0$. The characteristic equation is $\lambda^2 + 5\lambda + 4 = 0$. Hence

$$y_1 = e^{-x} \quad \text{and} \quad y_2 = e^{-4x}.$$

A general solution y of the nonhomogeneous equation is

$$y = c_1 e^{-x} + c_2 e^{-4x} + \frac{e^{2x}}{6}.$$

Since $y(0) = c_1 + c_2 + \frac{1}{6}$ and $y'(0) = -c_1 - 4c_2 + \frac{2}{6}$, we require

$$c_1 + c_2 + \tfrac{1}{6} = 1$$

and

$$-c_1 - 4c_2 + \tfrac{2}{6} = 0.$$

This system of linear equation can be solved to obtain $c_1 = 1$ and $c_2 = -\frac{1}{6}$. The required solution is

$$y = e^{-x} - \frac{e^{-4x}}{6} + \frac{e^{2x}}{6}. \qquad \blacksquare$$

We see that a general solution of (6.2) can be determined if any one particular solution of (6.2) can be found and if two linearly independent solutions y_1 and y_2 of the corresponding homogeneous problem $Ly = 0$ can be found. We then form the linear combination

(6.4) $y_c = c_1 y_1 + c_2 y_2$

and add y_p to it. We note that the solution (6.4) is usually called the **complementary solution** or **complementary function**, while y_p is called a **particular solution** of (6.2).

The same technique can be used to decompose the solution of the equation $Ly = g_1 + g_2$ into three parts. Let $\{y_1, y_2\}$ be a fundamental set of solutions of the homogeneous equation $Ly = 0$. Let y_{p_1} and y_{p_2} be particular solutions of the two nonhomogeneous equations

$$Ly_{p_1} = g_1 \quad \text{and} \quad Ly_{p_2} = g_2.$$

Then a general solution of $Ly = g_1 + g_2$ is

$$y = c_1 y_1 + c_2 y_2 + y_{p_1} + y_{p_2}.$$

Similarly, to solve a nonhomogeneous equation of the form

(6.5) $$Ly = g_1 + g_2 + \ldots + g_m,$$

we may first find solutions y_{p_j} of $Ly = g_j$ for $j = 1, 2, 3, \ldots, m$, then find a fundamental set $\{y_1, y_2\}$ of solutions of $Ly = 0$, and form the general solution

(6.6) $$y = c_1 y_1 + c_2 y_2 + \sum_{j=1}^{m} y_{p_j}.$$

EXAMPLE 6.3   Find a general solution of $y'' + 5y' + 4y = 3e^{2x} + 8$.

The complementary solution is $y_c = c_1 e^{-x} + c_2 e^{-4x}$. From Example 6.2 we know that $y_{p_1} = e^{2x}/6$ solves

$$y'' + 5y' + 4y = 3e^{2x}.$$

It is easy to verify that $y_{p_2} = 2$ solves

$$y'' + 5y' + 4y = 8.$$

Thus a general solution is

$$y = c_1 e^{-x} + c_2 e^{-4x} + \frac{e^{2x}}{6} + 2. \quad \blacksquare$$

The method of solution of (6.5) embodied in (6.6) is called the **principle of superposition**. By this we mean that (6.5) is decomposed into the subproblems

$$Ly = 0$$

and

$$Ly = g_i \qquad \text{for } i = 1, 2, \ldots, m,$$

the subproblems are solved, and the resulting solutions are added together (or superimposed) to obtain the solution (6.6). Superposition is an effective and useful technique when it works. It always works for linear equations. It should not be tried when solving nonlinear equations.

PROBLEMS   In Problems 1–9, verify that the function given is a particular solution of the nonhomogeneous equation. Then find a general solution of the equation.

1. $y'' + 3y' + 2y = e^x$, $y_p = \dfrac{e^x}{6}$.

2. $y'' - 3y' + 2y = e^x$, $y_p = -xe^x$.

3. $y'' - 4y' + 4y = 3$, $y_p = \frac{3}{4}$.

4. $y'' + y' + 2y = e^{-x}$, $y_p = \dfrac{e^{-x}}{2}$.

5. $y'' + 3y' + 2y = 6$, $y_p = 3$.

6. $y'' + 4y = 5e^x$, $y_p = e^x$.

7. $y'' + 3y = e^x$, $y_p = \dfrac{e^x}{4}$.   **8.** $y'' + y' + y = 3$, $y_p = 3$.

9. $y'' + y' + y = e^{2x}$, $y_p = \dfrac{e^{2x}}{7}$.

10. Solve $y'' - 2y' + y = e^{2x}$, $y(0) = 1$, $y'(0) = -1$ given $y_p = e^{2x}$.

11. Solve $y'' + 4y = \sin x$, $y(0) = 1$, $y'(0) = 2$ given $y_p = \dfrac{\sin x}{3}$.

12. Solve $y'' + y = 3$, $y(0) = 0$, $y'(0) = 0$ given $y_p = 3$.

13. Solve $y'' + 3y' + 2y = e^{3x}$, $y(0) = 0$, $y'(0) = 0$ given $y_p = \dfrac{e^{3x}}{20}$.

14. Solve $y'' - 4y = 3$, $y(0) = 1$, $y'(0) = 0$ given $y_p = -\tfrac{3}{4}$.

15. Solve $y'' - 4y = 3e^x$, $y(0) = y'(0) = 0$, given $y_p = -e^x$.

16. Verify that $e^{2x}/12$ solves $y'' + 3y' + 2y = e^{2x}$. Then solve

$$y'' + 3y' + 2y = e^x + e^{2x}, \qquad y(0) = y'(0) = 0.$$

     Hint: Use Problem 1.

17. Verify that $e^{-x}/6$ solves $y'' - 3y' + 2y = e^{-x}$. Then find a general solution of $y'' - 3y' + 2y = 3e^{-x} - 2e^x$.

18. (a) Solve $y' = y^2$, $y(0) = 2$. Call the solution y_c.

     (b) Verify that $y_p = 1$ solves $y' = y^2 - 1$, $y(0) = 1$.

     (c) Does $y_c + y_p$ solve $y' = y^2 - 1$, $y(0) = 3$?

     (d) Is $y' = y^2 - 1$, $y(0) = 3$ a linear or a nonlinear problem?

3.7   UNDETERMINED COEFFICIENTS: I

From the results in Section 3.6 we see that in order to find a general solution of

(7.1) $$ay'' + by' + cy = g(x),$$

it is necessary to find a general solution of the corresponding homogeneous equation and then add to it any particular solution of (7.1). We now show how, for a large class of forcing functions $g(x)$, a particular solution of (7.1) may be found. This solution technique, called the method of undetermined coefficients, is based on judicious guesses of the probable form of particular solutions. It is applicable to any function g that can be written in one of the following ways:

(7.2) $g(x) = e^{\alpha x} p(x) \sin \beta x$ or $g(x) = e^{\alpha x} p(x) \cos \beta x$

where $p(x)$ is any polynomial in x while α and β are any real numbers. The special cases $\alpha = 0$ or $\beta = 0$ or $p(x) \equiv$ constant are allowed.

We shall illustrate this method by several examples and then develop the method in general.

EXAMPLE 7.1   Find a general solution of $y'' + 3y' + 2y = 3e^x$.

The nonhomogeneous term is $g(x) = 3e^x$. We shall try to find a solution of the form $y = Ae^x$, where A is some constant that is not yet determined. Substitute this trial solution into the equation to obtain

$$Ae^x + 3Ae^x + 2Ae^x = 3e^x.$$

After dividing by e^x we find that $6A = 3$ or $A = \frac{1}{2}$. Thus $y_p = e^x/2$ is a particular solution. A general solution of this equation is

$$y = c_1 e^{-x} + c_2 e^{-2x} + \frac{e^x}{2}. \quad \blacksquare$$

EXAMPLE 7.2   Find a general solution of $y'' - 3y' + 2y = 4e^x$.

Since the forcing function is $g(x) = 4e^x$, we shall again attempt to find a solution of the form $y = Ae^x$, where A is a constant that must be determined. Substituting this trial solution into the equation gives

$$Ae^x - 3Ae^x + 2Ae^x = 4e^x,$$

or $0 = 4e^x$. This is clearly impossible! Hence there can be no solution of the form Ae^x. The reason for this is that the characteristic polynomial for the associated homogeneous equation is

$$\lambda^2 - 3\lambda + 2 = (\lambda - 1)(\lambda - 2) = 0.$$

Thus Ae^x is a solution of this homogeneous equation for any constant A.

We take as a second trial solution $y = Axe^x$. On substituting into the equation, we find that

(7.3) $$(2Ae^x + Axe^x) - 3(Ae^x + Axe^x) + 2Axe^x = 4e^x.$$

Notice that the terms involving xe^x sum to zero. Thus (7.3) reduces to

$$(2A - 3A)e^x = 4e^x$$

and $A = -4$. The required general solution can be written as

$$y = c_1 e^x + c_2 e^{2x} - 4xe^x. \quad \blacksquare$$

Exponential Case. Examples 7.1 and 7.2 suggest the following procedure for solving equations of the form

(7.4) $$ay'' + by' + cy = de^{\alpha x}.$$

Suppose that the associated homogeneous equation has characteristic roots λ_1 and λ_2. If α is not equal to λ_1 or λ_2, then take as a trial solution

$$y = Ae^{\alpha x}.$$

On substituting into (7.4) we obtain

$$(a\alpha^2 + b\alpha + c)Ae^{\alpha x} = de^{\alpha x}.$$

Hence $A = d/(a\alpha^2 + b\alpha + c)$. If α is a simple root of the characteristic equation

(7.5) $$a\lambda^2 + b\lambda + c = 0,$$

then the trial solution will be

$$y = Axe^{\alpha x}.$$

If α is a double root of (7.5), then $e^{\alpha x}$ and $xe^{\alpha x}$ are both solutions of the homogeneous equation. In this case the trial solution will have the form

$$y = Ax^2 e^{\alpha x}.$$

Polynomial Case. Now consider the problem

$$ay'' + by' + cy = p(x),$$

where $p(x) = a_0 + a_1 x + a_2 x^2 + \ldots + a_m x^m$ is a polynomial of degree m. Assume for the moment that $c \neq 0$. Then zero is not a root of the characteristic equation of the associated homogeneous equation. Since the derivative of a polynomial is again a polynomial, we shall use the trial solution

(7.6) $$y = A_0 + A_1 x + A_2 x^2 + \ldots + A_m x^m,$$

where $A_0, A_1, \ldots, A_m$ are constants that must be determined. If $\lambda = 0$ is a simple characteristic root of (7.5), the trial solution will be

$$y = x(A_0 + A_1 x + \ldots + A_m x^m).$$

If $\lambda = 0$ is a double root of (7.5), then (7.5) has the form $y'' = p(x)$ and the trial solution will be

$$y = x^2(A_0 + A_1 x + \ldots + A_m x^m).$$

EXAMPLE 7.3   Find a particular solution of $y'' - 5y' + 4y = x^2$.
 The characteristic polynomial of the associated homogeneous equation is $\lambda^2 - 5\lambda + 4 = 0$. It has roots $\lambda = 1$ or 4. Neither of these characteristic roots is zero. Hence the trial solution will be

$$y = A_0 + A_1 x + A_2 x^2.$$

On substituting this trial solution into the equation, we obtain

$$2A_2 - 5(A_1 + 2A_2 x) + 4(A_0 + A_1 x + A_2 x^2) = x^2.$$

or

$$(2A_2 - 5A_1 + 4A_0) + (-10A_2 + 4A_1)x + (4A_2)x^2 = 0 + 0 \cdot x + 1 \cdot x^2.$$

Equate powers of x on each side of the equation to obtain

$$2A_2 - 5A_1 + 4A_0 = 0, \qquad -10A_2 + 4A_1 = 0, \qquad 4A_2 = 1.$$

This is a system of three equations in three unknowns. These equations can be solved starting with the last and working backward. The solution is $A_2 = \frac{1}{4}$, $A_1 = \frac{5}{8}$, and $A_0 = \frac{21}{32}$. Thus a particular solution is

$$y_p = \frac{21}{32} + \frac{5}{8}x + \frac{x^2}{4}.$$

The nonhomogeneous term $g(x) = x^2$ has no power of x and no constant term. In spite of this the trial solution must have a constant term A_0 and a linear term A_1x. These two terms cannot be left out.   ∎

The following case includes and generalizes the cases discussed above.

EXPONENTIAL POLYNOMIAL CASE

Consider the problem

$$ay'' + by' + cy = e^{\alpha x}p(x),$$

where $p(x) = a_0 + a_1x + \ldots + a_mx^m$ is a polynomial of degree m. If α is not a root of the characteristic equation (7.5), the trial solution will be of the form

$$y = e^{\alpha x}(A_0 + A_1x + A_2x^2 + \ldots + A_mx^m),$$

where the constants $A_0, A_1, \ldots, A_m$ must be determined. If α is a simple root of (7.5), the trial solution will be of the form

$$y = xe^{\alpha x}(A_0 + A_1x + \ldots + A_mx^m).$$

If α is a double root of (7.5), the trial solution will be of the form

$$y = x^2e^{\alpha x}(A_0 + A_1x + \ldots + A_mx^m).$$

EXAMPLE 7.4   Solve $y'' + 3y' + 2y = 6xe^x$, $y(0) = 1$, $y'(0) = 0$.
   The characteristic roots of the associated homogeneous equation $y'' + 3y' + 2y = 0$ are $\lambda_1 = -1$ and $\lambda_2 = -2$. Neither of these is 1. Hence we try a solution of the form

$$y = (A_0 + A_1x)e^x.$$

Substituting into the given equation we find that

$$2A_1e^x + (A_0 + A_1x)e^x + 3(A_1e^x + (A_0 + A_1x)e^x) + 2(A_0 + A_1x)e^x = 6xe^x.$$

On simplifying, the result is

$$(6A_0 + 5A_1)e^x + 6A_1xe^x = 6xe^x$$

or

$$(6A_0 + 5A_1) + 6A_1x = 6x.$$

Hence $6A_1 = 6$ and $6A_0 + 5A_1 = 0$, so $A_1 = 1$, $A_0 = -\frac{5}{6}$. Thus a particular solution is

$$y_p = (-\tfrac{5}{6} + x)e^x.$$

A general solution is

$$y = c_1e^{-x} + c_2e^{-2x} + (x - \tfrac{5}{6})e^x.$$

The initial conditions $y(0) = 1$ and $y'(0) = 0$ yield

$$c_1 + c_2 - \tfrac{5}{6} = 1 \quad \text{and} \quad -c_1 - 2c_2 + 1 - \tfrac{5}{6} = 0.$$

Thus $c_1 = \tfrac{21}{6}$ and $c_2 = -\tfrac{5}{3}$. ∎

EXAMPLE 7.5   Find a general solution of $y'' - 2y' + y = e^x + 4$.
　　　　The characteristic equation $\lambda^2 - 2\lambda + 1 = 0$ has the double root $\lambda = 1$. Hence for the equation

$$y'' - 2y' + y = e^x$$

we try $y = x^2 A e^x$. On substituting in the equation, we find that

$$(2Ae^x + 4xAe^x + x^2 A e^x) - 2(2xAe^x + x^2 A e^x) + Ax^2 e^x = e^x,$$

or $2Ae^x = e^x$. Thus $A = \tfrac{1}{2}$ and $y_{p_1} = x^2 e^x / 2$.
　　　　For the equation

$$y'' - 2y' + y = 4$$

we try $y_{p_2} = A$ and quickly find that $A = 4$. Hence a particular solution is $y_p = x^2 e^x / 2 + 4$. The complementary solution is $y_c = (c_1 + c_2 x)e^x$. A general solution is

$$y = c_1 e^x + c_2 x e^x + 4 + \left(\frac{x^2}{2}\right) e^x. \quad ∎$$

　　　　Be sure to remember that the method of undetermined coefficients works only when the equation is *linear with constant coefficients* and the nonhomogeneous term $g(x)$ of the *special form* (7.2). The method should not be attempted unless these special properties are true.
　　　　The form of the trial solution probably seems a bit mysterious. In many simple situations it is not hard to see why the given trial form was used. For example, consider the equation

(7.7) $$Ly = ay'' + by' + cy = d e^{\alpha x}.$$

Suppose that $L_1 y = (D - \alpha)y = y' - \alpha y$. Then for any function y that has three continuous derivatives

$$\begin{aligned}
L_1(Ly) &= (D - \alpha)(aD^2 y + bDy + cy) \\
&= aD^3 y + bD^2 y + cDy - (a\alpha D^2 y + b\alpha Dy + \alpha c y) \\
&= (aD^2 + bD + c)Dy - (aD^2 + bD + c)\alpha y \\
&= (aD^2 + bD + c)(D - \alpha)y = L(L_1 y).
\end{aligned}$$

Define $w = L_1 y$. Apply L_1 to both sides of (7.7). Since

$$L_1(d e^{\alpha x}) = (D - \alpha)(d e^{\alpha x}) = 0,$$

then

$$L_1(Ly) = L(L_1 y) = Lw = L_1(d e^{\alpha x}) = 0$$

or $Lw = 0$. Let λ_1 and λ_2 be the roots of the characteristic equation $a\lambda^2 + b\lambda + c = 0$. What happens next depends on the values α, λ_1, and λ_2.

Case 1. $\lambda_1 \neq \lambda_2$ and α is not λ_1 or λ_2.
In this case $Lw = 0$ has solution

$$w = c_1 e^{\lambda_1 x} + c_2 e^{\lambda_2 x}.$$

Since $w = L_1 y$, then y must solve the equation

$$y' - \alpha y = c_1 e^{\lambda_1 x} + c_2 e^{\lambda_2 x}.$$

This first-order linear equation has integrating factor $e^{-\alpha x}$. Hence

$$(e^{-\alpha x} y)' = c_1 e^{(\lambda_1 - \alpha)x} + c_2 e^{(\lambda_2 - \alpha)x},$$

$$e^{-\alpha x} y = \frac{c_1}{\lambda_1 - \alpha} e^{(\lambda_1 - \alpha)x} + \frac{c_2}{\lambda_2 - \alpha} e^{(\lambda_2 - \alpha)x} + c_3,$$

and

$$y = \left(\frac{c_1}{\lambda_1 - \alpha} e^{\lambda_1 x} + \frac{c_2}{\lambda_2 - \alpha} e^{\lambda_2 x} \right) + c_3 e^{\alpha x}.$$

The term in parentheses is a solution of the homogeneous equation. The last term $y_p = c_3 e^{\alpha x}$ is a particular solution of (7.7) when the coefficient c_3 is correctly determined.

Case 2. $\lambda_1 \neq \lambda_2$, $\alpha = \lambda_1$.
The case $Lw = 0$ has a solution

$$w = c_1 e^{\lambda_1 x} + c_2 e^{\lambda_2 x}.$$

Since $\alpha = \lambda_1$, then y must solve the equation

$$y' - \lambda_1 y = c_1 e^{\lambda_1 x} + c_2 e^{\lambda_2 x}.$$

This is a first-order linear equation with integrating factor $e^{-\lambda_1 x}$. Hence

$$(e^{-\lambda_1 x} y)' = c_1 + c_2 e^{(\lambda_2 - \lambda_1)x},$$

$$e^{-\lambda_1 x} y = c_1 x + \frac{c_2 e^{(\lambda_2 - \lambda_1)x}}{\lambda_2 - \lambda_1} + c_3,$$

and

$$y = c_1 x e^{\lambda_1 x} + \left(\frac{c_2}{\lambda_2 - \lambda_1} e^{\lambda_2 x} + c_3 e^{\lambda_1 x} \right).$$

The term in parentheses is a solution of the homogeneous equation. The term $y_p = c_1 x e^{\lambda_1 x}$ is a particular solution of (7.7) when the coefficient c_1 is correctly determined.

The remaining cases are

Case 3. $\lambda_1 = \lambda_2 = \alpha$, $y_p = cx^2 e^{\alpha x}$.

Case 4. $\lambda_1 = \lambda_2$, $\alpha \neq \lambda_1$, $y_p = ce^{\alpha x}$.

In these two cases the form of y_p can be obtained by similar computations.

A complete justification of the method of undetermined coefficients can be found at the end of Section 4.3. The analysis found there uses the theory developed in Chapter 4 for nth-order equations plus the **annihilator technique.**

PROBLEMS   In Problems 1–16, find a general solution.

1. $y'' + y = 1 + x$.

2. $y'' + 4y = e^{3x}$.

3. $y'' + y' + 3y = e^{2x}$.

4. $y'' - y' + 2y = x$.

5. $y'' - 5y' + 6y = e^{-x}$.

6. $y'' - y = 5 - 3x$.

7. $y'' + y' = 4$.

8. $(D^2 + 1)y = xe^{2x}$.

9. $(D^2 + 1)y = xe^x$.

10. $y'' + 2y' + y = x^3$.

11. $y'' + 2y' = x$.

12. $y'' + 4y = x + 2x^3$.

13. $\dfrac{d^2N}{dt^2} - 3\dfrac{dN}{dt} + 2N = e^{-t}$.

14. $y'' - 4y = e^{2x}$.

15. $y'' - 4y' + 4y = e^{2x}$.

16. $\dfrac{d^2S}{dt^2} - 9S = 3t + e^t$.

In Problems 17–23, solve the initial value problem.

17. $y'' - y = e^{2x}$, $y(0) = -1$, $y'(0) = 1$.   **18.** $y'' + y = 2e^x$, $y(0) = 1$, $y'(0) = -1$.

19. $B'' - 4B' + 4B = x$, $B(0) = 0$, $B'(0) = 1$.   **20.** $y'' - 4y' + 3y = e^x$, $y(0) = 0$, $y'(0) = 0$.

21. $\dfrac{d^2B}{dt^2} - B = t^2$, $B(0) = 0$, $B'(0) = 1$.

22. $\dfrac{d^2N}{ds^2} - 9N = 1 + e^{3s}$, $N(0) = 1$, $\dfrac{dN}{ds}(0) = 1$.

23. $y'' - 4y' + 4y + e^{2x} = 0$, $y(0) = y'(0) = 0$.

In Problems 24–28, write down the *correct form* for a trial solution. Do *not* solve.

24. $y'' + 4y' + 4y = x^4 + x^2e^{-2x}$.

25. $y'' - 3y' + 2y = x^2(e^x + e^{-x})$.

26. $y'' + 3y' + 2y = x^2(e^x + e^{-x})$.

27. $2y'' + 8y = x^3 + e^{2x}$.

28. $\dfrac{d^2N}{dt^2} + \pi^2N = t^2 + e^t + 1$.

29. Let $L = aD^2 + bD + c$ with $c \neq 0$ and let $p(x) = a_0 + a_1x + \ldots + a_mx^m$ be a given polynomial of degree m. Show that the equation $Ly = p$ has a solution of the form $y_p = A_0 + A_1x + \ldots + A_mx^m$, where the constants A_j satisfy the equations

$$cA_m = a_m, \qquad cA_{m-1} + bmA_m = a_{m-1},$$

$$cA_{m-2} + b(m-1)A_{m-1} + cm(m-1)A_m = a_{m-2}, \ldots, cA_0 + bA_1 + cA_2 = a_0.$$

Hint: Put the trial solution into the equation and equate powers of x.

30. Let $L = aD^2 + bD + c$ and let $p(x) = a_0 + a_1x + \ldots + a_mx^m$ be a given polynomial of degree m.

(a) Show that if $y = e^{\alpha x}P(x)$, where $P(x) = A_0 + A_1x + \ldots + A_mx^m$, then

$$Ly = e^{\alpha x}((a\alpha^2 + b\alpha + c)P(x) + (2a\alpha + b)P'(x) + aP''(x)).$$

(b) Show that $y = e^{\alpha x}P(x)$ solves $Ly = e^{\alpha x}p(x)$ if $P(x)$ satisfies

$$(a\alpha^2 + b\alpha + c)P(x) + (2a\alpha + b)P'(x) + aP''(x) = p(x).$$

(c) Show that if $a\alpha^2 + b\alpha + c \neq 0$, then $Ly = e^{\alpha x}p(x)$ has a solution of the form $y = e^{\alpha x}P(x)$. *Hint:* Use Problem 29.

In Problems 31–34 find all solutions of the given **boundary value problem** by first finding a general solution in the form $y = c_1\varphi_1(x) + c_2\varphi_2(x) + y_p(x)$. Then use the two boundary conditions to determine c_1 and c_2. Each problem may have no solution, one solution, or infinitely many solutions.

31. $y'' + y = 1$, $y(0) = 1$, $y'(2) = -1$.

32. $y'' + 2y' + y = -2$, $y(0) = -2$, $y'(1) = 0$.

33. $y'' + 4y = x$, $y(0) = 0$, $y(\pi) = 0$.

34. $y'' - 2y' + y = e^x$, $y(0) = 1/2$, $y(1) = 0$.

3.8   UNDETERMINED COEFFICIENTS: II

We now consider the solution of

(8.1) $$ay'' + by' + cy = g(x)$$

in case $g(x)$ has one of the following two forms:

(8.2) $$e^{\alpha x}p(x) \cos \beta x \quad \text{or} \quad e^{\alpha x}q(x) \sin \beta x.$$

Here α and β are any real numbers and $p(x)$ and $q(x)$ are real polynomials of degree m or less. Recall that Euler's formula states that

$$e^{(\alpha + i\beta)x} = e^{\alpha x} \cos \beta x + ie^{\alpha x} \sin \beta x.$$

Equivalently, one can write

$$e^{\alpha x} \cos \beta x = \text{Re}\,(e^{(\alpha + i\beta)x})$$

$$= \frac{e^{(\alpha + i\beta)x} + e^{(\alpha - i\beta)x}}{2}$$

and

$$e^{\alpha x} \sin \beta x = \text{Im}\,(e^{(\alpha + i\beta)x})$$

$$= \frac{e^{(\alpha + i\beta)x} - e^{(\alpha - i\beta)x}}{2i}.$$

Hence, if $g(x) = e^{\alpha x} \cos \beta x = e^{(\alpha + i\beta)x}/2 + e^{(\alpha - i\beta)x}/2$, and if $\alpha + i\beta$ is not a root of the characteristic equation

$$(8.3) \qquad\qquad a\lambda^2 + b\lambda + c = 0,$$

then it is natural to try a solution of the form

$$(8.4) \qquad\qquad y_p = Ae^{\alpha x} \cos \beta x + Be^{\alpha x} \sin \beta x,$$

where A and B are constants that must be determined. Notice that (8.4) has both a sine and a cosine term even though the forcing function g contains only a cosine term.

If $\alpha + i\beta$ is a root of (8.3), the trial solution has the form

$$(8.5) \qquad\qquad y_p = x(Ae^{\alpha x} \cos \beta x + Be^{\alpha x} \sin \beta x).$$

If $g(x) = e^{\alpha x} \sin \beta x$, the trial solution will have the form (8.4) when $\alpha + i\beta$ is not a root of (8.3) and will have the form (8.5) when $\alpha + i\beta$ is a root of (8.3).

EXAMPLE 8.1   Find a general solution of $y'' + y' + y = e^x \sin 2x$.
   The characteristic equation $\lambda^2 + \lambda + 1 = 0$ has roots $(-1 \pm \sqrt{3}i)/2$. Neither of these roots equals $1 \pm 2i$. Hence the trial solution is of the form

$$(8.6) \qquad\qquad y_p = Ae^x \cos 2x + Be^x \sin 2x.$$

On substituting (8.6) into the given equation, we find that

$$(8.7) \qquad (-A + 6B)e^x \cos 2x - (6A + B)e^x \sin 2x = e^x \sin 2x,$$

so that $-A + 6B = 0$ and $-(6A + B) = 1$. Hence $A = -\frac{6}{37}$ and $B = -\frac{1}{37}$. The general solution is

$$y = e^{-x/2}\left(c_1 \cos \frac{\sqrt{3}x}{2} + c_2 \sin \frac{\sqrt{3}x}{2}\right) - \frac{e^x(6 \cos 2x + \sin 2x)}{37}. \qquad \blacksquare$$

EXAMPLE 8.2   Find a particular solution of $y'' + y' + y = -e^x \cos 2x$.
   The trial solution is again of the form (8.6). Here (8.7) will be replaced by

$$(-A + 6B)e^x \cos 2x - (6A + B)e^x \sin 2x = -e^x \cos 2x.$$

Hence $-A + 6B = -1$ and $-(6A + B) = 0$. It follows that $A = \frac{1}{37}$ and $B = -\frac{6}{37}$. The solution is

$$y_p = \frac{e^x(\cos 2x - 6 \sin 2x)}{37}. \qquad \blacksquare$$

EXAMPLE 8.3   Find a particular solution of

$$y'' + y' + y = 2e^x \cos 2x - 3e^x \sin 2x.$$

Again the trial solution will have the form (8.6). The constants A and B must satisfy

$$-A + 6B = 2 \quad \text{and} \quad -(6A + B) = -3.$$

Hence $A = \frac{16}{37}$, $B = \frac{15}{37}$ and

$$y_p = \frac{e^x(16 \cos 2x + 15 \sin 2x)}{37}.$$

This particular solution can also be found by using the results obtained in Examples 8.1 and 8.2 together with superposition. Let $g_1(x) = e^x \sin 2x$ be the forcing function used in Example 8.1 and let y_{p_1} be the particular solution obtained in Example 8.1. Let $g_2(x) = -e^x \cos 2x$ be the forcing function used in Example 8.2 and let y_{p_2} be the particular solution obtained there. Since the current forcing function $g(x)$ has the form

$$g(x) = -3g_1(x) - 2g_2(x),$$

then a particular solution is

$$y_p = -3y_{p_1} - 2y_{p_2}$$

$$= -3\left[\frac{-e^x(6 \cos 2x + \sin 2x)}{37}\right] - 2\left[\frac{e^x(\cos 2x - 6 \sin 2x)}{37}\right]$$

$$= \frac{e^x(16 \cos 2x + 15 \sin 2x)}{37},$$

as expected. ■

Now consider the general case where

$$g(x) = e^{\alpha x}p(x) \cos \beta x + e^{\alpha x}q(x) \sin \beta x,$$

and $p(x)$ and $q(x)$ are polynomials in x of maximum degree m. If $\alpha + i\beta$ is not a root of (8.3), the trial solution will have the form

$$y_p = e^{\alpha x}(A_0 + A_1 x + \ldots + A_m x^m) \cos \beta x$$
$$+ e^{\alpha x}(B_0 + B_1 x + \ldots + B_m x^m) \sin \beta x.$$

If $\alpha + i\beta$ is a root of (8.3), the trial solution will have the form

$$y_p = xe^{\alpha x}(A_0 + A_1 x + \ldots + A_m x^m) \cos \beta x$$
$$+ xe^{\alpha x}(B_0 + B_1 x + \ldots + B_m x^m) \sin \beta x.$$

The method of undetermined coefficients is summarized in the following table.

TABLE 3.1 $Ly = g(x)$

Form of $g(x)$	Form of $y_p(x)$
1. $p_n(x) = a_0 + a_1x + \ldots + a_nx^n$	I. $x^sP_n(x) = x^s(A_0 + A_1x + \ldots + A_nx^n)$
2. $p_n(x)e^{\alpha x}$	II. $x^sP_n(x)e^{\alpha x}$
3. $p_n(x)e^{\alpha x}\cos \beta x$	III. $x^s(P_n(x)\cos \beta x + Q_n(x)\sin \beta x)$
	where $Q_n(x) = B_0 + B_1x + \ldots + B_nx^n$
4. $p_n(x)e^{\alpha x}\sin \beta x$	IV. Same as III
5. $g_1(x) + g_2(x)$	V. $y_{1p} + y_{2p}$

The number s is the smallest nonnegative integer so that no term in $y_p(x)$ is a solution of the corresponding homogeneous equation $Ly = 0$.

EXAMPLE 8.4   What is the proper form for the trial solution of

(8.8) $$y'' + 2y' + 3y = x \cos 3x - \sin 3x?$$

The characteristic equation $\lambda^2 + 2\lambda + 3 = 0$ has roots $-1 \pm \sqrt{2}i$. These roots are not equal to $\pm 3i$. Hence the trial solution has the form

$$y_p = (A_0 + A_1x)\cos 3x + (B_0 + B_1x)\sin 3x.$$

The constants A_0, A_1, B_0, and B_1 must be determined by substituting this trial solution into (8.8).   ∎

EXAMPLE 8.5   What is the form of the trial solution of

$$y'' + 2y' + 5y = x^2e^x \sin x?$$

The characteristic roots of the associated homogeneous equation are $-1 \pm 2i$. They are not equal to $1 \pm i$. Hence we try

$$y_p = (A_0 + A_1x + A_2x^2)e^x \cos x + (B_0 + B_1 + B_2x^2)e^x \sin x.$$ ∎

EXAMPLE 8.6   What is the form of the trial solution of

$$y'' + 2y' + 5y = xe^{-x} \cos 2x?$$

As in Example 8.5, the characteristic roots are $-1 \pm 2i$. These roots are the same as $\alpha \pm i\beta = -1 \pm 2i$. Hence we try

$$y_p = x\{(A_0 + A_1x)e^{-x} \cos 2x + (B_0 + B_1x)e^{-x} \sin 2x\}.$$ ∎

PROBLEMS

In Problems 1–14, find the general solution.

1. $y'' + 4y = e^x \cos x$.

2. $y'' + y = e^x \sin x$.

3. $y'' + 2y' + y = \sin x$.

4. $(D^2 - 3D + 2)y = \cos x - \sin x$.

5. $y'' = y + e^x \sin 2x$.

6. $y'' + y = e^{2x} \cos x$.

7. $(D^2 - 5)y = \cos x$.

8. $(D^2 + 5)y = \cos x$.

9. $R'' + R = \sin x$.

10. $N'' + 4N = \cos 2x$.

11. $y'' + 2y' + 4y = \cos 2x$.

12. $y'' + 2y' + 4y = e^x \cos x$.

13. $y'' - 2y' + 4y = e^x \sin x$.

14. $y'' + 2y' + y = x \sin x$.

In Problems 15–20, find the correct form for a trial solution y_p. Do not solve.

15. $y'' - 5y' + 6y = xe^x \cos 2x$.

16. $y'' + 3y' + 2y = \cos x + xe^{2x} \sin x$.

17. $y'' + y = x^2 \sin x$.

18. $y'' + 2y' + 4y = e^{-x} \cos x$.

19. $y'' - 4y' + 5y = xe^{2x} \sin x$.

20. $y'' + 25y = x \cos x + x \sin 5x$.

In Problems 21–27, solve the initial value problems.

21. $\dfrac{d^2 y}{dt^2} + 4y = \sin t$, $y(0) = 2$, $y'(0) = -1$.

22. $y'' + 4y' + y = e^x \cos x$, $y(0) = \frac{5}{61}$, $y'(0) = \frac{11}{61}$.

23. $B'' + B = 2 \cos x$, $B(0) = 1$, $B'(0) = 0$.

24. $\dfrac{d^2 N}{dt^2} + 5 \dfrac{dN}{dt} + 6N = 1 + \sin t$, $N(0) = N'(0) = 0$.

25. $y'' - 6y' + 9y = e^{3x} + \cos x$, $y(0) = 1$, $y'(0) = 0$.

26. $y'' - 4y = \sinh 2x$, $y(0) = 1$, $y'(0) = 0$.

27. $\dfrac{d^2 y}{ds^2} + 3 \dfrac{dy}{ds} + 2y = 3 - 2e^s$, $y(0) = y'(0) = 0$.

28. (a) Given $\omega > 0$ with $\omega \neq 2$, find a general solution of the equation

$$y'' + 4y = \cos \omega x.$$

(b) When $\omega = 4$, find all periodic solutions of this equation. What are the periods of the solutions found?

3.9　VARIATION OF PARAMETERS

The solution of the nonhomogeneous linear equation

(9.1)　　　　　　　　　$y' + b(x)y = g(x)$

can be obtained as follows. The general solution of the corresponding homogeneous equation

$$y' + b(x)y = 0$$

is $y = c_1 y_1(x)$, where $y_1(x) = e^{-\int b(x)\,dx}$. We shall replace the parameter c_1 by an unknown function $v_1(x)$ and take as a trial solution of (9.1) the expression

(9.2) $$y = v_1(x)y_1(x).$$

On substituting (9.2) into (9.1) we see that

$$v_1' y_1 + v_1 y_1' = v_1' y_1 + v_1(-by_1)$$
$$= -b(v_1 y_1) + g.$$

Thus

$$v_1' = \frac{g}{y_1} = g(x)e^{\int b(x)\,dx}$$

and

$$v_1(x) = \int g(x)e^{\int b(x)\,dx}\,dx + c.$$

Since the parameter c_1 in $y = c_1 y_1(x)$ is replaced by the function $v_1(x)$ to obtain the trial solution, this method of solution is known as *variation of parameters*.

EXAMPLE 9.1   Solve $y' - 2xy = x$ using variation of parameters.

A solution of the corresponding homogeneous equation is $y_1 = e^{\int 2x\,dx} = e^{x^2}$. The trial solution of the nonhomogeneous equation is $y = v_1(x)e^{x^2}$. Thus

$$v_1' e^{x^2} + v_1(2xe^{x^2}) = 2x(v_1 e^{x^2}) + x$$

or $v_1' e^{x^2} = x$. Thus $v_1(x) = (-\tfrac{1}{2})e^{-x^2} + c$. The required solution is

$$y(x) = v_1(x)e^{x^2} = ce^{x^2} - \tfrac{1}{2}. \quad\blacksquare$$

We now return to the nonhomogeneous second-order linear equation

(9.3) $$y'' + b_1(x)y' + b_0(x)y = g(x),$$

where b_0, b_1, and g are defined and continuous on some interval J. Assume that two linearly independent solutions of the associated homogeneous equation are known. If these two solutions are called y_1 and y_2, then on J,

$$W(y_1, y_2) = \begin{vmatrix} y_1 & y_2 \\ y_1' & y_2' \end{vmatrix} \neq 0,$$

and a general solution of the associated homogeneous equation

(9.4) $$y'' + b_1(x)y' + b_0(x)y = 0$$

is

(9.5) $$y = c_1 y_1(x) + c_2 y_2(x).$$

We shall replace the parameters c_1 and c_2 in (9.5) by functions $v_1(x)$ and $v_2(x)$ and take as a trial solution of (9.3)

$$(9.6) \qquad\qquad y = v_1(x)y_1(x) + v_2(x)y_2(x).$$

On substituting (9.6) into (9.3), we shall obtain one differential equation that the functions v_1 and v_2 must satisfy. Since there are two unknowns, v_1 and v_2, a second equation is needed to determine these unknowns. The second condition will be imposed in such a way that the calculations are simplified. This is done as follows.

From (9.6) it follows that

$$y' = v_1y_1' + v_2y_2' + v_1'y_1 + v_2'y_2.$$

To keep the calculation simple, we now require that

$$(9.7) \qquad\qquad v_1'y_1 + v_2'y_2 = 0.$$

Thus $y' = v_1y_1' + v_2y_2'$ and

$$y'' = v_1y_1'' + v_2y_2'' + v_1'y_1' + v_2'y_2'.$$

Substitute y' and y'' into (9.3) and rearrange to see that

$$(9.8) \quad v_1(y_1'' + b_1y_1' + b_0y_1) + v_2(y_2'' + b_1y_2' + b_0y_2) + v_1'y_1' + v_2'y_2' = g(x).$$

Since y_1 and y_2 are solutions of (9.4), the first two terms in (9.8) are zero. Thus

$$(9.9) \qquad\qquad v_1'y_1' + v_2'y_2' = g(x).$$

Thus v_1 and v_2 must be solutions of (9.7) and also of (9.9); that is, v_1' and v_2' solve the pair of simultaneous equations

$$v_1'y_1 + v_2'y_2 = 0,$$
$$v_1'y_1' + v_2'y_2' = g(x).$$

This pair of equations is solved to obtain

$$v_1' = \frac{-gy_2}{y_1y_2' - y_2y_1'} = \frac{-gy_2}{W(y_1, y_2)} \quad \text{and} \quad v_2' = \frac{gy_1}{W(y_1, y_2)}.$$

These expressions can be integrated to obtain v_1 and v_2. Hence

$$(9.10) \qquad y = y_1(x)\int \frac{-gy_2}{W(y_1, y_2)}\, dx + y_2(x)\int \frac{gy_1}{W(y_1, y_2)}\, dx.$$

Our derivation can be summarized as follows:

METHOD OF VARIATION OF PARAMETERS

To solve the nonhomogeneous equation $y'' + b_1(x)y' + b_2(x)y = g(x)$:

1. Determine two linearly independent solutions y_1 and y_2 of the corresponding homogeneous equation $y'' + b_1(x)y' + b_2(x)y = 0$.
2. Take a trial solution of the form

$$y = v_1(x)y_1(x) + v_2(x)y_2(x),$$

where v_1 and v_2 are to be determined.
3. Find v_1' and v_2' by solving the pair of equations (9.7) and (9.9). Integrate the resulting expressions to obtain v_1 and v_2.
4. Substitute v_1 and v_2 into the trial solution to obtain y. [Your answer will be equivalent to (9.10).]

EXAMPLE 9.2   Find a general solution of

(9.11) $$y'' + y = \tan x, \qquad -\frac{\pi}{2} < x < \frac{\pi}{2}.$$

A fundamental set of solutions of the homogeneous problem is $y_1 = \cos x$ and $y_2 = \sin x$. A trial solution for (9.11) is

$$y_p = v_1 \cos x + v_2 \sin x.$$

The derivative of y_p is

$$y_p' = (v_1' \cos x + v_2' \sin x) - v_1 \sin x + v_2 \cos x.$$

The term in parentheses is set equal to zero, that is,

(9.12) $$v_1' \cos x + v_2' \sin x = 0,$$

so that

$$y_p'' = -v_1' \sin x + v_2' \cos x - v_1 \cos x - v_2 \sin x.$$

On substituting y_p into (9.11) and simplifying, we get

(9.13) $$-v_1' \sin x + v_2' \cos x = \tan x.$$

Solving (9.12) and (9.13) gives

$$v_1' = -\sin x \tan x = \frac{\cos^2 x - 1}{\cos x} = \cos x - \sec x,$$

and

$$v_2' = \cos x \tan x = \sin x.$$

Integration gives

$$v_1(x) = \sin x - \log |\sec x + \tan x|$$

and

$$v_2(x) = -\cos x.$$

The constants of integration have been dropped since any integral will do. Our particular solution is

$$y_p = -\cos x \log |\sec x + \tan x|,$$

and a general solution is

$$y = c_1 \cos x + c_2 \sin x + y_p. \quad \blacksquare$$

In problems where the method of undetermined coefficients can be applied, it may be easier to use the method of undetermined coefficients rather than variation of parameters. The advantage of variation of parameters is that it can be applied to a larger class of nonhomogeneous terms $g(x)$ and also to equations with nonconstant coefficients.

PROBLEMS

In Problems 1–9, use variation of parameters to find a particular solution.

1. $y'' + y = \sec x$.

2. $y'' + 4y = 2 \cot 2x$.

3. $Q'' - 4Q' + 4Q = \dfrac{e^{2x}}{x}, 0 < x < \infty$.

4. $e^{3x}(y'' + 6y' + 9y) = x^{-2}, 0 < x < \infty$.

5. $e^{3x}(R'' + 6R' + 9R) = x^{-2}, -\infty < x < 0$.

6. $\dfrac{d^2 y}{dt^2} + y = \sec t \tan t, -\dfrac{\pi}{2} < t < \dfrac{\pi}{2}$.

7. $(D^2 + 1)y = \sec^3 x, -\dfrac{\pi}{2} < x < \dfrac{\pi}{2}$.

8. $y'' + 2y' + y = e^{-x} \log x, 0 < x < \infty$.

9. $(D^2 - 2D + 1)y = e^x x^{1/2}, 0 < x < \infty$.

In Problems 10–16, solve by the easiest method available.

10. $R'' + R = \tan x, R(0) = 1, R'(0) = -1$.

11. $y'' - 2y' + y = e^x \sqrt{x} + 1, y(0) = 1, y'(0) = 0$.

12. $\dfrac{d^2 N}{dt^2} + 2\dfrac{dN}{dt} + 5N = 3t^2 + 1, N(0) = 2, N'(0) = -1$.

13. $x^2 y'' - 2xy' + 2y = 3, y(1) = -1, y'(1) = 1$. *Hint:* $y_1 = x$ and $y_2 = x^2$.

14. $x^2 y'' - 2xy' + 2y = x, y(1) = 0, y'(1) = 1$. *Hint:* See Problem 13.

15. $x^2 y'' - 2xy' + 2y = x \log x, y(1) = 1, y'(1) = 1$. *Hint:* See Problem 13.

16. $y'' - 5y' + 4y = xe^{-x}, y(0) = y'(0) = 0$.

17. Let $h(x)$ be the unique solution of the initial value problem

$$y'' + by' + cy = 0, \qquad y(x_0) = 0, \qquad y'(x_0) = 1.$$

Show that

$$y(x) = \int_{x_0}^{x} h(x - s)g(s)\, ds$$

solves

$$y'' + by' + cy = g(x), \qquad y(x_0) = y'(x_0) = 0.$$

Hint: Differentiate $y(x)$. Then verify that $y(x)$ is the solution of the initial value problem.

3.10 REDUCTION OF ORDER

Given an nth-order linear differential equation, if one nontrivial solution is known, then a technique very similar to variation of parameters can be used to reduce the equation to an $(n - 1)$st-order linear equation. This fact is particularly interesting when $n = 2$, since the resulting first-order equation can always be solved by the method of Section 2.6.

Consider a second-order linear homogeneous equation

$$(10.1) \qquad\qquad y'' + b_1(x)y' + b_0(x)y = 0,$$

where b_0 and b_1 are defined and continuous on some interval J. Suppose that one solution of (10.1) is known, say $y_1(x)$, where $y_1(x)$ is not identically zero. Then $y = cy_1(x)$ is a solution for any constant c. We shall replace the constant c by an unknown function $v(x)$ and make a trial solution of the form

$$(10.2) \qquad\qquad y = v(x)y_1(x).$$

On substituting (10.2) into (10.1) it follows that

$$y' = v'y_1 + vy_1',$$

$$y'' = v''y_1 + 2v'y_1' + vy_1'',$$

and

$$(10.3) \qquad v''y_1 + v'(2y_1' + b_1y_1) + v(y_1'' + b_1y_1' + b_0y_1) = 0.$$

Since y_1 is a solution of (10.1), the last term in (10.3) is zero. Therefore, (10.3) can be written as

$$(10.4) \qquad\qquad v''y_1(x) + v'(2y_1'(x) + b_1(x)y_1(x)) = 0.$$

Since (10.4) is a first-order linear equation in v', it can be solved by the methods of Sections 2.6 and 3.1. Define $w = v'$ so that

$$w' + \frac{2y_1' + b_1 y_1}{y_1} w = 0.$$

Since

$$\int \frac{2y_1' + b_1 y_1}{y_1} \, dx = 2 \log y_1 + \int b_1(x) \, dx,$$

then

$$w(x) = v'(x) = c_1 \exp\left[-\log y_1^2 - \int b_1(x) \, dx \right]$$

$$= c_1 y_1^{-2} \exp\left[-\int b_1(x) \, dx \right].$$

A second integration gives $v(x)$. Since any antiderivative will do, the integration constants in $v(x)$ can be chosen in any manner that makes the computations simple.

EXAMPLE 10.1   Given $y_1(x) = x$, find a general solution of

(10.5) $x^2 y'' - xy' + y = 0,$ $0 < x < \infty.$

Note that $y_1 = x$ does indeed solve (10.5). To find a second solution, we put $y = xv(x)$. Then $y' = xv' + v$, $y'' = xv'' + 2v'$ and (10.5) becomes

$$x^2(xv'' + 2v') - x(xv' + v) + xv = 0.$$

This simplifies to

$$x^3 v'' + x^2 v' = 0,$$

or if $w = v'$, then

$$w' + \frac{1}{x} w = 0.$$

Thus $w = v' = c_1 x^{-1}$ and $v = c_1 \log x + c_2$. On multiplying v by x, we obtain the general solution

$$y = x(c_1 \log x + c_2).$$

If we chose $c_1 = 1$ and $c_2 = 0$, this expression reduces to the second linearly independent solution $y_2 = x \log x$.   ∎

The technique can be used to solve either homogeneous or nonhomogeneous equations.

SOLUTION VIA REDUCTION OF ORDER

Given a second-order linear equation of the form

$$y'' + b_1(x)y' + b_2(x)y = g(x),$$

(with $g \equiv 0$ allowed) we proceed as follows:

1. Find a solution $y_1(x)$ of the corresponding homogeneous equation. Form a trial solution of the form

$$y = v(x)y_1(x).$$

2. Substitute the trial solution into the second-order equation, and simplify the resulting expression to obtain a linear equation for v'.
3. Substitute $w = v'$, and solve the resulting first-order linear differential equation for w. Integrate $w = v'$ to find v. This v is used in the trial solution to obtain y.

EXAMPLE 10.2   Find a general solution of

(10.6) $$x^2 y'' - xy' + y = x^{1/2}, \qquad 0 < x < \infty.$$

From Example 10.1 we know that $y_1(x) = x$ is a solution of the corresponding homogeneous equation. Take as a trial solution for (10.6) $y = xv(x)$. Substituting into (10.6) gives

$$x^3 v'' + x^2 v' = x^{1/2}$$

or

$$w' + \frac{1}{x}w = x^{-5/2}.$$

This is a linear equation. It can be solved by finding an integrating factor $\mu(x)$ as explained in Chapter 2. One finds that $\mu(x) = e^{\int x^{-1}dx} = e^{\log x} = x$. Thus

$$xw' + x = x^{-3/2},$$

or $(xw)' = x^{-3/2}$. Thus $xw = -2x^{-1/2} + c_1$ and

$$w = v' = c_1 x^{-1} - 2x^{-3/2}.$$

Hence $v = c_1 \log x + 4x^{-1/2} + c_2$ and

$$y = xv = c_1 x \log x + c_2 x + 4x^{1/2}$$

is a general solution of (10.6). If we specialize to $c_1 = c_2 = 0$, we obtain the particular solution $y_p = 4x^{1/2}$.   ∎

PROBLEMS

In Problems 1–4, find a general solution. Use reduction of order.

1. $x^2 y'' + 2xy' - 6y = 0, \ 0 < x < \infty, \ y_1 = x^2.$

2. $x^2 y'' - 3xy' + 4y = 0, \ 0 < x < \infty, \ y_1 = x^2.$

3. $t^2 \dfrac{d^2 y}{dt^2} + 2t \dfrac{dy}{dt} - 2y = 0, \ 0 < t < \infty, \ y_1 = t.$

4. $(1 - x^2)y'' - 2xy' + 2y = 0, \ -1 < x < 1, \ y_1 = x.$ (Hard!)

In Problems 5–12, find a particular solution. Use any method from this chapter that you wish.

5. $y'' - 2y' - 24y = 3 + 2e^{3x}, \ -\infty < x < \infty.$

6. $x^2 y'' - 3xy' + 3y = x^2, \ 0 < x < \infty, \ y_1 = x.$

7. $x^2 y'' + 5xy' - 5y = x^{-1/2}, \ 0 < x < \infty, \ y_1 = x.$

8. $x^2 y'' - xy' + y = x^{-1}, \ 0 < x < \infty, \ y_1 = x, \ y_2 = x \log x.$

9. $(D^2 - 8D + 16)y = -e^{2x}, \ -\infty < x < \infty.$

10. $\dfrac{d^2 B}{dx^2} + B = \csc^3 x, \ 0 < x < \pi, \ B_1 = \sin x.$

11. $(D^2 - 8D + 16)y = 3e^{4x}, \ -\infty < x < \infty.$

12. $t^2 \dfrac{d^2 y}{dt^2} - 5t \dfrac{dy}{dt} + 9y = t^4 \log t, \ 0 < t < \infty, \ y_1 = t^3.$

In Problems 13–16, find a general solution.

13. $x^2 \dfrac{d^2 B}{dx^2} = 2B, \ 0 < x < \infty, \ B_1 = x^2.$

14. $(1 - s^2)\dfrac{d^2 y}{ds^2} - 2s \dfrac{dy}{ds} + 2y = 1 - 3s^2, \ 0 < s < 1, \ y_1 = s.$

15. $r \dfrac{d^2 R}{dr^2} - (r + 1)\dfrac{dR}{dr} + R = 0, \ 0 < r < \infty, \ R_1 = e^r.$

16. $t^2 \dfrac{d^2 M}{dt^2} - 3t \dfrac{dM}{dt} + 4M = 0, \ -\infty < t < 0, \ M_1 = t^2.$

3.11 *EULER–CAUCHY EQUATIONS*

The reader has seen that for linear second-order homogeneous or nonhomo-geneous equations with constant coefficients a reasonably satisfactory method of solution exists. For a general linear equation with variable coefficients the problem of finding solutions is much more difficult. The solution of this type of equation will be the topic of Chapter 5. However, one special type of equation with variable coefficients, the Euler equation, readily admits solution by simple methods. The Euler equation is important because it comes up in the course of solving certain interesting partial differential equations.

Any second-order equation of the form

(11.1) $$x^2 y'' + bxy' + cy = 0,$$

where b and c are real constants, is called an **Euler equation.** (The names **Cauchy equation** and **Euler–Cauchy equation** are also used.) By dividing by x^2 we can put (11.1) in standard form

$$y'' + \frac{b}{x} y' + \frac{c}{x^2} y = 0, \qquad x \neq 0.$$

The coefficients are defined and continuous on the interval $0 < x < \infty$ and also on the interval $-\infty < x < 0$. Thus solutions of this equation can be defined on $-\infty < x < 0$ or $0 < x < \infty$ but are not necessarily defined at $x = 0$. We shall take the interval J to be the interval $0 < x < \infty$ and shall first seek solutions on this interval.

The Euler equation is readily solved after first using the change variables $x = e^t$, or equivalently $t = \log x$. To express (11.1) in terms of the new variable, we first compute

$$y' = \frac{dy}{dx} = \frac{dy}{dt} \frac{dt}{dx} = \frac{dy}{dt} \frac{1}{x} = \frac{dy}{dt} e^{-t}$$

and

$$y'' = \frac{d}{dx}\left(\frac{dy}{dx}\right) = \left(\frac{d}{dt}\left(\frac{dy}{dx}\right)\right)\frac{dt}{dx} = \left(\frac{d}{dt}\left(\frac{dy}{dt} e^{-t}\right)\right)e^{-t}$$

$$= \left(\frac{d^2y}{dt^2} e^{-t} - \frac{dy}{dt} e^{-t}\right)e^{-t} = \left(\frac{d^2y}{dt^2} - \frac{dy}{dt}\right)e^{-2t}.$$

Hence (11.1) can be expressed, in terms of y and t, as

$$x^2\left(\frac{d^2y}{dt^2} - \frac{dy}{dt}\right)e^{-2t} + bx\left(\frac{dy}{dt} e^{-t}\right) + cy$$

$$= e^{2t}\left(\frac{d^2y}{dt^2} - \frac{dy}{dt}\right)e^{-2t} + be^t\left(\frac{dy}{dt} e^{-t}\right) + cy = 0,$$

or

(11.2) $$\frac{d^2y}{dt^2} + (b - 1)\frac{dy}{dt} + cy = 0.$$

Thus the substitution $x = e^t$ has the effect of replacing an equation with variable coefficients [i.e., (11.1)] by an equation with constant coefficients [i.e., (11.2)]. If we solve (11.2) by using the methods developed for equations with constant coefficients and then use the substitution $t = \log x$, we will obtain solutions of (11.1).

For the interval $-\infty < x < 0$ the method of solution is almost the same. The substitution $|x| = e^t$, or equivalently $x = -e^t$, will again reduce (11.1) to (11.2). Once (11.2) is solved we use the inverse substitution $t = \log|x|$ to obtain solutions of the original problem.

THEOREM 11.1: SOLUTION OF EULER'S EQUATION

Let λ_1 and λ_2 be the roots of the equation

$$\lambda^2 + (b-1)\lambda + c = 0.$$

Then a general solution of (11.1) is obtained as follows.

(a) If λ_1 and λ_2 are real and not equal, then

$$y = c_1|x|^{\lambda_1} + c_2|x|^{\lambda_2}.$$

(b) If λ_1 and λ_2 are real and equal (i.e., $\lambda_1 = \lambda_2 = \lambda$), then

$$y = c_1|x|^{\lambda} + c_2|x|^{\lambda}\log|x|.$$

(c) If $\lambda_1 = \alpha + i\beta$ and $\lambda_2 = \alpha - i\beta$, then

$$y = c_1|x|^{\alpha}\cos(\beta\log|x|) + c_2|x|^{\alpha}\sin(\beta\log|x|).$$

For example, if $\lambda^2 + (b-1)\lambda + c = 0$ has two real roots λ_1 and λ_2, then a general solution of (11.2) is

$$y(t) = c_1 e^{\lambda_1 t} + c_2 e^{\lambda_2 t}.$$

Since $x = e^t$ when $x > 0$, then $\log x = t$ and

$$\begin{aligned} y(x) &= c_1 e^{\lambda_1 \log x} + c_2 e^{\lambda_2 \log x} \\ &= c_1(e^{\log x})^{\lambda_1} + c_2(e^{\log x})^{\lambda_2} \\ &= c_1 x^{\lambda_1} + c_2 x^{\lambda_2}. \end{aligned}$$

The other cases are handled in a similar manner.

EXAMPLE 11.2   Solve $x^2 y'' + 4xy' + 2y = 0$, $y(1) = 0$, $y'(1) = 2$.

Note that the equation has variable coefficients but is of the correct form to be an Euler equation. From Theorem 11.1 we see that a good trial solution is $y = x^{\lambda}$. Then $y' = \lambda x^{\lambda-1}$, $y'' = \lambda(\lambda-1)x^{\lambda-2}$ and the equation is satisfied when

$$x^2(\lambda(\lambda-1)x^{\lambda-2}) + 4x(\lambda x^{\lambda-1}) + 2x^{\lambda} = x^{\lambda}(\lambda^2 + 3\lambda + 2) = 0.$$

Hence $\lambda = -1$ and $\lambda = -2$ will do. By Theorem 11.1, part (a) it follows that a general solution is

$$y = c_1 x^{-1} + c_2 x^{-2}.$$

Since $y' = -c_1 x^{-2} - 2c_2 x^{-3}$, then c_1 and c_2 must satisfy the two equations

$$c_1 + c_2 = 0 \quad\text{and}\quad -c_1 - 2c_2 = 2.$$

Hence $c_1 = 2$, $c_2 = -2$, and $y = 2x^{-1} - 2x^{-2}$ for $0 < x < \infty$. ∎

EXAMPLE 11.3   Find a general solution of

(11.3) $$x^2y'' - 5xy' + 13y = 0.$$

The equation has variable coefficients. It is an Euler equation. We try a solution of the form $y = x^\lambda$ for $0 < x < \infty$. (Absolute values can be added later for the solution over the interval $-\infty < x < 0$.) Thus

$$x^2(\lambda(\lambda - 1)x^{\lambda - 2}) - 5x(\lambda x^{\lambda - 1}) + 13x^\lambda = 0$$

or

$$x^\lambda(\lambda^2 - 6\lambda + 13) = 0.$$

Hence $\lambda = 3 \pm 2i$. Since $x^p = (e^{\log x})^p = e^{p \log x}$ for any number p, then

$$x^{3 + 2i} = x^3 x^{2i} = x^3 e^{2i \log x} = x^3[\cos (2 \log x) + i \sin (2 \log x)],$$

and two linearly independent real-valued solutions over $0 < x < \infty$ are

$$y_1 = x^3 \cos (2 \log x) \quad \text{and} \quad y_2 = x^3 \sin (2 \log x).$$

A real-valued general solution is

$$y = x^3[c_1 \cos (2 \log x) + c_2 \sin (2 \log x)]. \quad \blacksquare$$

Notice that our technique of solution is also useful for solving the non-homogeneous Euler equation

$$x^2y'' + bxy' + cy = g(x).$$

Since two solutions of the homogeneous equation can be found, then either variation of parameters or reduction of order can be used.

EXAMPLE 11.4   Find a general solution of

(11.4) $$x^2y'' - 2xy' + 2y = 2x^3, \qquad 0 < x < \infty.$$

First compute a fundamental set of solutions of the corresponding homogeneous equation. With $y = x^\lambda$ we find that $\lambda^2 - 3\lambda + 2 = 0$. Hence $\lambda = 1$ or $\lambda = 2$, so that $y_1 = x$ and $y_2 = x^2$ will do. Next compute a particular solution of (11.4). Using reduction of order we try $y_p = xv(x)$. Then

$$x^2(xv'' + 2v') - 2x(xv' + v) + 2xv = 2x^3.$$

Hence $x^3v'' = 2x^3$ or $v'' = 2$. Therefore, $v = x^2$ is a particular solution. A general solution of (11.4) is now seen to be

$$y = c_1x + c_2x^2 + x^3. \quad \blacksquare$$

PROBLEMS   In Problems 1–14, find a general solution over $0 < x < \infty$.

1. $x^2y'' - 4xy' + 6y = 0.$ 2. $x^2y'' + 2xy' - 6y = 0.$

3. $x^2y'' + 3xy' - 8y = 0.$ 4. $x^2y'' + 5xy' + 4y = 0.$

5. $2x^2y'' - xy' + y = 0.$

6. $x^2y'' + 9xy' + 16y = 0.$

7. $x^2y'' + y = 0.$

8. $x^2y'' - xy' + 4y = 0.$

9. $x^2y'' - 6y = 1.$

10. $x^2y'' - xy' + y = x.$

11. $x^2y'' + 3xy' + y = x^{1/2}.$

12. $x^2y'' - 3xy' + 3y = x^2.$

13. $x^2y'' + 5xy' - 5y = x^2.$

14. $x^2y'' - 6y = \log x.$

In Problems 15–20, solve the initial value problem.

15. $x^2y'' - 6xy' + 10y = 0,\ y(1) = 1,\ y'(1) = 0.$

16. $x^2y'' + 8xy' + 10y = 0,\ y(2) = 0,\ y'(2) = 2.$

17. $x^2y'' - 12y = 0,\ y(-1) = 1,\ y'(-1) = -1.$

18. $2x^2y'' + 6xy' + 2y = 1,\ y(-2) = 1,\ y'(-2) = 0.$

19. $x^2y'' - 6y = x,\ y(1) = 2,\ y'(1) = 2.$

20. $x^2y'' + 2xy' + y = \log x,\ y(1) = y'(1) = 0.$ *Hint:* Let $x = e^t.$

21. Show that under the substitution $x - \alpha = e^t$, the equation

$$(x - \alpha)^2 y'' + b(x - \alpha)y + cy = 0$$

is transformed into the equation

$$\frac{d^2y}{dt^2} + (b - 1)\frac{dy}{dt} + cy = 0.$$

Use this substitution to solve each problem.

(a) $(x + 1)^2 y'' - (x + 1)y' + y = 0,\ y(0) = 1,\ y'(0) = 0.$

(b) $(x - 2)^2 y'' + y = 0,\ y(1) = 3,\ y'(1) = 1.$

(c) $(x - 1)^2 y'' - 5(x - 1)y' + 9y = 0,\ y(0) = y'(0) = 1.$

(d) $(x + 1)^2 y'' - 12y = 6,\ y(0) = 1,\ y'(0) = -1.$

22. Find a general solution of each problem.

(a) $t^2 \dfrac{d^2y}{dt^2} + 2t\dfrac{dy}{dt} - 6y = 0,\ 0 < t < \infty.$

(b) $(t - 2)^2 \dfrac{d^2B}{dt^2} + (t - 2)\dfrac{dB}{dt} + 4B = 0,\ -\infty < t < 2.$

(c) $4s^2 \dfrac{d^2N}{ds^2} + N = 0,\ 0 < s < \infty.$

(d) $9(x + \pi)^2 \dfrac{d^2R}{dx^2} + 7(x + \pi)\dfrac{dR}{dx} + \dfrac{1}{9}R = 0,\ -\pi < x < \infty.$

(e) $(u - 1)^2 \dfrac{d^2V}{du^2} + 3(u - 1)\dfrac{dV}{du} + V = 0,\ 1 < u < \infty.$

3.12 VIBRATIONS OF MECHANICAL SYSTEMS

Translational mechanical systems were introduced in Section 2.8. A linear mass–spring problem was discussed and solved. Since we can now discuss this problem, and related problems, much more easily and efficiently, we consider the mechanical system depicted in Figure 3.3. This system consists of an elastic spring with a point mass M attached. For now it will be assumed that all frictional forces can be neglected. When the spring is elongated or compressed it will produce an opposing force $-f(z)$ which depends on the amount z of elongation or compression. We shall take the convention that deformation z is positive when the spring is elongated and is negative when the spring is compressed. Hence $f(z) > 0$ when $z > 0$ and $f(z) < 0$ when $z < 0$. Moreover, we assume that $f'(z)$ is always positive.

At equilibrium the elongation z_0 produces a force that exactly balances the gravitational force on the mass, that is,

(12.1) $$Mg = f(z_0),$$

where g is the gravitational constant (in correct units). If the system is disturbed from equilibrium by compressing or elongating the spring and then removing the disturbing force, the system will begin to oscillate. Our problem is to describe the resulting oscillations. According to Newton's second law,

(12.2) $$M\frac{d^2z}{dt^2} = Mg - f(z).$$

If $z = y + z_0$, then (12.1) and (12.2) imply that

$$M\frac{d^2z}{dt^2} = M\frac{d^2y}{dt^2} = Mg - f(y + z_0) = f(z_0) - f(y + z_0).$$

Define $F(y) = f(y + z_0) - f(z_0)$. Then

(12.3) $$M\frac{d^2y}{dt^2} + F(y) = 0.$$

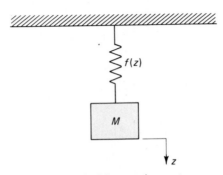

Figure 3.3. Mass–spring system.

Here F is a function satisfying $F(y) > 0$ for $y > 0$ and $F(y) < 0$ for $y < 0$.

For small oscillations and common elastic materials **Hooke's law** is true (or is at least a very good approximation). Hooke's law states that the force produced by the spring is proportional to the deformation, that is,

(12.4) $$f(z) = Kz.$$

A spring that satisfies (12.4) is called a **linear spring.** The proportionally constant K is positive. It is called the **stiffness coefficient** of the spring. For very stiff springs K is large and for weak springs K is near zero. If (12.4) is used in (12.3), then $F(y) = f(y + z_0) - f(z_0) = K(y + z_0) - Kz_0 = Ky$. Hence y solves the equation

(12.5) $$M\frac{d^2y}{dt^2} + Ky = 0.$$

This equation is linear, homogeneous, and has constant coefficients. The characteristic equation for this differential equation is $M\lambda^2 + K = 0$. The characteristic roots $\lambda_1 = i\sqrt{K/M}$ and $\lambda_2 = -i\sqrt{K/M}$ are complex. Hence two linearly independent solutions of (12.5) on $(-\infty, \infty)$ are

$$y_1 = \cos at \quad \text{and} \quad y_2 = \sin at, \qquad a = \sqrt{\frac{K}{M}}.$$

A general solution is

(12.6) $$y(t) = c_1 \cos at + c_2 \sin at, \qquad a = \sqrt{\frac{K}{M}}.$$

The constants c_1 and c_2 can be determined when initial conditions a_0 and a_1 are given. Since the sine and cosine functions are periodic of period 2π, then y given by (12.6) is a periodic function of period T, where

$$T = \frac{2\pi}{a} = 2\pi\sqrt{\frac{M}{K}}.$$

This period depends on the size of the mass and on the stiffness of the spring. We can draw the reasonable conclusions that the system oscillates more rapidly as the spring is made stiffer (i.e., K larger) or the mass smaller.

The solution (12.6) is often written in **amplitude-phase form.** This is accomplished as follows. Define $A = (c_1^2 + c_2^2)^{1/2}$ and choose φ in the range $0 \le \varphi < 2\pi$ so that $c_1/A = \sin \varphi$ and $c_2/A = \cos \varphi$. If the numbers c_1 and c_2 are known, then φ can be determined using a calculator. The solution (12.6) can be written as

$$y(t) = A\left(\cos at \frac{c_1}{A} + \sin at \frac{c_2}{A}\right) = A(\cos at \sin \varphi + \sin at \cos \varphi),$$

or

$$y(t) = A \sin(at + \varphi).$$

Thus we see that $y(t)$ is a multiple of the sine function which has been shifted along the t-axis by an amount φ. The constant A is the **amplitude** of $y(t)$ while φ is the **phase shift** of the solution $y(t)$.

EXAMPLE 12.1   If $M = 1$ kilogram and $K = 4$ newtons per meter, determine the period of the resulting oscillations of the system in Figure 3.3. If $y_0 = 0.2$ meter and $y_0' = -0.1$ meter per second, write the solution in amplitude-phase form.

In this case the initial value problem is

$$\frac{d^2 y}{dt^2} + 4y = 0, \qquad y(0) = 0.2, \qquad y'(0) = -0.1.$$

The period is π and the solution is

$$y(t) = 0.2 \cos 2t - 0.05 \sin 2t.$$

Thus the amplitude is $A = (0.2^2 + 0.05^2)^{1/2} \cong 0.20616$. The constant φ must satisfy $\sin \varphi = 0.97014$ and $\cos \varphi = -0.24254$. Thus $\varphi \cong 1.81577$ radians. ∎

EXAMPLE 12.2   Consider the system depicted in Figure 3.3 and assume that (12.4) is true. If a force of 0.5 newton will stretch the spring 0.01 meters, compute the stiffness of the spring. What mass will cause the spring to oscillate at the rate of 10 cycles per second?

Since the spring satisfies Hooke's law, a deformation z produces a force $F = Kz$. Hence $0.5 = 0.01K$ or $K = 50$. Since the period of solutions of (12.5) is $T = 2\pi \sqrt{M/K}$ and since a frequency of 10 cycles per second corresponds to $T = 1/10$ second, M must satisfy $\frac{1}{10} = 2\pi \sqrt{M/50}$. Hence $M \cong 0.01267$ kilogram. ∎

Next consider the mass–spring system depicted in Figure 3.4. This system is the same as that in Figure 3.3 except that we assume that there is friction in the system. This friction might be caused by air resistance acting on the

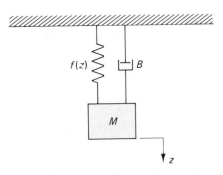

Figure 3.4. Mass–spring–damper system.

mass M, internal friction in the spring, or a combination of both. The friction is assumed to be viscous friction; that is, it exerts a retarding force $-Bv$ on the mass, where v is the velocity of the mass and B is a positive constant. While (12.1) is still true, (12.2) must be replaced by

$$(12.7) \qquad M\frac{d^2z}{dt} = Mg - Bv - f(z), \qquad v = \frac{dz}{dt}.$$

Let $z = y + z_0$ so that $v = dz/dt = dy/dt$ and

$$M\frac{d^2z}{dt^2} = M\frac{d^2y}{dt^2} = Mg - Bv - f(y + z_0) = f(z_0) - Bv - f(y + z_0).$$

Hence, if $F(y) = f(y + z_0) - f(z_0)$ as before, then

$$(12.8) \qquad M\frac{d^2y}{dt^2} + B\frac{dy}{dt} + F(y) = 0.$$

Again it will be assumed that Hooke's law [see (12.4)] applies. Hence the displacement y solves the linear equation

$$(12.9) \qquad \frac{d^2y}{dt^2} + 2b\frac{dy}{dt} + c^2y = 0,$$

where $b = B/(2M)$ and $c = \sqrt{K/M}$. This equation has constant coefficients. The characteristic equation $\lambda^2 + 2b\lambda + c^2 = 0$ has roots $-b \pm \sqrt{b^2 - c^2}$. The solutions will have different properties depending on whether $b^2 > c^2$, $b^2 = c^2$, or $b^2 < c^2$. We consider these three cases in turn.

Case 1. $b^2 > c^2$. The characteristic equation is

$$\lambda^2 + 2b\lambda + c^2 = 0.$$

The roots $\lambda_1 = -b + \sqrt{b^2 - c^2}$ and $\lambda_2 = -b - \sqrt{b^2 - c^2}$ are negative and $\lambda_1 \neq \lambda_2$. Hence solutions have the form

$$y(t) = c_1 e^{\lambda_1 t} + c_2 e^{\lambda_2 t}.$$

The derivative of such a solution will have at most one change of sign. After that the solution tends monotonically to zero as $t \to \infty$. Some typical solutions are graphed in Figure 3.5.

Case 2. $b^2 = c^2$. In this case the characteristic equation has a double root $\lambda_1 = \lambda_2 = -b$. A general solution has the form

$$y(t) = (c_1 + c_2 t)e^{-bt}.$$

Again solutions tend to zero as $t \to \infty$ after at most one change of sign.

Case 3. $b^2 < c^2$. This is the most interesting case. The characteristic roots are complex numbers, that is, $\lambda_1 = -b + i\sqrt{c^2 - b^2}$ and $\lambda_2 = \bar{\lambda}_1$. A general solution has the form

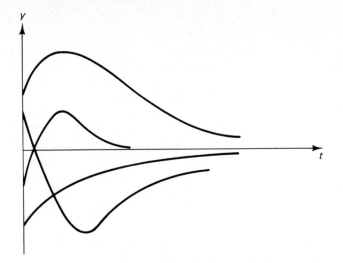

Figure 3.5. Solutions of an overdamped equation.

$$y(t) = e^{-bt}[c_1 \cos (\sqrt{c^2 - b^2} \ t) + c_2 \sin (\sqrt{c^2 - b^2} \ t)].$$

The term in brackets can be written in amplitude-phase form, that is

(12.10) $$y(t) = e^{-bt} A \sin (\sqrt{c^2 - b^2} \ t + \varphi),$$

where $A = (c_1^2 + c_2^2)^{1/2}$, $A \sin \varphi = c_1$, and $A \cos \varphi = c_2$. Hence we see that (12.10) represents an oscillatory motion whose amplitude $e^{-bt} A$ is exponentially decaying to zero. Typical solutions are shown in Figure 3.6.

Clearly, the presence of the friction term Bv alters the behavior of solutions of the linear mass–spring system. The presence of this term is said to cause

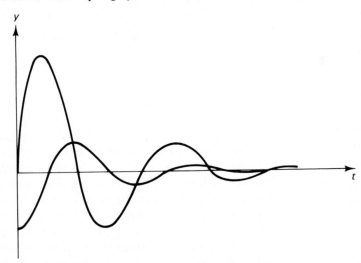

Figure 3.6. Typical solutions of an underdamped equation.

damping. Equation (12.9) is called **overdamped** when $b^2 > c^2$, or equivalently when $B^2 > 4MK$. In this case solutions of (12.9) tend rapidly to zero without much wiggling. This type of behavior is typical of the suspension system of a car. (Near each wheel is a heavy spring and a shock absorber that acts as a damper. If the system is operating properly, the damping coefficient B will be so large that the system is overdamped.) When $b^2 < c^2$, or equivalently when $B^2 < 4MK$, then (12.9) is called **underdamped.** The motion in this case is oscillatory but eventually dies out. This is what we usually see with simple mass–spring systems. The intermediate case $b^2 = c^2$, or $B^2 = 4MK$, is called **critically damped.** If $B = 0$, then (12.8) reduces to (12.5) and is called **undamped.** In this case the system will oscillate indefinitely. This type of behavior is typical of the pendulum motion of a grandfather clock in good working order. There the damping is so small that for time periods of an hour or so it can be ignored completely.

Translational symbols and units are given in Table 3.2.

TABLE 3.2   Translational Symbols and Units

Symbol	Quanity	English Units	Metric Units
f	Force	pounds	newtons
y	Distance	feet	meters
v	Velocity	feet/second	meters/second
a	Acceleration	feet/second²	meters/second²
M	Mass	slugs = pound-second²/foot	kilograms
K	Stiffness coefficient	pounds/foot	newtons/meter
B	Damping constant	pounds/(foot/second)	newtons/(meter/second)

Some Useful Constants

Standard gravity (at 45° latitude and sea level) $g_0 = 9.80665$ meters/second²

1 slug	$= 14.5939$ kilograms
1 foot	$= 0.304801$ meter
1 gallon	$= 0.13368$ cubic foot
1 pound (force)	$= 4.44822$ newtons

EXAMPLE 12.3
Model
Railroading

Many systems that may not at first look like mass–spring systems can be put in the form (12.9). For example, consider the train depicted in Figure 3.7. The train is ascending a hill with constant grade whose angle of elevation is θ. The train consists of a locomotive of mass M_l and one car of mass M_c. We idealize by assuming these are point masses. The locomotive engine is used to exert a constant forward force u on the locomotive. The coupling between the locomotive and the railway car is modeled as a spring that exerts a restoring force $-F(z)$ when the distance between the locomotive and the car is z and a viscous frictional force $-B\,dz/dt$. We shall neglect air resistance.

Let y_l and y_c be the positions of the locomotive and of the car as measured from some fixed reference point on the hill. According to Newton's second law,

Photo 9. A multi-car system. (Courtesy of Thrall Car Manufacturing Co.)

$$M_l \frac{d^2 y_l}{dt^2} = -g M_l \sin \theta - F(y_l - y_c) - B\left(\frac{dy_l}{dt} - \frac{dy_c}{dt}\right) + u,$$

(12.11)

$$M_c \frac{d^2 y_c}{dt^2} = -g M_c \sin \theta + F(y_l - y_c) + B\left(\frac{dy_l}{dt} - \frac{dy_c}{dt}\right),$$

where g is the gravitational constant. We assume that the spring in the railway coupling is linear (i.e., it satisfies Hooke's law), so that for some $K > 0$

(12.12) $F(z) = Kz.$

If the locomotive and the car are moving at a constant velocity v_0, then $y_l = v_0 t + a_0$, $y_c = v_0 t + a_1$, and (12.11) reduces to

$$0 = -g M_l \sin \theta - K(a_0 - a_1) - B\cdot 0 + u,$$

(12.13)

$$0 = -g M_c \sin \theta + K(a_0 - a_1) + B\cdot 0.$$

From the second equation it follows that

(12.14) $K(a_0 - a_1) = g M_c \sin \theta.$

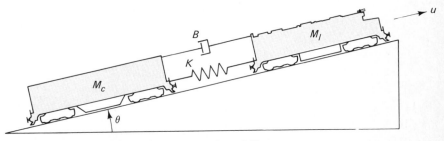

Figure 3.7. One car train uphill.

This expression can be substituted into the first equation in (12.13) to see that

(12.15) $$u = (M_l + M_c)g \sin \theta.$$

This means that at constant velocity v_0 the engine exerts a force u which just balances the backward acceleration on the train due to gravity. The number $a_0 - a_1$ can be computed from (12.14).

It will be assumed that u, a_0, and a_1 are chosen so that (12.14) and (12.15) are true and that the train is traveling in such a way that v_l and v_c are nearly equal to v_0. Let

$$w_l = y_l - v_0 t - a_0, \qquad w_c = y_c - v_0 t - a_1$$

be the deviations of the locomotive and the car from the uniform motion. Define $w = w_l - w_c$. Then

$$w = (y_l - v_0 t - a_0) - (y_c - v_0 t - a_1) = y_l - y_c + (a_1 - a_0).$$

From (12.11) and (12.13)–(12.15) it follows that

$$M_l \frac{d^2 y_l}{dt^2} = -g M_l \sin \theta - K(y_l - y_c) - B(v_l - v_c) + (M_l + M_c)g \sin \theta$$

$$= -g M_l \sin \theta - [Kw + K(a_0 - a_1)] - B\frac{dw}{dt} + (M_l + M_c)g \sin \theta$$

or

$$M_l \frac{d^2 y_l}{dt^2} = -Kw - B\frac{dw}{dt}.$$

Similarly,

$$M_c \frac{d^2 y_c}{dt^2} = -g M_c \sin \theta + [K(w) + K(a_0 - a_1)] - B\left(\frac{dy_c}{dt} - \frac{dy_l}{dt}\right)$$

$$= K(w) - B(v_c - v_l)$$

$$= Kw + B\frac{dw}{dt}.$$

Hence

$$\frac{d^2 w}{dt^2} = \frac{d^2}{dt^2}(y_l - y_c) = -\left(\frac{K}{M_l} + \frac{K}{M_c}\right)w - \left(\frac{B}{M_l} + \frac{B}{M_c}\right)\frac{dw}{dt}.$$

Let M be the number defined by the relation

$$\frac{1}{M} = \frac{1}{M_l} + \frac{1}{M_c}.$$

Then w satisfies the equation

(12.16) $$\frac{d^2 w}{dt^2} = -\frac{K}{M}w - \frac{B}{M}\frac{dw}{dt}.$$

This equation has the form (12.9). Hence it can be analyzed in the same way. In particular, since $B > 0$ we see that $w(t)$ tends to zero as t tends to positive infinity. Hence as $t \to \infty$,

$$y_l(t) - y_c(t) = w(t) + (a_0 - a_1) \to a_0 - a_1.$$

The motion of the train consists of two pieces, the motion of the train as a whole at uniform velocity v_0 and with locomotive-car spacing $a_0 - a_1$ plus a damped oscillation of the car and the locomotive about this uniform motion. The damped portion of the motion will eventually decay to zero as t goes to $+\infty$.

The railway model (12.1) is, of course, a bit too simple to be of practical interest. More realistic models can be derived. Those who are interested in advanced modeling should try the following projects:

1. Write out the equations for a two and then a three car train. (This is Problem 24 of Section 7.1.)
2. Write out the equations for an n car train.
3. The actual coupling between railway cars is more complicated than that described here. Read the description of *springs with dead zones* in Section 3.13. Then write out the equations for an n car train with this type of coupler. (See Section 3.13, Problem 12 for related material.)

PROBLEMS

1. In the spring problem in Figure 3.3, suppose that $M = 3$ kilograms and that the spring is linear with $K = 12$ newtons per meter. Determine the period at which the system oscillates. For each of the following initial conditions find the solution of (12.5) and write it in amplitude-phase form.

   (a) $y(0) = 1$ (meter), $y'(0) = 0$ meters per second.

   (b) $y(0) = 0$, $y'(0) = 2$.

   (c) $y(0) = 1$, $y'(0) = 2$.

   (d) $y(0) = -3$, $y'(0) = -1$.

2. In the spring problem in Figure 3.3, suppose that $M = \frac{1}{50}$ slug and that the spring is linear with $K = 2$ pounds per foot. Determine the period at which the system oscillates. For each of the following initial conditions find the solution and write it in amplitude-phase form.

   (a) $y(0) = 1$ foot, $y'(0) = 0$ feet per second.

   (b) $y(0) = 0$, $y'(0) = \frac{1}{2}$.

   (c) $y(0) = 1$, $y'(0) = -2$.

   (d) $y(0) = \frac{1}{2}$, $y'(0) = 1$.

3. A linear spring will stretch 0.01 meter under a force of 0.01 newton. A mass of 0.2 kilogram is suspended from the spring. Find the resulting oscillation if the mass is pulled down 0.05 meter and then released. (Assume that there is no damping.) What is the period of this oscillation? What is its amplitude?

4. A linear spring will stretch 1 inch under a force of $\frac{3}{16}$ pound. A mass weighing 1 pound (i.e., $M = 1/32.2$ slugs) is suspended from the spring. Find the resulting

oscillation if the mass is pushed up 3 inches and then released from rest. (Assume that there is no damping.) What is the period of this oscillation? What is its amplitude?

5. Two masses, each 0.1 kilogram, are suspended from the spring described in Problem 3. (There is still no damping.) One mass is firmly attached while the second is loosely attached. If at time zero the mass–spring system is at rest and if at that time one mass suddenly falls off, determine the motion of the remaining mass.

6. A linear spring will stretch 0.5 inch under a force of 0.8 pound. A 1-pound weight is suspended from the spring. Find the resulting motion, assuming no damping, if the mass is pulled down 2 inches and then released. What is the period of the resulting oscillation?

7. Two 1-pound weights are suspended from the spring described in Problem 6. One is firmly attached and the second is loosely attached. If at time zero, the mass–spring system is at rest and if at that time one mass suddenly falls off, determine the motion of the remaining mass.

8. Consider the mass–spring arrangement in Figure 3.8. Suppose that both springs are linear and that they have stiffness coefficients K_1 and K_2. Assume no damping. If x is the displacement of the mass from equilibrium (with displacements to the right considered positive):

   (a) Show that the equation of motion governing the problem is

   $$M \frac{d^2 x}{dt^2} + (K_1 + K_2)x = 0.$$

   (b) Show that for any initial displacement x_0 and any initial velocity v_0 the solution is periodic. Compute the period.

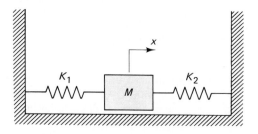

Figure 3.8. Mass–double spring system.

9. Given the mass–spring–damper system depicted in Figure 3.4, suppose that $M = 3$ kilograms and that the spring is linear with $K = 12$ newtons per meter. Find the motion of the system in each situation.

   (a) $B = 3$ (newton-seconds) per meter, $y(0) = \frac{1}{5}$ meter, $y'(0) = 0$ meters per second.

   (b) $B = 12$, $y(0) = \frac{1}{5}$, $y'(0) = 0$.   (c) $B = 15$, $y(0) = \frac{1}{5}$, $y'(0) = 0$.

   (d) $B = 3$, $y(0) = 0$, $y'(0) = 1$.   (e) $B = 12$, $y(0) = 0$, $y'(0) = 1$.

   (f) $B = 15$, $y(0) = 0$, $y'(0) = 2$.   (g) $B = 3$, $y(0) = 0$, $y'(0) = 0$.

   (h) $B = 15$, $y(0) = \frac{1}{2}$, $y'(0) = -\frac{1}{2}$.   (i) $B = 0$, $y(0) = \frac{1}{2}$, $y'(0) = -\frac{1}{2}$.

In which of these cases is the system undamped? underdamped? overdamped? critically damped?

10. Given the mass–spring–damper system depicted in Figure 3.4, suppose that $M = \frac{1}{4}$ slug and the spring is linear with $K = 4$ pounds per foot. Find the motion of the system in each case.

   (a) $B = 1$ pound-seconds per foot, $y(0) = 1$ foot, $y'(0) = 0$ feet per second.

   (b) $B = 2$, $y(0) = 1$, $y'(0) = 0$.   (c) $B = 3$, $y(0) = 1$, $y'(0) = 0$.

   (d) $B = 1$, $y(0) = 0$, $y'(0) = -1$.   (e) $B = 2$, $y(0) = 0$, $y'(0) = -1$.

   (f) $B = 3$, $y(0) = 0$, $y'(0) = -1$.   (g) $B = 1$, $y(0) = 1$, $y'(0) = -1$.

   (h) $B = 2$, $y(0) = -1$, $y'(0) = 2$.   (i) $B = 3$, $y(0) = 0$, $y'(0) = 0$.

   (j) $B = 0$, $y(0) = \frac{1}{2}$, $y'(0) = -\frac{1}{2}$.

   In which of these cases is the system undamped? underdamped? overdamped? critically damped?

11. Do Problem 5 assuming a frictional force Bv where $B = 0.01$ (newton-second) per meter.

12. Do Problem 7 assuming a frictional force Bv where $B = 0.06$ (pound-second) per foot.

13. A mass of 1 kilogram is suspended from a linear spring with $K = 20$ pounds per foot. Assume that there is no damping. Find the resulting motion if the mass is pushed upward 6 inches and then released from rest. *Hint:* Convert everything to English units.

14. A mass of 0.5 kilogram is suspended from a linear spring with $K = 20$ pounds per foot. Assume a frictional retarding force Bv on the mass where $B = 0.01$ (newton-second) per meter. If the mass is pulled down 3 inches and then released from rest, find the resulting motion.

15. Do Problem 5 assuming a frictional force Bv, where $B = 0.02$ (pound-second) per meter.

16. Do Problem 7 assuming a frictional force Bv where $B = 0.01$ (newton-second) per foot.

17. For the mass–spring–damper system in Figure 3.4, suppose that $B = 0$, M is 2 ± 0.01 pounds (i.e., $1.99 \le M \le 2.01$) and the spring is linear with $K = 50 \pm 0.5$ pound per foot. Give upper and lower esimates of the period of the system.

18. For the mass–spring–damper system in Figure 3.4, suppose that the spring is linear, $B = 0$, $M = 2 \pm 0.02$ pounds, and the period of the solutions of the system is $T = 1.25 \pm 0.02$ seconds. Give upper and lower estimates for K, the stiffness coefficient of the spring.

19. Consider the train depicted in Figure 3.7. Suppose that when the train is traveling with velocity near v_0 air resistance exerts a retarding force $B_l v_0$ on the locomotive and a retarding force $B_c v_0$ on the car.

   (a) Find the value u which is just sufficient for the train to have constant velocity v_0.

(b) Let u be determined by part (a). Let $w_l = y_l - v_0 t - a_0$ and $w_c = y_c - v_0 t - a_1$. Find two second-order differential equations that w_l and w_c satisfy. Show that $w = w_l - w_c$ satisfies an equation of the form (12.9).

20. Consider the train depicted in Figure 3.9. This train is descending a hill of constant grade whose angle of elevation is θ. The locomotive has mass M_l and the car mass M_c. The locomotive brakes are used to exert a constant backward force $-u$ on the locomotive. The coupling between the locomotive and the car is modeled as a linear spring with constant $K > 0$ plus a viscous friction term with constant $B > 0$. Air resistance is neglected.

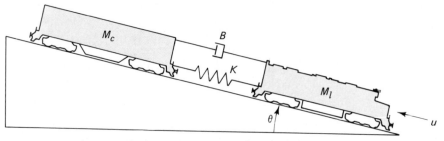

Figure 3.9. One car train downhill.

(a) Write a system of two second-order differential equations that describe the motion of this train.

(b) Find the value of u that is just sufficient for the train to travel with constant velocity v_0.

(c) Given the value of u from part (b), show that as $t \to \infty$ the velocities of the locomotive and the railway car tend to v_0 and the distance between the two tends to a constant value.

21. In Figure 3.7, suppose that instead of neglecting air resistence we assume that air exerts a frictional force $-B_a \, dy_l/dt$ on the locomotive and a frictional force $-B_a \, dy_c/dt$ on the car. Find the values of u and $a_0 - a_1$ necessary in order that the train can travel at the uniform velocity $v_0 > 0$.

22. Consider the mass–spring–damper system of Figure 3.4. The potential energy stored in the spring when it is displaced by an amount y from equilibrium is

$$E_p(y) = \int_0^y F(u) \, du$$

(where $y = 0$ at equilibrium). The kinetic energy stored in the mass when its velocity is v is

$$E_k(u) = M \frac{v^2}{2}.$$

The total energy in the system is $E(y, u) = E_p(y) + E_k(v)$. Assume that F is a continuous, monotone increasing function with $F(0) = 0$.

(a) Show that $E_p(y) > 0$ for all $y \neq 0$.

(b) Show that $E(y, v) > 0$ except when $y = v = 0$.

(c) Let $y = \varphi(t)$ be a nonconstant solution of (12.8). Show that

$$\frac{d}{dt}E(\varphi(t), \varphi'(t)) = -B\varphi'(t)^2.$$

Show that $E(\varphi(t), \varphi'(t))$ is a monotone strictly decreasing function of t.

(d) Does the total energy decrease faster or slower as B grows larger? Does this make sense physically?

3.13   NONLINEAR VIBRATIONS

Consider the mass–spring arrangement depicted in Figure 3.10. Two identical linear springs with stiffness coefficients $K/2$ are attached to a plate of mass M. If the mass moves to the right a distance d (i.e., if $y = d$), it will engage a third linear spring with stiffness coefficient K_1. For $y > d$ three springs are engaged. Similarly, if M moves to the left a distance d (i.e., if $y = -d$), then M will engage the fourth linear spring. Let $F(y)$ be the force of this multiple spring

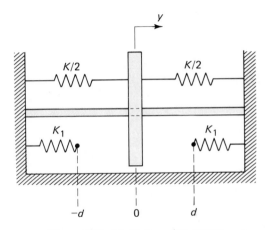

Figure 3.10. Multiple spring system.

system acting on M due to a displacement y from equilibrium. Then

$$(13.1) \qquad F(y) = \begin{cases} Ky & \text{if } -d < y < d, \\ Ky + K_1(y - d) & \text{if } y > d, \\ Ky + K_1(y + d) & \text{if } y < -d. \end{cases}$$

The function F is graphed in Figure 3.11. By Newton's second law of motion the behavior of the plate M is described by the equation

$$(13.2) \qquad M\frac{d^2y}{dt^2} + F(y) = 0.$$

In other words, the system in Figure 3.10 can be viewed as a system with a single mass and a single spring. The spring, which is characterized by (13.1), is a **nonlinear spring.** (By a nonlinear spring we mean a spring that does not

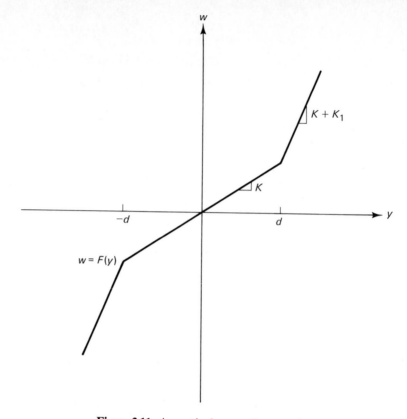

Figure 3.11. An equivalent nonlinear spring.

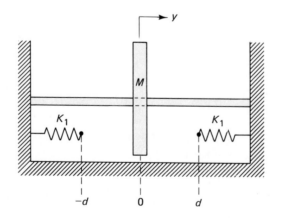

Figure 3.12. Spring system with dead zone.

obey Hooke's law.) Moreover, if K_1 is not small, it will not usually be satisfactory to approximate (13.1) by a linear function.

A second example of a nonlinear spring is the spring arrangement depicted in Figure 3.12. A plate of mass M slides freely on a frictionless horizontal rod when y, the displacement of M from equilibrium, is between $-d$ and d. If $z \geq d$, then M will engage the right hand spring. This spring is linear with stiffness coefficient K_1. If $y \leq -d$, then M will engage the left hand spring, a linear spring with stiffness coefficient K_1. Hence the force $F(y)$ exerted by the spring system on the mass M due to a displacement y is given by

(13.3)
$$F(y) = \begin{cases} K_1(y - d) & \text{if } y \geq d, \\ 0 & \text{if } -d < y < d, \\ K_1(y + d) & \text{if } y \leq -d. \end{cases}$$

This function is graphed in Figure 3.13. A spring that satisfies the relation $F(y) = 0$ for $|y| \leq d$, $F(y) > 0$ for $y > d$, and $F(y) < 0$ for $y < -d$ is called a **spring with dead zone.** The dead zone is the interval $[-d, d]$. Such a spring is nonlinear (i.e., it does not satisfy Hooke's law). Moreover, if d is not small, one

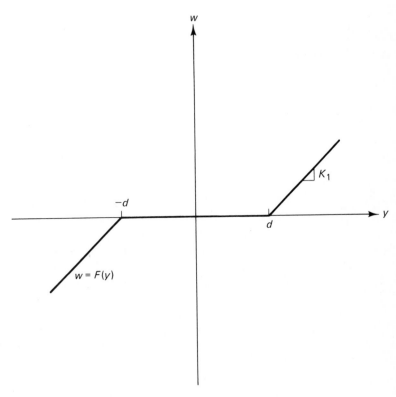

Figure 3.13. Equivalent nonlinear spring with dead zone.

cannot usually satisfactorily approximate (13.3) by a linear spring. A common and practical example of a device containing a spring with dead zone is a railway car coupler (see Photo 10). The constant d is determined by the length of the internal slot (see the right end of the detail, Photo 11).

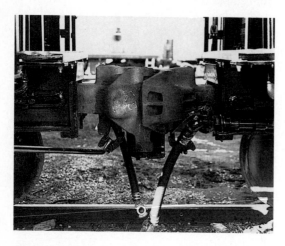

Photo 10. Railway car coupling. (Courtesy of Thrall Car Manufacturing Co.)

Photo 11. Detail of a car coupling. (Courtesy of McConway and Torley Corporation.)

A third example of a nonlinear spring is:

(13.4)
$$F(y) = \begin{cases} Ky & \text{if } |y| \le d, \\ Kd & \text{if } y > d, \\ -Kd & \text{if } y < -d. \end{cases}$$

The function defined by (13.4) is graphed in Figure 3.14. In the mathematical literature this function is usually called a **ramp function**. In the engineering literature it is usually called a **saturation function**. The **linear region** for $F(y)$ is the interval $[-d, d]$. There the spring responds as a linear spring would. Once $y = \pm d$ is reached the function **saturates;** that is, it becomes constant. In many situations (e.g., when $|y|$ is expected to get significantly above d) the saturation function cannot be satisfactorily approximated by a linear function. Equation (13.2) with $F(y)$ given by (13.1), (13.3), or (13.4) is a nonlinear equation. We shall now consider the solution of such equations.

Consider a frictionless spring problem with mass M and nonlinear spring. The spring function will be denoted by $F(y)$. Hence we are considering the equation

(13.5)
$$M \frac{d^2 y}{dt^2} + F(y) = 0.$$

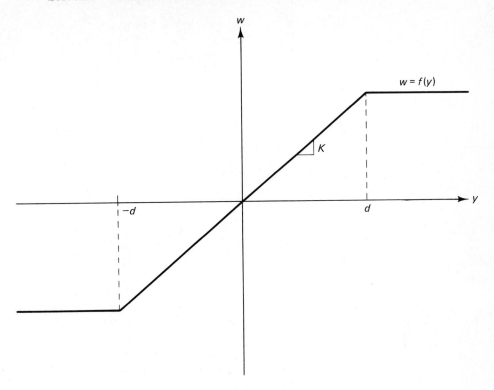

Figure 3.14. Ramp or saturation function.

We shall assume that F is a continuous function, that $F(y) > 0$ for all $y > 0$ and $F(y) < 0$ for all $y < 0$. Following the discussion in Section 3.1 for the equation (1.2), we set $p = dy/dt$ so that

$$\frac{d^2y}{dt^2} = \frac{dp}{dt} = \frac{dp}{dy}\frac{dy}{dt} = \frac{dp}{dy}p.$$

On substituting this into (13.5), we obtain the separable equation

$$M\frac{dp}{dy}p + F(y) = 0.$$

Hence

(13.6)
$$\frac{Mp^2}{2} = -\int_0^y F(u)\,du + c_1$$

or

(13.7)
$$\frac{M}{2}\left(\frac{dy}{dt}\right)^2 + \int_0^y F(u)\,du = c_1.$$

The constant c_1 can be determined from the initial conditions. This result has the following interesting interpretation. First $Mp^2/2 = M(dy/dt)^2/2$ is the **kinetic energy** stored in the mass M when it is moving with velocity p. The integral

$$\int_0^y F(u)\,du$$

determines the **potential energy** stored in the spring when it suffers a deformation y. The left-hand side of (13.7) is an expression for the total energy in the system at the given y and p. Hence (13.7) is the statement that along any solution of (13.5) the energy of the system *remains constant*.

To find solutions, one would need to integrate (13.7) one more time; that is, one must solve

$$\frac{dy}{dt} = \pm \left[\frac{2\left(c_1 - \int_0^y F(u)\,du\right)}{M}\right]^{1/2}.$$

Normally, it is not possible to carry out this second integration. However, the energy integral (13.7) can be used to obtain interesting general information about solutions of (13.5). This is done as follows. Graph (13.6) in the (y, p) plane. We assume that $\int_0^y F(u)\,du \to \infty$ as $y \to \pm\infty$. Thus for any $c_1 > 0$ this graph is a simple closed curve that surrounds the origin (see Figure 3.15). If $y = \varphi(t)$ is a solution such that $A = (\varphi(t_0), \varphi'(t_0))$ is a point on this curve, then $(\varphi(t), \varphi'(t))$ moves along this curve in a clockwise direction as t increases. To see this, consider the curve in Figure 3.15 determined by c_1. Define

$$\theta = \arctan\left(\frac{p}{y}\right)$$

where $-\pi/2 < \theta < \pi/2$ or else $\pi/2 < \theta < 3\pi/2$. Then

$$\frac{d\theta}{dt} = \frac{1}{1 + (p/y)^2} \frac{y\,dp/dt - p\,dy/dt}{y^2} = \frac{y(-F(y)/M) - p^2}{y^2 + p^2} < 0.$$

Since $yF(y)$ is always positive when $y \neq 0$, then $-(yF(y)/M + p^2)/(y^2 + p^2)$ is always negative on this curve. Indeed, the maximum of this expression over the curve is a negative constant $-m$. Hence

$$\frac{d\theta}{dt} = -\frac{yF(y)/M + p^2}{y^2 + p^2} \leq -m < 0.$$

Thus the solution starting at any point on the curve must traverse the curve, in a clockwise direction, with angular speed of m or more.

If $A = (\varphi(t_0), \varphi'(t_0))$ is a point on the curve (Figure 3.15), then $(y, p) = (\varphi(t), \varphi'(t))$ will move around the curve as t increases until it returns to A at some time $t_1 > t_0$. Define $T = t_1 - t_0$. Then (y, p) returns to A in time $t_0 + T$. The solution will then start a second trip around the curve and will return to A at time $t_0 + 2T$, and so on. The solution $y = \varphi(t)$ is periodic in time t with

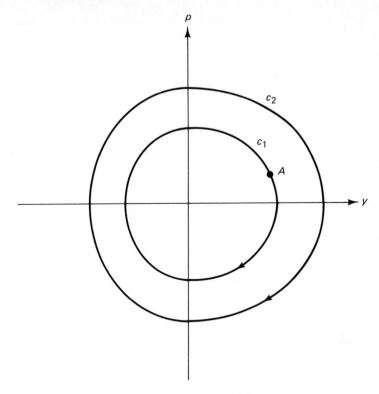

Figure 3.15. Energy curves with $0 < c_1 < c_2$.

period T. To see this, define $\psi(t) = \varphi(t + T)$. Since

$$M \frac{d^2\psi(t)}{dt^2} = M \frac{d^2\varphi(t + T)}{dt^2} = -F(\varphi(t + T)) = -F(\psi(t)),$$

then $y = \varphi(t)$ and $y = \psi(t) = \varphi(t + T)$ are solutions of (13.5) that satisfy the same initial conditions, that is,

$$(\varphi(t_0), \varphi'(t_0)) = A = (\varphi(t_0 + T), \varphi'(t_0 + T)).$$

By the basic existence and uniqueness theorem $\varphi(t) = \varphi(t + T)$. Hence all nonconstant solutions of (13.5) are periodic. The following theorem has been proved.

THEOREM 13.1

If $F(y)$ is a continuous function such that $F(y) > 0$ for $y > 0$ and $F(y) < 0$ for $y < 0$ and such that $\int_0^y F(u)\,du \to \infty$ as $y \to \pm\infty$, then all nonconstant solutions of (13.5) are periodic.

Thus solutions of (13.5) and of the linear problem

$$(13.8) \qquad M\frac{d^2y}{dt^2} + Ky = 0$$

have similar behavior. Each equation has one constant solution, namely the equilibrium $y = 0$. Each nonconstant solution $y = \varphi(t)$ is periodic and oscillates above and below the equilibrium. However, solutions of (13.8) can be found in terms of sines and cosines, while the formula for solutions of (13.5) cannot usually be found. Moreover, all solutions of (13.8) will have the same period $T = 2\pi\sqrt{M/K}$. The periods of solutions of (13.5) cannot usually be determined. Moreover, the periods of solutions of (13.5) can vary from one solution to another.

EXAMPLE 13.2   Analyze $y'' + y + y^3 = 0$.

For this equation $F(y) = y + y^3$. Hence

$$\int_0^y F(u)\, du = \frac{y^2}{2} + \frac{y^4}{4}.$$

For any $c > 0$ the constant energy curve

$$(13.9) \qquad E(y, p) = \frac{p^2}{2} + \frac{y^2}{2} + \frac{y^4}{4} = c$$

determines a solution. Since $p = dy/dt$, then from (13.9) we see that

$$\frac{dy}{dt} = \pm\sqrt{2c - y^2 - \frac{y^4}{2}}.$$

There is no easy way to obtain $y(t)$. Of course, all solutions are periodic, but it can be shown that the period T gets steadily smaller as c grows larger. ∎

The foregoing discussion will not apply to (13.5) when $F(y)$ is a spring with dead zone since $F(y) = 0$ for $-d \le y \le d$. A modified version of this discussion will apply. Consider (13.5) when $F(y)$ is the spring with dead zone given by (13.3). We shall divide the (y, p) plane into the three regions $R_1 = \{(y, p): y < -d\}$, $R_2 = \{(y, p): -d < y < d\}$, and $R_3 = \{(y, p): y > d\}$ (see Figure 3.16). In the region R_2 (13.5) reduces to $My'' = 0$. Hence we can solve for $p \equiv p_0$ and $y = p_0 t + y_0$, where $|y| \le d$. When $p_0 = 0$, then $y \equiv y_0$. In this case the mass is a rest in some position y_0 between $-d$ and d. If $p_0 \ne 0$, the mass coasts through the dead zone until it reaches $\pm d$, where the spring is engaged. Since in R_1 the equation is

$$(13.10) \qquad My'' + K(y + d) = 0,$$

and since in R_3 the equation is

$$(13.11) \qquad My'' + K(y - d) = 0,$$

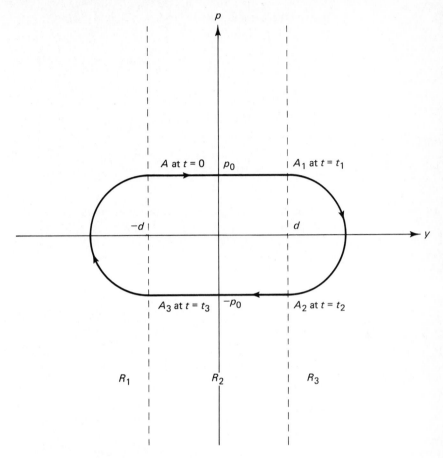

Figure 3.16. Solution of $My'' + f(y) = 0$, dead zone case.

the equation can be solved separately in the regions R_1 and R_3. The problem is to put the solutions in the three regions together in the proper manner.

Consider the initial conditions $y(0) = -d$, $y'(0) = p_0 > 0$ (point A in Figure 3.16). The solution has just reached the dead zone and it will coast across this dead zone, that is,

$$(13.12) \qquad\qquad p = p_0 \quad \text{and} \quad y = p_0 t - d, \qquad 0 \le t \le t_1.$$

y will reach the end of the dead zone at A_1 when $p_0 t - d = d$, that is, when $t = t_1 = 2d/p_0$. Now the solution enters the region R_3, where (13.5) has the form (13.11). We must solve (13.11) subject to the initial conditions

$$y(t_1) = d, \qquad y'(t_1) = p_0, \qquad \text{that is,} \quad A_1 = (d, p_0).$$

A particular solution of (13.11) is $y_p = d$. Hence in R_3

$$y(t) = c_1 \sin\left(\sqrt{\frac{K}{M}}(t + c_2)\right) + d.$$

Since $y(t_1) = c_1 \sin(\sqrt{K/M}(t_1 + c_2)) + d = d$, then $c_2 = -t_1$ will do. From $y'(t) = \sqrt{K/M}\, c_1 \cos(\sqrt{K/M}[t - t_1])$ we see that $y'(t_1) = \sqrt{K/M}\, c_1 = p_0$ or $c_1 = p_0\sqrt{M/K}$. Hence

$$y(t) = d + p_0 \sqrt{\frac{M}{K}} \sin\left(\sqrt{\frac{K}{M}}(t - t_1)\right), \qquad t_1 \le t \le t_2.$$

This solution segment is graphed in Figure 3.16. The number t_2 is chosen so that the solution reenters the dead zone at A_2 at time t_2, that is, $y(t_2) = d$. Hence $t_2 = t_1 + \pi\sqrt{M/K}$. Now the solution will coast across the dead zone from right to left, that is,

$$p = -p_0, \qquad y(t) = d - p_0(t - t_2), \qquad t_2 \le t \le t_3,$$

where $t_3 = t_2 + 2d/p_0$. At time t_3 the solution enters the region R_1 at the point A_3. To continue the solution we must solve

$$M\frac{d^2y}{dt^2} + K(y + d) = 0, \qquad y(t_3) = -d, \qquad y'(t_3) = -p_0.$$

A particular solution is $y_p = -d$, so that

$$y(t) = c_3 \sin\left(\sqrt{\frac{K}{M}}(t + c_4)\right) - d.$$

From the initial conditions we see that $c_4 = -t_3$, $c_3 = -\sqrt{M/K}\, p_0$ and

$$y(t) = -\sqrt{\frac{M}{K}}\, p_0 \sin\left(\sqrt{\frac{K}{M}}(t - t_3)\right) - d, \qquad t_3 \le t \le t_4.$$

This solution is valid until the solution returns to the starting point A (i.e., until $t_4 = t_3 + \pi\sqrt{M/K}$). For $t > t_4$ the solution will now repeat its course around the curve graphed in Figure 3.16. The solution is periodic with period $T = t_4$, where

$$t_4 = \pi\sqrt{\frac{M}{K}} + t_3 = \pi\sqrt{\frac{M}{K}} + \frac{2d}{p_0} + t_2$$

$$= \pi\sqrt{\frac{M}{K}} + \frac{2d}{p_0} + \pi\sqrt{\frac{M}{K}} + t_1$$

$$= \pi\sqrt{\frac{M}{K}} + \frac{2d}{p_0} + \pi\sqrt{\frac{M}{K}} + \frac{2d}{p_0}$$

or

$$T = 2\pi \sqrt{\frac{M}{K} + \frac{4d}{p_0}}.$$

Notice that the period depends on the initial condition p_0. This sort of thing must be expected when dealing with nonlinear equations (13.5).

PROBLEMS

1. Consider the nonlinear problem

(13.2) $M \dfrac{d^2 y}{dt^2} + F(y) = 0,$

where $F(y)$ is given (13.1). Assume that $M = 1$, $K = 2$, $K_1 = 2$, and $d = 3$. Find the solution of (13.2) that satisfies the following initial conditions:

(a) $y(0) = 1$, $y'(0) = 0$.   (b) $y(0) = 0$, $y'(0) = -2$.

(c) $y(0) = 4$, $y'(0) = 0$.   (d) $y(0) = 0$, $y'(0) = 0$.

Solve over $0 \le t \le T$, where T is the period of the solution.

2. Show that if $y = \varphi(t)$ solves (13.2), then for any $\tau > 0$ so does $y = \varphi(t - \tau)$. Use this information to solve Problem 1 for the following initial conditions:

(a) $y(1) = 1$, $y'(1) = 0$.   (b) $y(-1) = 0$, $y'(-1) = -2$.

(c) $y(3) = 4$, $y'(3) = 0$.   (d) $y(\pi) = 1$, $y'(\pi) = 0$.

Find the solution over $\tau \le t \le T + \tau$, where T is the period of the solution.

3. Consider (13.2) when F is the ramp function defined by (13.4). With $M = 2$, $K = 2$, and $d = 2$ find the solution (over one period) that satisfies each of the following initial conditions:

(a) $y(0) = 1$, $y'(0) = 0$.   (b) $y(0) = 0$, $y'(0) = 0$.

(c) $y(0) = 2$, $y'(0) = 0$.   (d) $y(\pi) = 2$, $y'(\pi) = 0$.

(e) $y(0) = 3$, $y'(0) = 0$.

4. Let $F(y)$ in (13.2) be continuous, $F(y) > 0$ and $F(-y) = -F(y)$. Let $y = \varphi(t)$ be a nonconstant solution of (13.2) with period T.

(a) Show that $y = \varphi(-t)$ is a solution of (13.2).

(b) Show that $y = -\varphi(t)$ is a solution of (13.2).

(c) Show that the curves depicted in Figure 3.15 are symmetric with respect to the p-axis, the y-axis, and the origin.

(d) Show that $\varphi(t + T/2) = -\varphi(t)$.

5. When $c_1 = 0$ in (13.6), what solution is obtained?

6. For the ramp function (13.4), compute the total energy in the system (13.5) when $M = 1$, $K = 4$, $d = 1$, and

(a) $y(0) = 2$, $y'(0) = 0$.   (b) $y(0) = 0$, $y'(0) = 3$.

(c) $y(0) = y'(0) = 1$.   (d) $y(0) = -1$, $y'(0) = 2$.

7. For $F(y) = Ky$ compute the total energy of the system (13.5) when $y(0) = a_0$, $y'(0) = a_1$. Show that for any $c_1 > 0$ the curve in Figure 3.15 is an ellipse.

8. For $F(y) = e^y - 1$ and $M = 1$ compute the total energy in the system (13.5) when

   (a) $y(0) = 1$, $y'(0) = 1$.   (b) $y(0) = -1$, $y'(0) = 1$.

   (c) $y(1) = 2$, $y'(1) = -1$.   (d) $y(-1) = y'(-1) = 1$.

   (e) $y(0) = -1$, $y'(0) = 1$.

9. Look up the definition of a piecewise continuous function. Suppose that F is a continuous function whose derivative $F'(y)$ is piecewise continuous. Show that

$$M \frac{d^2 y}{dt^2} + F(y) = 0, \qquad y(t_0) = y_0, \qquad y'(t_0) = p_0$$

has a unique solution for any t_0, y_0, and p_0.

10. In (13.5) suppose that $F(y) = Ky$ when $|y| \leq d$. Show that for any initial conditions $y(t_0) = a_0$, $y'(t_0) = a_1$ such that

$$\frac{Ma_1^2}{2} + \frac{Ka_0^2}{2} \leq \frac{Kd^2}{2},$$

the solution of (13.5) is a solution of the linear problem

$$M \frac{d^2 y}{dt^2} + Ky = 0.$$

11. Let $y = \varphi(t)$ be a solution of

$$M \frac{d^2 y}{dt^2} + B \frac{dy}{dt} + F(y) = 0,$$

where $B > 0$ and F is a continuous function such that $yF(y) > 0$ for $y \neq 0$.

   (a) Let

$$E(y, y') = \frac{M}{2} \left(\frac{dy}{dt} \right)^2 + \int_0^y F(u)\, du.$$

   Show that $(d/dt) \left[E(\varphi(t), \varphi'(t)) \right] = -B\varphi'(t)^2$.

   (b) Show that $E(\varphi(t), \varphi'(t))$ is a monotone decreasing function of t.

12. In the train problem (12.11) we replace (12.12) by a more realistic assumption about the railway coupling. Indeed, we assume that F is given by (13.3); that is, F is a spring with dead zone.

   (a) Find the value of u which is necessary in order that the train can travel at a constant velocity $v_0 > 0$.

   (b) Given u as determined in part (a) show that if $y_l = v_0 t + a_0$ and $y_c = v_0 t + a_1$, then $|a_1 - a_0| > d$, where $[-d, d]$ is the dead zone of the spring F.

(c) Define $w = (y_l - v_0 t - a_0) - (y_c - v_0 t - a_1)$. Show that w satisfies the equation

$$\frac{d^2 w}{dt^2} = \left(\frac{1}{M_l} + \frac{1}{M_c} \right) \left[-B \frac{dw}{dt} - G(w) \right]$$

for some function $G(w)$.

(d) Show that G is a continuous function such that $G(w) > 0$ when $w > 0$ and $G(w) < 0$ when $w < 0$.

(e) Show that for w small, $G(w) = K_1 w$.

3.14 ROTATIONAL MECHANICAL SYSTEMS

We shall now consider mechanical systems in which the only motion is rotation about a fixed axis. About this fixed axis we set up a coordinate system by assigning the angle $\theta = 0$ and assigning a positive direction. The equations that describe mechanical rotational systems are similar to those used to describe translational mechanical systems. Displacements are now angular displacements θ measured in radians, velocities are now angular velocities w measured in radians per second, acceleration is angular acceleration α, forces are replaced by torques T, and masses are replaced by inertial elements with moment of inertia J. We shall consider only inertial elements whose moment of inertia J is fixed.

When a torque is applied to an inertial element with moment of inertia J, it produces an angular acceleration α and a reaction torque T_J, where

$$T_J = J\alpha = J \frac{dw}{dt} = J \frac{d^2 \theta}{dt^2}.$$

When a torque T is applied to a spring at equilibrium, the spring is twisted by an angle θ and the torque is transmitted through the spring to produce a reaction torque $T_K = F(\theta)$ at the opposite end (see Figure 3.17). A rotational spring is called a **linear spring** when

$$F(\theta) = K\theta$$

for some constant K. The constant K is called the **stiffness coefficient** of the spring since the larger is K the stiffer is the spring. We shall consider only **linear**

Figure 3.17. A rotational spring.

(or **viscous**) dampers, that is, dampers where the damping torque T_B satisfies the relation

$$T_B = Bw.$$

The constant B is called the **damping coefficient** (see Table 3.3).

Consider the rotational system depicted in Figure 3.18. This system consists of a linear spring, an inertial element, a linear damper, and an applied tor-

TABLE 3.3. Rotational Symbols and Units

Symbol	Quantity	English Units	Metric Units
T	Torque	pound-feet	newton-meters
θ	Angle	radians	radians
W	Angular velocity	radians per second	radians per second
α	Angular acceleration	radians per second^2	radians per second^2
J	Moment of inertia	slug-feet^2	kilogram-meters^2
K	Stiffness coefficient	(pound-feet) per radian	(newton-meters) per radian
B	Viscous damping coefficient	(pound-feet) per (radian/second)	(newton-meters) per (radian/second)

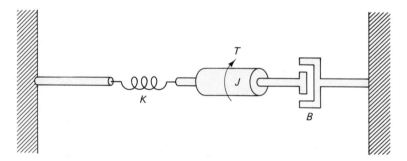

Figure 3.18. Rotational system.

que T. For such systems **Newton's second law** states that the applied torque T equals the sum of the reaction torques. For the system under consideration this means that $T_J + T_B + T_K = T$ or

(14.1)
$$J\frac{d^2\theta}{dt^2} + B\frac{d\theta}{dt} + K\theta = T.$$

The description of the system is completed by giving two initial conditions

(14.2)
$$\theta(t_0) = a_0, \qquad \frac{d\theta}{dt}(t_0) = a_1.$$

EXAMPLE 14.1   When $B = 0$ and $T = 0$, find a general solution of (14.1).

There is no applied torque and no damping. Hence we would expect the system to oscillate. The equation

$$J \frac{d^2\theta}{dt^2} + K\theta = 0$$

has constant coefficients. The characteristic polynomial $p(\lambda) = J\lambda^2 + K$ has roots $\pm i\sqrt{K/J}$. Two linearly independent real-valued solutions are $\theta_1 = \cos(\sqrt{K/J}\,t)$ and $\theta_2 = \sin(\sqrt{K/J}\,t)$, and a general solution is

(14.3) $$\theta(t) = c_1 \cos\left(\sqrt{\frac{K}{J}}\,t\right) + c_2 \sin\left(\sqrt{\frac{K}{J}}\,t\right).$$

The solution (14.3) can be written in **amplitude-phase form** as follows. Let $A = (c_1^2 + c_2^2)^{1/2}$. Let φ be that number in the range $0 \le \varphi < 2\pi$ such that $c_1/A = \sin\varphi$ and $c_2/A = \cos\varphi$. (You may need a calculator to find φ.) The solution (14.3) can be written as

$$\theta(t) = A\left[\cos\left(\sqrt{\frac{K}{J}}\,t\right)\frac{c_1}{A} + \sin\left(\sqrt{\frac{K}{J}}\,t\right)\frac{c_2}{A}\right]$$

$$= A\left[\cos\left(\sqrt{\frac{K}{J}}\,t\right)\sin\varphi + \sin\left(\sqrt{\frac{K}{J}}\,t\right)\cos\varphi\right]$$

$$= A\sin\left(\sqrt{\frac{K}{J}}\,t + \varphi\right).$$

Hence we see that θ is a multiple of the sine function which has been shifted along the t-axis by an amount φ. The number $A \ge 0$ is the **amplitude** of the solution while φ is its **phase shift.** In particular, it is clear that each solution is a periodic function with period

$$T = \frac{2\pi}{\sqrt{K/J}} = 2\pi\sqrt{\frac{J}{K}}. \quad \blacksquare$$

EXAMPLE 14.2   Suppose that $J = 4$ kilogram-meters^2, $K = 9$ newtons per (meter per radian), $T = 0$ newton-meters, and $B = 0$ newton-meters per (radian per second). Find the solution of (14.1) that satisfies $\theta(0) = 0.05$ radian and $d\theta(0)/dt = -0.1$ radian per second. Put the solution in amplitude-phase form and determine the period of the solution.

The initial value problem is

$$4\frac{d^2\theta}{dt^2} + 9\theta = 0, \qquad \theta(0) = 0.05, \qquad \frac{d\theta}{dt}(0) = -0.1.$$

The equation is homogeneous with constant coefficients. The characteristic equation $4\lambda^2 + 9 = 0$ has roots $\pm i(\frac{3}{2})$. Hence

$$\theta(t) = c_1 \cos\left(\frac{3t}{2}\right) + c_2 \sin\left(\frac{3t}{2}\right),$$

and

$$\frac{d\theta}{dt} = -\frac{3}{2} c_1 \sin\left(\frac{3t}{2}\right) + \frac{3}{2} c_2 \cos\left(\frac{3t}{2}\right).$$

At $t = 0$, $\theta(0) = c_1 = 0.05$ and $d\theta(0)/dt = \frac{3}{2}c_2 = -0.1$. Hence

$$\theta = 0.05 \cos\left(\frac{3t}{2}\right) - \frac{2}{30} \sin\left(\frac{3t}{2}\right).$$

The amplitude $A = [0.05^2 + (\frac{2}{30})^2]^{1/2} = 0.08333 \dots$. The phase shift φ must satisfy

$$\sin\varphi = \frac{0.05}{A} = 0.6 \quad \text{and} \quad \cos\varphi = \frac{-2}{30A} = -0.8.$$

With the help of a calculator one can compute $\varphi = 2.49809 \dots$ and

$$\theta(t) \cong 0.08333 \sin\left(\frac{3t}{2} + 2.49809\right).$$

The period T must satisfy the relation $3T/2 = 2\pi$. Hence one has $T = 4\pi/3 \cong 4.18879$. ∎

If the torque T is zero but $B > 0$ in (14.1), the system is **damped.** It has the form of (12.9), that is, the form

(14.4) $$\frac{d^2\theta}{dt^2} + 2b \frac{d\theta}{dt} + c^2\theta = 0,$$

where $b = B/(2J)$ and $c = \sqrt{K/J}$. The discussion in Section 3.12 applies equally well to (14.4). If $b^2 > c^2$, then (14.4) is **overdamped.** Typical solutions are graphed in Figure 3.5 (with y replaced by θ on the vertical axis). When $b^2 = c^2$, the system is **critically damped.** If $b^2 < c^2$, then (14.4) is said to be **underdamped.** In this case solutions have the form (12.10) (see also Figure 3.6). When $B = 0$, then $b = 0$ and (14.4) is called **undamped.** The undamped case was discussed in Example 14.1.

EXAMPLE 14.3   Suppose that $J = 4$, $K = 9$, and $T = 0$ in (14.4). For what values of B is the equation underdamped? overdamped? critically damped?

The equation is

$$\frac{d^2\theta}{dt^2} + \frac{B}{4}\frac{d\theta}{dt} + \frac{9}{4}\theta = 0.$$

The characteristic equation $\lambda^2 + (B/4)\lambda + \frac{9}{4} = 0$ has roots

$$\left(-\frac{B}{4} \pm \sqrt{\frac{B^2}{16} - 9}\right)\bigg/2.$$

The type of solution depends on the sign of the expression $B^2/16 - 9$. Overdamping occurs when $(B/4)^2 - 9 > 0$ (i.e., $B^2 > 144$ or $B > 12$). Critical damping occurs when $(B/4)^2 - 9 = 0$ (i.e., $B = 12$). Underdamping occurs when $(B/4)^2 - 9 < 0$ (i.e., $0 < B < 12$).   ∎

Consider a body of fixed mass M attached to a stiff, thin rod of length l (see Figure 3.19). Assuming that the mass can be considered a point mass and that the connecting rod is inflexible and weightless, the moment of inertia of the resulting inertial element is $J = l^2M$. If k point masses $M_1, M_2, \ldots, M_k$ are distributed (using inflexible, weightless rods) at distances $l_1, l_2, \ldots, l_k$, the moment of inertia of such an inertial system is $J = l_1^2M_1 + l_2^2M_2 + \ldots + l_k^2M_k$.

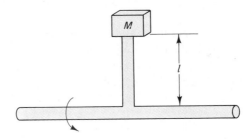

Figure 3.19. Moment of inertia.

EXAMPLE 14.4   Write the equation of motion for the inertial system (see Figure 3.20) consisting of four point masses, M_1, M_2, M_3, and M_4, suspended by thin inflexible rods of length l, plus two linear springs with stiffness coefficients K_1 and K_2.

The moment of inertia of the inertial element is

$$J = l^2M_1 + l^2M_2 + l^2M_3 + l^2M_4 = l^2(M_1 + M_2 + M_3 + M_4).$$

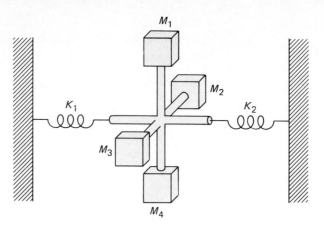

Figure 3.20. Compound rotational system.

Since the applied torque is zero, then by Newton's second law of motion,

$$l^2(M_1 + M_2 + M_3 + M_4)\frac{d^2\theta}{dt^2} + K_1\theta + K_2\theta = 0$$

or

$$\frac{d^2\theta}{dt^2} + c^2\theta = 0, \qquad c = \left[\frac{K_1 + K_2}{l^2(M_1 + M_2 + M_3 + M_4)}\right]^{1/2}.$$

Solutions of this system have the form $\theta = A \sin(ct + \varphi)$, where A and φ are arbitrary constants with $A \geq 0$ and $0 \leq \varphi \leq 2\pi$. ■

Rotational systems can lead to nonlinear equations. As an example, consider the pendulum depicted in Figure 3.21. A point mass M is suspended from

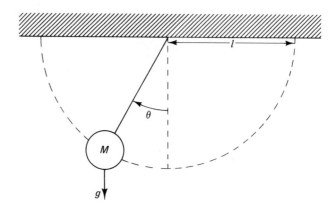

Figure 3.21. Pendulum.

a fixed pivot by a weightless, inflexible rod of length l. The angle θ is measured so that the vertical equilibrium point corresponds to $\theta = 0$ and positive rotation is clockwise. We neglect all frictional forces. The moment of inertia is $J = l^2 M$. There is a downward gravitational force M_g exerted on the mass. The component of force in the direction of motion can be shown to be $-Mg \sin \theta$, where g is the gravitational constant in correct units. Hence the applied torque due to gravitational action on this mass is $-l(Mg \sin \theta)$. By Newton's second law of motion

$$(l^2 M)\frac{d^2\theta}{dt^2} + Mgl \sin \theta = 0$$

or

(14.5) $$\frac{d^2\theta}{dt^2} + \frac{g}{l} \sin \theta = 0.$$

Equation (14.5) is nonlinear. The methods of Section 3.1 can be applied. Define $w = d\theta/dt$ and change the independent variable from t to θ. Hence

$$\frac{d^2\theta}{dt} = \frac{dw}{dt} = \frac{dw}{d\theta}\frac{d\theta}{dt} = \frac{dw}{d\theta} w,$$

and (14.5) becomes

$$w \frac{dw}{d\theta} + \frac{g}{l} \sin \theta = 0.$$

This equation separates. Hence it is possible to solve for w, that is,

$$w \, dw = -\frac{g}{l} \sin \theta \, d\theta$$

and

(14.6) $$\frac{w^2}{2} = \frac{g}{l} \cos \theta + c_1.$$

Since $w = d\theta/dt$, (14.6) separates to obtain

$$\frac{d\theta}{dt} = \sqrt{\frac{2}{l}} \sqrt{g \cos \theta + lc_1}$$

or

(14.7) $$\int \frac{d\theta}{\sqrt{g \cos \theta + lc_1}} = \sqrt{\frac{2}{l}} t + c_2.$$

Since there is no effective way to evaluate the integral on the left in (14.7), this is not a practical method of solution. It is practical to use the methods of Section 3.13 to obtain properties of solutions. Multiply (14.6) by M, use $w = d\theta/dt$, and rearrange to obtain

(14.8) $$\frac{M}{2}\left(\frac{d\theta}{dt}\right)^2 + \frac{Mg}{l}(1 - \cos\theta) = d_1,$$

where $d_1 = Mc_1 + Mg/l$ is an arbitrary nonnegative constant. Since

$$\frac{Mg}{l}\int_0^\theta \sin u \, du = \frac{Mg}{l}(1 - \cos\theta)$$

is the potential energy stored in the mass M when it has angle of deviation θ, then (14.8) is the statement that the energy in the pendulum system,

$$E(\theta, w) = \frac{M}{2}w^2 + \frac{Mg}{l}(1 - \cos\theta),$$

is a constant of the motion (14.5). This useful fact can be used to derive interesting properties of the solution of (14.5) (see the problem section).

PROBLEMS   A wheel with moment of inertia J is suspended on a wire as shown in Figure 3.22. The wire acts as a linear spring with stiffness coefficient K. Damping Bw is present where $B \geq 0$. Problems 1–5 concern this mechanical system.

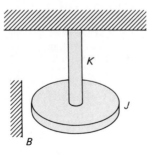

Figure 3.22. Wheel on a wire.

1. Suppose that $K = 0.09$ pound-feet per radian, $J = 0.01$ slug-feet^2, and $B = 0$. Determine the period of the oscillation. For each of the following initial conditions find the solution and write it in amplitude-phase form.

   (a) $\theta(0) = 0.3$ (radian), $\dfrac{d\theta}{dt}(0) = 0$ (radians per second).

   (b) $\theta(1) = 0.3$, $\dfrac{d\theta}{dt}(1) = 0$.

   (c) $\theta(0) = 0$, $\dfrac{d\theta}{dt}(0) = 2$.

   (d) $\theta(-3) = 0$, $\dfrac{d\theta}{dt}(-3) = 2$.

   (e) $\theta(0) = 0$, $\dfrac{d\theta}{dt}(0) = 0$.

   (f) $\theta(0) = 0.2$, $\dfrac{d\theta}{dt}(0) = 1$.

2. Suppose that a torque of 0.04 newton-meter results in a deformation $\theta = 0.09$ radian. Find the stiffness coefficient K. If $J = 2$ and $B = 0$, determine the solution for each of the following initial conditions. Write it in amplitude-phase form.

(a) $\theta(0) = 0.3, \dfrac{d\theta}{dt}(0) = 0$.

(b) $\theta(0) = 0, \dfrac{d\theta}{dt}(0) = 3$.

(c) $\theta(4) = 0, \dfrac{d\theta}{dt}(4) = 3$.

(d) $\theta(0) = 0.2, \dfrac{d\theta}{dt}(0) = 0.1$.

(e) $\theta(2\pi) = 0, \dfrac{d\theta}{dt}(2\pi) = 0$.

(f) $\theta(0) = 0.2, \dfrac{d\theta}{dt}(0) = -0.1$.

3. Suppose that $J = 2$ and $K = 1$. Solve for the following values of B and the following initial conditions. State whether the system is underdamped, critically damped, or overdamped.

(a) $B = 2, \theta(0) = 1, \dfrac{d\theta}{dt}(0) = 0$.

(b) $B = 2, \theta(0) = 0, \dfrac{d\theta}{dt}(0) = -1$.

(c) $B = 4, \theta(0) = 1, \dfrac{d\theta}{dt}(0) = -1$.

(d) $B = 2\sqrt{2}, \theta(0) = \pi, \dfrac{d\theta}{dt}(0) = 1$.

(e) $B = 2\sqrt{2}, \theta(1) = \pi, \dfrac{d\theta}{dt}(1) = 1$.

(f) $B = 5, \theta(-2\pi) = \dfrac{d\theta}{dt}(-2\pi) = 0$.

4. For $J = 2$ and $B = 0$ suppose that $K = 1 \pm 0.05$. Give bounds for the period of the solution.

5. Suppose that $B = 0$ and $K = 9$. If the period of solutions is 5, determine J.

6. For the system depicted in Figure 3.18 suppose that $J = 1$ and $K = 4$. Find $\theta(t)$ under the following conditions.

(a) $B = 1, T = 3, \theta(0) = 0, \dfrac{d\theta}{dt}(0) = 0$.

(b) $B = 0, T = 1, \theta(0) = 0, \dfrac{d\theta}{dt}(0) = 1$.

(c) $B = 2, T = -2, \theta(0) = 1, \dfrac{d\theta}{dt}(0) = 0$.

(d) $B = 2, T = -2, \theta(1) = 1, \dfrac{d\theta}{dt}(1) = 0$.

(e) $B = 2, T = t + 1, \theta(0) = 0, \dfrac{d\theta}{dt}(0) = 0$.

(f) $B = 4, T = -1, \theta(0) = \dfrac{d\theta}{dt}(0) = 0$.

(g) $B = 5, T = 1, \theta(0) = \dfrac{d\theta}{dt}(0) = 0$.

7. For the system depicted in Figure 3.20 suppose that $M_1 = 1$, $M_2 = 2$, $M_3 = 1$, $M_4 = 5$, and $l = 2$. Let $K_1 = K_2 = 3$. Find the solution that satisfies $\theta(0) = 0.25$, $d\theta(0)/dt = 3$. Write the solution in amplitude-phase form.

8. Consider the pendulum system in Figure 3.21.

(a) If $M = 1$ kilogram and $l = \frac{1}{2}$ meter. What value would you use for g?

(b) If M is a 2-pound weight and $l = 3$ feet, what values would you use for M and for g?

(c) Show that if $|\theta(0)|$ and $|d\theta(0)/dt|$ are both nearly zero, then the solution is periodic.

(d) If $\theta(0) = a_0$, $d\theta(0)/dt = a_1$, and if $E(a_0, a_1) > 2Mg/l$, show that either w is always positive or else w is always negative. Does such a solution make sense physically?

9. Determine all constant solutions of (14.5). Is there a difference between the number of physical equilibrium positions and the number of mathematically constant solutions? Explain.

10. When θ is small, $\sin \theta$ is nearly equal to θ. Hence for small oscillations (14.5) is often replaced by the linear approximation

$$\frac{d^2\theta}{dt^2} + \frac{g}{l}\theta = 0.$$

(a) Show that all solutions of this approximate equation are periodic and determine the period.

(b) If $l = 2$ feet and M is a 5-pound weight, what period is predicted by the linear approximation? What is the predicted period if M is an 8-pound weight?

11. In the pendulum problem (14.5) add a damping term Bw and replace $\sin \theta$ by the linear approximation θ. Let $M = 1$ kilogram, $l = 0.3$ meter, and $B = 0.2$ newton-meter per (radian per second).

(a) Solve using the initial values $\theta(0) = \pi/30$ radian, $\theta'(0) = 0$ radians per second.

(b) Write the solution in amplitude-phase form.

(c) Find a time t_1 after which the pendulum will deviate no more than 3 degrees from the vertical.

12. Repeat Problem 11 for the following initial values.

(a) $\theta(0) = 20$ degrees, $\dfrac{d\theta}{dt}(0) = 0.$

(b) $\theta(0) = 0$ degrees, $\dfrac{d\theta}{dt}(0) = \frac{1}{2}$ degree per second.

Hint: Be careful to use correct units.

13. (a) Show that the equation of motion of an ice skater spinning about a fixed point on the ice is $J\theta'' + B\theta' = 0$.

(b) What is J? Do you expect B to be large or small?

(c) If the skater is first spinning with arms extended and then tucks her arms up against her body, she will spin faster. Why?

3.15 FORCED OSCILLATIONS

The mechanical system in Figure 3.23 contains a mass, a linear spring, and a linear viscous damper. We assume that an external force $f(t)$ is applied to the mass. In this case Newton's second law implies that

$$M\frac{d^2y}{dt^2} + B\frac{dy}{dt} + Ky = f(t).$$

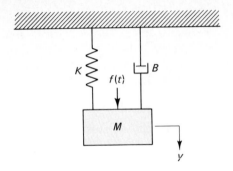

Figure 3.23. Forced–damped system.

We wish to solve this equation when $f(t) = F \cos ct$, where $c > 0$; that is, we wish to solve the equation

(15.1)
$$M \frac{d^2 y}{dt^2} + B \frac{dy}{dt} + Ky = F \cos ct.$$

Two cases are of interest, the damped case $B > 0$ and the undamped case $B = 0$. It will always be assumed that M, K, and F are positive constants.

Undamped Case. If $B = 0$, then the characteristic equation for the corresponding homogeneous equation is $M\lambda^2 + K = 0$. Define $c_0 = (K/M)^{1/2}$. Then a general solution of the homogeneous equation is

$$y_c(t) = A \cos (c_0 t + \varphi),$$

where $A \geq 0$ and $0 \leq \varphi < 2\pi$. If $c \neq c_0$, a particular solution of (15.1) will be of the form

$$y_p(t) = B_1 \cos ct + B_2 \sin ct,$$

where B_1 and B_2 must be determined. Since

$$y_p''(t) = -c^2 B_1 \cos ct - c^2 B_2 \sin ct,$$

then y_p solves (15.1) when

$$M(-c^2 B_1) + KB_1 = F, \qquad M(-c^2 B_2) + KB_2 = 0.$$

Thus $B_2 = 0$, $B_1 = F/(K - Mc^2) = F/[M(c_0^2 - c^2)]$ and a general solution of (15.1) is

(15.2)
$$y(t) = A \cos (c_0 t + \varphi) + \frac{F}{M(c_0^2 - c^2)} \cos ct.$$

This solution is the sum of two periodic functions with different periods. These periods are $2\pi/c_0$ and $2\pi/c$. Such functions will be periodic when c/c_0 is a rational number. If p and q are positive integers with no common factor and if $c/c_0 = p/q$, then the period of the function on the right-hand side of (15.2) will be $T = 2\pi q/c_0 = 2\pi p/c$. If c/c_0 is not a rational number, the solution is not periodic. In this case it is called **almost periodic.**

When $c = c_0$ the forcing function in (15.1) is periodic with the same period as the period of the complementary solution. In this case a particular solution will have the form

$$y_p(t) = t(B_1 \cos c_0 t + B_2 \sin c_0 t),$$

where B_1 and B_2 must be determined. Since

$$y_p'(t) = (B_1 \cos c_0 t + B_2 \sin c_0 t) + tc_0(-B_1 \sin c_0 t + B_2 \cos c_0 t)$$

and

$$y_p''(t) = 2(-c_0 B_1 \sin c_0 t + c_0 B_2 \cos c_0 t) + tc_0^2(-B_1 \cos c_0 t - B_2 \sin c_0 t),$$

then $-2c_0 B_1 = 0$ and $2Mc_0 B_2 = F$. Hence $B_1 = 0$, $B_2 = F/2c_0 M$ and a general solution of (15.1) is

$$(15.3) \qquad\qquad y(t) = A \cos (c_0 t + \varphi) + \frac{Ft}{2c_0 M} \sin (c_0 t).$$

The character of the solution (15.3) is very different from the character of the solution of (15.1) in case $c \neq c_0$. The solution (15.3) still oscillates above and below zero, but these oscillations grow with time and become unbounded as $t \to \infty$. This type of growth behavior occurs when (15.1) is **in resonance** (i.e., $c = c_0$). The term $c_0/2\pi$ is called the **resonance frequency** for the mechanical system. Of course in actual practice the solution could not grow indefinitely. Instead, the system would fail (perhaps break) when $y(t)$ or $dy(t)/dt$ became sufficiently large. Notice that when c is close to c_0, certain solutions (15.2) and (15.3) are close in the sense that

$$\lim_{c \to c_0} \left[\frac{F}{M(c_0^2 - c^2)} \cos ct - \frac{F}{M(c_0^2 - c^2)} \cos c_0 t \right]$$

$$= \lim_{c \to c_0} \frac{F}{M(c_0 + c)} \left(\frac{\cos ct - \cos c_0 t}{c_0 - c} \right) = \frac{Ft}{2Mc_0} \sin c_0 t$$

for all $t \geq 0$.

Damped Case. If $B > 0$, we first look at the corresponding homogeneous system

$$M \frac{d^2 y}{dt^2} + B \frac{dy}{dt} + Ky = 0.$$

The form of the solution depends on whether the equation is overdamped, critically damped, or underdamped. This was explained in Section 3.12. In all cases the complementary solution $y_c(t)$ tends to zero as t goes to infinity. A general solution of (15.1) has the form

$$(15.4) \qquad\qquad y(t) = y_c(t) + B_1 \cos ct + B_2 \sin ct.$$

Using the method of undetermined coefficients, we see that B_1 and B_2 are solutions of the pair of simultaneous equations

$$(-c^2M + K)B_1 + cBB_2 = F$$

and

$$(-c^2M + K)B_2 - cBB_1 = 0.$$

The solution of this pair of simultaneous equations is

$$B_1 = \frac{F(K - c^2M)}{(K - c^2M)^2 + c^2B^2}, \qquad B_2 = \frac{FBc}{(K - c^2M)^2 + c^2B^2}.$$

Hence

(15.5) $\quad y(t) = y_c(t) + \dfrac{F}{(K - c^2M)^2 + (cB)^2} \left[(K - c^2M) \cos ct + Bc \sin ct\right].$

The solution $y(t)$ is made up of a periodic function with period $2\pi/c$ plus a complementary solution $y_c(t)$ which tends to zero as $t \to \infty$. $y_c(t)$ is often called the **transient solution.** It depends on the initial conditions. That the transient solution disappears as t tends to ∞ implies that the eventual behavior of the system is periodic and this periodic behavior is independent of the initial conditions. The periodic portion of the solution is called the **steady-state** solution, or more precisely the **harmonic steady-state** solution.

The periodic portion of the solution (15.5) is

(15.6) $\qquad\qquad y_p(t) = \dfrac{F}{h(c)^2} \left[(K - c^2M) \cos ct + Bc \sin ct\right],$

where

$$h(c) = \left[(K - c^2M)^2 + (Bc)^2\right]^{1/2}.$$

This solution can be written in the form

$$y_p(t) = \frac{F}{h(c)} (\cos ct \cos \varphi + \sin ct \sin \varphi)$$

or

(15.7) $\qquad\qquad y_p(t) = \dfrac{F}{h(c)} \cos (ct - \varphi),$

where $\cos \varphi = (K - c^2M)/h(c)$ and $\sin \varphi = (cB)/h(c)$.

Consider the following experiment. We are given a black box that has an input port and an output port. We input a function $f(t) = F \cos ct$. Given this input the black box will produce an output $y(t)$, where y solves (15.1). We wait a short time to allow the transient solution to die away. The output is then $y_p(t)$, as given by (15.7). The black box has shifted the phase of the cosine by φ and has amplified its amplitude by an amount $h(c)^{-1}$. The maximum amplification will occur at a value c, where

$$\frac{d}{dc}\left[h(c)^{-1}\right] = \frac{-1}{h(c)^2}\frac{dh}{dc}(c) = 0$$

if $c > 0$. Now dh/dc is zero when

$$2(K - c^2 M)(-2cM) + 2B^2 c = 0.$$

The maximum occurs at $c = 0$ if $K/M - B^2/(2M^2) < 0$ and at

(15.8) $$c_m = \left[\frac{K}{M} - \frac{1}{2}\left(\frac{B}{M}\right)^2\right]^{1/2} \quad \text{if } \frac{K}{M} - \left(\frac{B}{M}\right)^2\frac{1}{2} \geq 0.$$

The value $c_m/2\pi$ is called the **resonance frequency** for the damped system (15.1). A damped system forced at this frequency is said to be **in resonance.** Forcing at this frequency will produce solutions $y_p(t)$ with large amplitudes if $B > 0$ is small.

The results of the black-box experiment have the following interesting interpretation. The input $f(t) = F \cos ct$ can be written as

$$f(t) = F \operatorname{Re}(\cos ct + i \sin ct) = F \operatorname{Re}(e^{ict}).$$

The output (15.6) can be written as

$$y_p(t) = F \operatorname{Re}\left[(\cos ct + i \sin ct)\left(\frac{K - c^2 M - icB}{(K - c^2 M)^2 + (cB)^2}\right)\right]$$

$$= F \operatorname{Re}\left[\frac{e^{ict}}{(K - c^2 M) + cBi}\right].$$

or

$$y_p(t) = F \operatorname{Re}\left[\frac{e^{ict}}{M(ic)^2 + B(ic) + K}\right].$$

This interesting formula will be explored further in the problem section.

PROBLEMS

1. Let $M = 3$, $B = 0$, and $K = 12$. Solve $My'' + Ky = f(x)$ for each set of initial data.

(a) $y(0) = 0$, $y'(0) = 2$, $f(x) = 2 \cos(3x)$.

(b) $y(0) = 1$, $y'(0) = -1$, $f(x) = 2 \cos(3x)$.

(c) $y(0) = 2$, $y'(0) = 0$, $f(x) = \cos(2x)$.

(d) $y(0) = 0$, $y'(0) = 0$, $f(x) = \cos(2x)$.

(e) $y(0) = -1$, $y'(0) = 1$, $f(x) = -\cos x$.

(f) $y(0) = 0$, $y'(0) = 0$, $f(x) = -\cos x$.

2. If in (15.1) $M = 2$, $B = 0$, and $K = 14$, find the resonance frequency c_0. Find a general solution when $c \neq c_0$.

3. In $2y'' + 32y = 15 \cos(cx)$, compute the resonance frequency c_0. Find a general solution for

(a) $c = c_0$.   (b) $c \neq c_0$.

4. (a) In $2y'' + 32y = 4\cos(cx)$ let $c = \frac{5}{4}$. Show that all solutions are periodic. Compute the period.

(b) Repeat part (a) when $c = \frac{4}{5}$.

5. For what values of c are all solutions of $y'' + 7y = F\cos(cx)$ periodic?

6. Solve $d^2y/dt^2 + dy/dt + 4y = 2\cos(ct)$ given the following data.

(a) $y(0) = 1, \dfrac{dy}{dt}(0) = 0, c = 2.$ $\qquad\qquad$ **(b)** $y(0) = 0, \dfrac{dy}{dt}(0) = 0, c = \frac{1}{2}.$

(c) $y(0) = 1, \dfrac{dy}{dt}(0) = -1, c = 4.$

7. Find the value of c for which the harmonic steady-state solution of $d^2y/dt^2 + dy/dt + 4y = F\cos ct$ receives maximum amplification.

8. (a) Given $d^2y/dt^2 + B(dy/dt) + y = F\cos(ct)$, for what values of B does the maximum amplification of the harmonic steady state occur at $c = 0$? At $c = 1/\sqrt{2}$? at $c = \frac{3}{4}$? at $c = 2$?

(b) Compute the limit of c_m as $B \to 0^+$.

9. (a) Find the periodic solution y_p of

$$M\frac{d^2y}{dt^2} + B\frac{dy}{dt} + Ky = F\sin ct.$$

(b) Show that $y_p = \text{Im}\,(e^{ict}/[M(ic)^2 + B(ic) + K])$.

10. (a) Find the (complex-valued) periodic solution z_p of

$$M\frac{d^2y}{dt^2} + B\frac{dz}{dt} + Kz = Fe^{ict}.$$

(b) Show that $z_p = p(ic)^{-1}Fe^{ict}$, where $p(\lambda) = M\lambda^2 + B\lambda + K$ is the characteristic polynomial for the corresponding homogeneous equation.

(c) Show that $\text{Re}\,z_p$ is the solution (15.6).

(d) Show that $\text{Im}\,z_p$ is the solution obtained in Problem 9.

11. (a) Show that for any complex numbers λ and F, $z_p = [F/p(\lambda)]e^{\lambda t}$ is a particular solution of

$$M\frac{d^2z}{dt^2} + B\frac{dz}{dt} + Kz = Fe^{\lambda t},$$

where $p(\lambda) = M\lambda^2 + B\lambda + K$ and when $p(\lambda) \neq 0$.

(b) Find a particular solution of

$$\frac{d^2z}{dt^2} + 2\frac{dz}{dt} + 3z = (3 + 4i)e^{(2+i)t}.$$

(c) Given your answer from part (b), find a particular solution of

$$\frac{d^2y}{dt^2} + 2\frac{dy}{dt} + 3y = 3e^{2t}\cos t - 4e^{2t}\sin t = \text{Re}\,(3 + 4i)e^{(2+i)t}.$$

12. If $B > 0$, show that (15.1) has only one periodic solution.

13. If $B > 0$, show that if y_p is the harmonic steady-state solution of (15.1) and if y is any other solution of (15.1), then

$$\lim_{t \to \infty} \left[y(t) - y_p(t) \right] = 0.$$

3.16 *ELECTRICAL NETWORKS*

Electrical circuits provide a large class of examples of differential equations. When discussing electrical circuits we use **Kirchhoff's voltage law** and **Kirchhoff's current law,** which state:

KIRCHHOFF'S LAW

(KVL) The algebraic sum of the potential differences around any closed loop equals zero.

(KCL) The algebraic sum of the currents at any junction or node in a circuit is zero.

We consider first linear elements; that is, we consider only voltage sources, linear capacitors, linear inductors, and linear resistors. These elements are described briefly below.

Voltage sources are modeled by batteries for dc currents and voltage generators for ac currents (see Figure 3.24). A linear resistor satisfies **Ohm's law.**

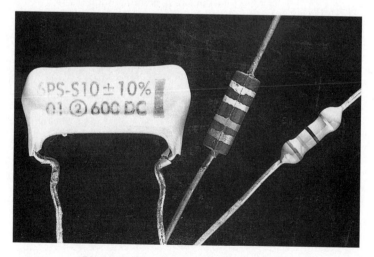

Photo 12. Linear electrical components.

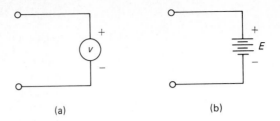

Figure 3.24. (a) ac voltage source; (b) dc voltage source.

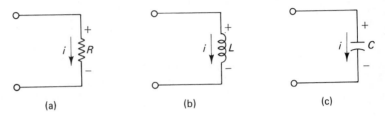

Figure 3.25. (a) A resistor; (b) an inductor; (c) a capacitor.

This law states that the voltage drop across a resistor is the product of the current i through the resistor and the resistance R (see Figure 3.25), that is, $v_R = Ri$ or $i = v_R/R$. The voltage drop across an inductor is the product of the inductance L and the derivative of the current (see Figure 3.25). In symbols this reads

$$v_L = L\frac{di}{dt} \quad \text{or} \quad i = \frac{1}{L}\int_0^t v_L(u)\,du + i_L(0).$$

The current i is assigned a positive direction. When i is negative, it means that the actual flow is in the opposite direction.

The voltage drop across a capacitor has magnitude equal to the ratio of the magnitude of the positive electric charge Q on its positive plate to the value C of its capacitance. Its direction is from the positive plate to the negative plate. Thus

$$v_c = \frac{Q}{C} = \frac{1}{C}\int_0^t i(u)\,du + \frac{Q_0}{C} = \frac{1}{C}\int_0^t i(u)\,du + v_c(0)$$

or $i = C\,dv_c/dt$.

A consistent set of units must be used. In the MKS system this means charge in coulombs, current in amperes, voltage in volts, inductance in henrys, capacitance in farads, and resistance in ohms (see Table 3.4).

Consider the simple RLC circuit depicted in Figure 3.26. We assume that the positive direction for the current is clockwise. Let $Q(t)$ denote the charge on the capacitor at time t. Then according to Kirchhoff's voltage law,

(16.1)
$$e(t) - \frac{Q}{C} - Ri - L\frac{di}{dt} = 0.$$

TABLE 3.4   *Electrical Units*

Symbol	Quantity	Metric Units
e or v	Voltage	volts
i	Current	amperes
L	Inductance	henrys
C	Capacitance	farads
R	Resistance	ohms

Since $i = dQ/dt$, this means that

(16.2)
$$L\frac{d^2Q}{dt^2} + R\frac{dQ}{dt} + \frac{1}{C}Q = e(t).$$

It is possible to write other equations which describe the behavior of the circuit in Figure 3.26. For example, in (16.1) we note that $Q/C = v_c$. Hence $Q = Cv_c$, $i = dQ/dt = C\,dv_c/dt$, and (16.1) can be written as

$$e(t) = v_c + Ri + L\frac{di}{dt}$$

$$= v_c + R\left(C\frac{dv_c}{dt}\right) + L\left(C\frac{d^2v_c}{dt^2}\right)$$

or

$$v_c'' + \frac{R}{L}v_c' + \frac{1}{LC}v_c = \frac{1}{LC}e(t).$$

If $e(t) \equiv 0$, then (16.2) takes the form

(16.3)
$$\frac{d^2Q}{dt^2} + \frac{R}{L}\frac{dQ}{dt} + \frac{1}{LC}Q = 0.$$

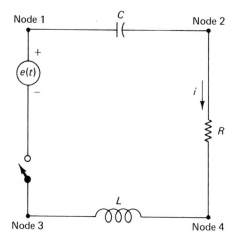

Figure 3.26. *RLC* circuit.

This equation has the form

(16.4)
$$\frac{d^2Q}{dt^2} + 2b\frac{dQ}{dt} + c^2Q = 0,$$

where $b = R/(2L) \geq 0$ and $c = (LC)^{-1/2} > 0$. Equation (16.4) for Q is the same equation as (12.9) for y. Thus the mechanical system depicted in Figure 3.4 has the same mathematical description as the electrical system depicted in Figure 3.26. The properties of the solutions of (16.4) were discussed in detail in Section 3.12. In particular, (16.4) is called **undamped** when $b = 0$ and **damped** when $b > 0$. Since $b = R/2L$, the presence or absence of a resistance R determines whether (16.3) is damped. When (16.3) is damped (i.e., when $R > 0$), all solutions of (16.3) tend to zero as t tends to infinity. When (16.3) is undamped (i.e., when $R = 0$), all nonzero solutions of (16.3) are periodic.

EXAMPLE 16.1 For the circuit in Figure 3.26 suppose that $C = 10^{-6}$, $L = 10^{-3}$, and $e(t) \equiv 7$. Then

(16.5)
$$10^{-3}Q'' + RQ' + 10^6Q = 7.$$

A particular solution is $Q_p = 7 \times 10^{-6}$. The corresponding homogeneous equation is $10^{-3}Q'' + RQ' + 10^6Q = 0$ or

(16.6)
$$Q'' + 10^3RQ' + 10^9Q = 0.$$

The characteristic roots of (16.6) are

$$-500R \pm \sqrt{(500R)^2 - 10^9}.$$

From the definitions in Section 3.12 we see that (16.6) is undamped when $R = 0$, underdamped when $(500R)^2 < 10^9$, critically damped when $(500R)^2 = 10^9$, and overdamped when $(500R)^2 > 10^9$. Whenever $R > 0$, all solutions of (16.5) tend to zero as $t \to \infty$.

Let us solve (16.5) assuming that $R = 20$, $Q(0) = 0$, and $i(0) = Q'(0) = 0$. A general solution of (16.5) is

$$Q(t) = e^{-10^4t}[B_1 \cos(30,000t) + B_2 \sin(30,000t)] + 7 \times 10^{-6}.$$

The initial conditions imply that $B_1 = (-7)10^{-6}$ and $B_2 = (-\frac{7}{3})10^{-6}$. ■

Kirchhoff's current law (KCL) can also be used to determine a mathematical description of simple circuits. One proceeds in the following manner.

1. Assign voltages v_i at each node in the circuit.
2. Choose one node in the circuit that will be assigned zero volts (i.e., ground potential).
3. Use (KCL) to write an equation for each node v_i whose voltage is not known. No equation is needed at the node that has been assigned ground potential.

EXAMPLE 16.2   Consider the system depicted in Figure 3.27. Note that the voltages at two of the nodes are known. Hence the unknowns in the problem are v_1 and v_2, the voltages at nodes 1 and 2. Using (KCL), we see that the equations at the two nodes are

$$(16.7) \qquad \frac{v_1 - e(t)}{R_1} + Cv_1' + \frac{v_1 - v_2}{R_2} = 0$$

and

$$(16.8) \qquad \frac{v_2 - v_1}{R_2} + i_L(0) + \frac{1}{L} \int_0^t v_2(s)\, ds = 0.$$

We solve for v_1' in (16.7). This gives

$$v_1' = \frac{v_2 - v_1}{R_2 C} + \frac{e(t) - v_1}{R_1 C}$$

or

$$(16.9) \qquad v_1' = -\left(\frac{1}{R_1} + \frac{1}{R_2}\right)\frac{1}{C} v_1 + \frac{1}{R_2 C} v_2 + \frac{e(t)}{R_1 C}.$$

From (16.8) we compute

$$\frac{v_2' - v_1'}{R_2} + \frac{1}{L} v_2 = 0$$

or

$$(16.10) \qquad v_2' = v_1' - \frac{R_2}{L} v_2.$$

Equations (16.9) and (16.10) form a system of two equations in the two unknowns v_1 and v_2. In order to complete the descriptions of the circuit we must specify the initial data $v_1(0)$ and $v_2(0)$. These two equations and the initial data can be used to obtain a single equation for v_1 or for v_2. For example, we can eliminate v_2 from (16.9) and (16.10) as follows. The derivative with respect to t of (16.9) is

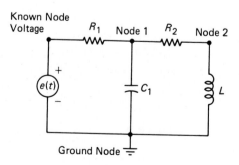

Figure 3.27. Electrical circuit.

(16.11) $v_1'' = -\left(\dfrac{1}{R_1} + \dfrac{1}{R_2}\right)\dfrac{1}{C}v_1' + \dfrac{1}{R_2 C}v_2' + \dfrac{e'(t)}{R_1 C}.$

We now use (16.10) in (16.11) to see that

$$v_1'' = -\left(\frac{1}{R_1} + \frac{1}{R_2}\right)\frac{1}{C}v_1' + \frac{1}{R_2 C}\left(v_1' - \frac{R_2}{L}v_2\right) + \frac{e'(t)}{R_1 C}$$

or

(16.12) $v_1'' = -\dfrac{1}{R_1 C}v_1' - \dfrac{1}{LC}v_2 + \dfrac{e'(t)}{R_1 C}.$

We now solve for v_2 in (16.9) and use the result in (16.12). The result of this is

$$v_1'' + \left(\frac{1}{R_1 C} + \frac{R_2}{L}\right)v_1' + \left(\frac{1}{R_1} + \frac{1}{R_2}\right)\frac{R_2}{CL}v_1 = \left[\frac{R_2 e(t)}{L} + e'(t)\right]\frac{1}{R_1 C}.$$

If $v_1(0)$ and $v_2(0)$ are known, then (16.9) can be used to compute $v_1'(0)$. Once $v_1(t)$ has been computed, the result can be substituted into (16.10) and $v_2(t)$ can then be computed. ∎

EXAMPLE 16.3   We analyze the circuit in Figure 3.26 using (KCL). Node 4 will be taken as the ground node. The voltage at node 1 is known, that is, $v_1 = e(t)$. The unknowns are v_2 and v_3. By (KCL) we have

$$C(v_2 - e(t))' + \frac{v_2 - v_3}{R} = 0$$

and

$$\frac{v_3 - v_2}{R} + i_L(0) + \frac{1}{L}\int_0^t v_3(s)\,ds = 0.$$

Hence

$$v_2' = e'(t) + \frac{v_3 - v_2}{RC}$$

and

$$v_3' - v_2' + \frac{R}{L}v_3 = 0. \quad ∎$$

In Examples 16.2 and 16.3, we obtain a system of two differential equations in two unknowns. One unknown can be eliminated in order to obtain a single second-order differential equation. The technique of elimination, as well as other methods of solution for systems, is discussed in Chapter 7. Complicated electrical circuits have complicated systems of differential equations to describe their behavior. Such complex systems are usually best solved using the methods of Chapters 6 and 7.

Many modern design problems are solved with the help of nonlinear circuits, that is, circuits that contain at least one nonlinear element. For example, for a nonlinear capacitor the capacitance $C(v)$ may be a function of v. In a nonlinear resistor the current and voltage drop may be related by a nonlinear relation such as $i = f(v)$ or $v = g(i)$.

EXAMPLE 16.4   Consider the circuit depicted in Figure 3.28. This circuit contains a nonlinear resistor characterized by the function $f(v) = v^3/3 - 3v^2/2 + 2v$ graphed in Figure 3.28. If v is the voltage drop across the capacitor and i the circuit through the inductor, then by (KVL)

$$L\frac{di}{dt} + v = E$$

and

$$C\frac{dv}{dt} + [f(v) - i] = 0.$$

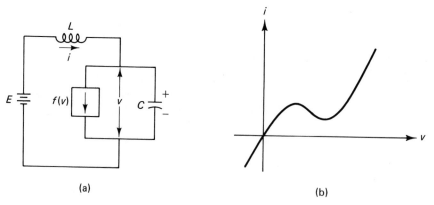

(a)   (b)

Figure 3.28. (a) Tunnel diode circuit; (b) graph of $i = f(v)$.

Since $f(v)$ is not a linear function, the system

(16.13)
$$\frac{di}{dt} = \frac{E - v}{L}$$
$$\frac{dv}{dt} = \frac{i - f(v)}{C}$$

is nonlinear.   ∎

PROBLEMS   1. (a) Find a general solution of (16.3) when $C = 10^{-6}$, $R = 10^2$, and $L = 10^{-2}$.
(b) Find the solution that satisfies $Q(0) = 1$, $i(0) = 0$.

2. Find a general solution of (16.2) when $C = 2 \times 10^{-6}$, $R = 50$, $L = 0.5$, and $e(t) = 100 \sin t$.

3. Let $C = 2 \times 10^{-6}$, $L = 0.6$, and $e(t) = 50 \cos t$. Find a general solution of (16.2) when

   (a) $R = 10$.   (b) $R = 0$.

4. In (16.2) let $C = 3 \times 10^{-6}$, $L = 0.5$, $R = 0$, and $e(t) = F \cos ct$. Find the resonance frequency for this equation. *Hint:* See Section 3.15.

5. Show that if L, R, and C in (16.2) are positive and $e(t) = F \cos ct$, then there is a periodic solution. Compute this solution. *Hint:* See (15.5).

6. No current is flowing in the circuit in Figure 3.29 before time zero. At time $t = 0$ the switch is closed. Find the current $i(t)$ when $t > 0$.

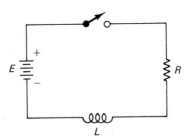

Figure 3.29. *RL* circuit.

7. Consider the circuit of Example 16.4.

   (a) Show that

   $$Cv'' + f'(v)v' + \frac{v}{L} = \frac{E}{L}.$$

   Find all constant solutions of this equation.

   (b) Show that if $v \neq E$, then

   $$\frac{dv}{di} = \frac{L}{C}\frac{i - f(v)}{E - v}.$$

   (c) Find all constant solutions of (16.13).

8. In Example 16.3, find a second-order differential equation that v_2 solves.

CHAPTER REVIEW

The reader must carefully distinguish between equations with constant coefficients and equations with variable coefficients. Among equations with variable coefficients the reader must recognize which are Euler equations and which are not. For example,

(17.1) $$\frac{d^2y}{dx^2} + 4y = 0$$

and

(17.2)
$$\frac{d^2y}{dt^2} + 3\frac{dy}{dt} + 2y = 0$$

are equations with constant coefficients, while

(17.3)
$$x^2\frac{d^2B}{dx^2} + x\frac{dB}{dx} + 4B = 0$$

and

(17.4)
$$t^2\frac{d^2y}{dt^2} + (\sin t)y = 0$$

are equations with variable coefficients. Note that (17.3) is an Euler equation, while (17.4) is not an Euler equation. The most common error made by students is to attempt to use constant-coefficient methods on equations that have variable coefficients.

The student must also carefully distinguish between the various types of nonhomogeneous equations and then apply a correct solution procedure. For example, the method of undetermined coefficients can be used for solution of all of the following equations. The form of the particular solution is given to the right of the equation.

(17.5)
$$\frac{d^2y}{dx^2} + 3\frac{dy}{dx} + 2y = e^x + e^{-x}, \qquad y_p = Ae^x + Bxe^{-x},$$

(17.6)
$$\frac{d^2y}{dt^2} + 4y = \sin t, \qquad y_p = A\cos t + B\sin t,$$

(17.7)
$$\frac{d^2R}{dt^2} + R = \cos t, \qquad R_p = t(A\cos t + B\sin t),$$

(17.8)
$$(D-1)^2 y = 1 + 3x^2, \qquad y_p = A + Bx + Cx^2.$$

The method of undetermined coefficients may not be applied to equations with variable coefficients.

Either variation of parameters or reduction of order can be used to solve the following equations:

(17.9)
$$(D^2 + 1)y = \tan x, \qquad \frac{-\pi}{2} < x < \frac{\pi}{2}.$$

(17.10)
$$s^2\frac{d^2B}{ds^2} - 2s\frac{dB}{ds} + 2B = s^3, \qquad 0 < s < \infty.$$

(17.11)
$$y'' + 4y' + 4y = e^{-2x}\sqrt{x}, \qquad 0 < x < \infty.$$

The student should be able to solve all of equations (17.1)–(17.11) except for (17.4).

**CHAPTER
REVIEW
PROBLEMS**

1. Review the methods of solution of nonlinear problems given in Section 3.1. Then solve each problem.

   (a) $y'' = 3y^2$, $y(0) = 1$, $y'(0) = \sqrt{2}$.

   (b) $\dfrac{dB}{dx}\dfrac{d^2B}{dx^2} = 1$, $B(0) = 2$, $B'(0) = 2$.

   (c) $y'y'' = x$, $y(0) = -1$, $y'(0) = 0$.

2. Find a general solution for (17.1), (17.2), and (17.3).

3. Find a general solution for each equation.

   (a) $\dfrac{d^2R}{dt^2} - 6\dfrac{dR}{dt} - 7R = 0.$ (b) $r\dfrac{dB}{dr} + B = 0.$

   (c) $(D^2 - 6D + 9)y = 0.$ (d) $t^2\dfrac{d^2y}{dt^2} - 6y = 0.$

   (e) $s^2\dfrac{d^2B}{ds^2} + 2B = 0.$

4. Solve each initial value problem. For some of these equations you will need methods from Chapter 2.

   (a) Equation (17.5) with $y(0) = 3$, $y'(0) = -1$.

   (b) Equation (17.6) with $y(0) = 0$, $y'(0) = -1$.

   (c) Equation (17.8) with $y(0) = 0$, $y'(0) = 0$.

   (d) $s\dfrac{d^2B}{ds^2} + \dfrac{dB}{ds} = s$, $B(-1) = 1$, $B'(-1) = 0$.

   (e) $\dfrac{dN}{dt} + N = N^2$, $N(0) = 2$.

   (f) $x^2y' + 3xy = 1$, $y(1) = 1$.

5. Find a particular solution for (17.10).

In Problems 6–12, find a general solution.

6. $(D^2 - 3D + 2)y = \cos 2x.$

7. $x^2\dfrac{d^2B}{dx^2} - 2x\dfrac{dB}{dx} + B = 0, 0 < x < \infty.$

8. $t^2\dfrac{d^2y}{dt^2} - 4t^2y = t^2e^t, 0 < t < \infty.$

9. $3y'' + y' + y = 1.$

10. $s^2\dfrac{d^2N}{ds^2} + 4s\dfrac{dN}{ds} + 2N = \log s, 0 < s < \infty.$

11. $2x^2\dfrac{d^2B}{dx^2} + 3B = 0, 0 < x < \infty.$

12. $y'' + 4y = \cos 2x.$

13. For what values of x_0, can you be sure (without solving) that the given equation has one and only one solution satisfying $y(x_0) = 1$, $y'(x_0) = \pi$?

    (a) $xy'' + 3y' + y = 0$.

    (b) $y'' + (\tan x)y = 2 \sin x$.

    (c) $(1 - x^2)y'' + 3y' + y = 0$.

    (d) $y'' + 2y' + y = 1 + x^2$.

14. Over what interval can you be sure (without solving) that the solution of the given initial value problem exists?

    (a) $(1 - x^2)y'' + 3y' + (\cos x)y = 0$, $y(0) = 0$, $y'(0) = \sqrt{3}$.

    (b) $(1 - x^2)y'' + 3y' + (\cos x)y = 0$, $y(2) = 1$, $y'(2) = -\pi$.

    (c) $(1 - x^2)y'' + 3y' + (\cos x)y = 0$, $y(-4) = 1$, $y'(-4) = 0$.

    (d) $y'' + (\tan x)y = 2 \sin x$, $y(0) = 3$, $y'(0) = 2$.

15. Show that the function 1, x, and $|x|$ are linearly independent over the interval $-\infty < x < \infty$ but are linearly dependent over $0 < x < \infty$.

16. Consider the mechanical system depicted in Figure 3.4. The spring is assumed to be linear with stiffness coefficient K. The system contains viscous friction, which is characterized by the constant B. The equation of motion is

$$M\frac{d^2y}{dt^2} + B\frac{dy}{dt} + Ky = 0.$$

    (a) For what values of B is the system overdamped? critically damped? underdamped? undamped?

    (b) Suppose that $M = 0.2$ kilogram, $K = 20$ newtons per meter, and $B = 0.01$ newton per (meter per second). Determine the solution that satisfies $y(0) = 0.03$ meter and $y'(0) = 0$ meters per second.

17. Given the rotational system pictured in Figure 3.18, suppose that $T(t) = T_0 \cos ct$.

    (a) If $B = 0$, what is the resonance frequency c_0 of the system?

    (b) If $B = 0$, for what values of c are all solutions periodic?

    (c) If $B > 0$, compute the harmonic steady-state solution.

CHAPTER FOUR

Linear Equations of Arbitrary Order

In this chapter we study nth-order linear differential equations of the form

(0.1) $$y^{(n)} + b_{n-1}(x)y^{(n-1)} + \ldots + b_1(x)y' + b_0(x)y = g(x),$$

where $g(x)$ and all of the $b_i(x)$ are given continuous functions on some basic interval J, $A_1 < x < A_2$, and $y^{(k)} = d^k y/dx^k$. The **existence and uniqueness theorem** for this equation states that there is one and only one solution of (0.1) which satisfies the n initial conditions

(0.2) $$y(x_0) = a_0, \quad y'(x_0) = a_1, \quad \ldots, \quad y^{(n-1)}(x_0) = a_{n-1}.$$

Since the equation is linear, then the solution of (0.1)–(0.2) will exist over the entire interval J.

4.1 GENERAL PROPERTIES

Linear systems of general order occur constantly in the design phase of many modern systems. Jet aircraft design is a particularly important example. Design and analysis of many components, subassemblies and control systems use the theory of such differential equations. These differential equations have the form

(N) $$y^{(n)} + b_{n-1}(x)y^{(n-1)} + \ldots + b_1(x)y' + b_0(x)y = g(x).$$

The coefficients $b_{n-1}, b_{n-2}, \ldots, b_0$ and the forcing function $g(x)$ are assumed to be continuous over the basic interval J. When $g(x)$ is not zero, the equation is called **nonhomogeneous** or **forced.** If $g(x)$ is identically zero on J, the equation reduces to

Photo 13. A 55C jet aircraft. (Courtesy of Learjet Corporation.)

(H) $$y^{(n)} + b_{n-1}(x)y^{(n-1)} + \ldots + b_1(x)y' + b_0(x)y = 0.$$

Equation (H) is called **homogeneous.** Equation (N) or (H) is said to have **constant coefficients** when all of the functions $b_j(x)$ are constant over J, that is,

(1.1) $$y^{(n)} + b_{n-1}y^{(n-1)} + \ldots + b_1 y' + b_0 y = g(x)$$

or

(1.2) $$y^{(n)} + b_{n-1}y^{(n-1)} + \ldots + b_1 y' + b_0 y = 0,$$

where $b_0, b_1, \ldots, b_{n-1}$ are real constants.

It will be useful to write (N) and (H) in operator notation. This is done as follows. Define

(1.3) $$L = \frac{d^n}{dx^n} + b_{n-1}(x)\frac{d^{n-1}}{dx^{n-1}} + \ldots + b_1(x)\frac{d}{dx} + b_0(x),$$

so that Lf is defined for any function f that is defined and has n continuous derivatives on the interval J. The operator L is linear; that is, $L(c\varphi_1) = cL(\varphi_1)$ and $L(\varphi_1 + \varphi_2) = L\varphi_1 + L\varphi_2$ for all constants c and all n times differential functions φ_1 and φ_2. The reader should check this. With this notation (N) can be written as $Ly = g$ and (H) as $Ly = 0$.

EXAMPLE 1.1   The equation $x^2 y''' + 3xy'' + y = 3 \sin x$ can be put in the form $Ly = g$. After dividing by x^2 we see that

$$L = \frac{d^3}{dx^3} + \frac{3}{x}\frac{d^2}{dx^2} + 0 \cdot \frac{d}{dx} + \frac{1}{x^2}.$$

The coefficients are $b_2(x) = 3/x$, $b_1(x) = 0$, and $b_0(x) = 1/x^2$, while the non-homogeneous term (or forcing term) is $g(x) = (3 \sin x)/x^2$. The interval J can be taken as $(0, \infty)$ or as $(-\infty, 0)$. The point $x = 0$ must be avoided. This equation has variable coefficients and is nonhomogeneous. ■

Operators can also be written using the notation $D = d/dx$.

EXAMPLE 1.2   The equation $y^{(4)} + 3y^{(3)} + y'' - y' + \sqrt{2}y = 3x$ can be written as $Ly = g(x)$, where $L = D^4 + 3D^3 + D^2 - D + \sqrt{2}$ and $g(x) = 3x$. This equation is nonhomogeneous and has constant coefficients. ■

EXAMPLE 1.3   The equation $y^{(4)} + 2y^{(3)} - y'' + 3y' - 7y = 0$ can be put in the form $Ly = 0$, where

$$L = D^4 + 2D^3 - D^2 + 3D - 7.$$

This equation is homogeneous and has constant coefficients. ■

Since L is a linear operator, the following result is true.

THEOREM 1.4

Let L be defined by (1.3). If $y_1, \ldots, y_k$ are solutions of $Ly = 0$ and if $c_1, \ldots, c_k$ are any real constants, then

$$y = c_1 y_1 + c_2 y_2 + \ldots + c_k y_k$$

also solves $Ly = 0$.

EXAMPLE 1.5   The equation $(D^3 - 4D^2 + 5D - 2)y = 0$ has solutions $y_1 = e^x$, $y_2 = xe^x$, and $y_3 = e^{2x}$. (The reader should check this assertion.) Hence

$$y = c_1 e^x + c_2 xe^x + c_3 e^{2x}$$

is also a solution for any constants c_1, c_2, and c_3. ■

Given k solutions $\{y_1, y_2, \ldots, y_k\}$ of $Ly = 0$ we say that the y_j's are **linearly independent over** J if from the equation

$$c_1 y_1 + c_2 y_2 + \ldots + c_k y_k = 0$$

for all x in the interval J, we can conclude that $c_1 = c_2 = \ldots = c_k = 0$. A linearly independent set of n solutions of (H) is also called a **fundamental set** of solutions. If a fundamental set of solutions is known, then a general solution of $Ly = 0$ can be written as

$$y = c_1 y_1 + \ldots + c_n y_n,$$

where $c_1, \ldots, c_n$ are arbitrary constants.

We can decide whether or not a set of n solutions is a fundamental set of solutions by computing the Wronskian. The **Wronskian** is defined by the determinant

$$W(y_1, y_2, \ldots, y_n) = \begin{vmatrix} y_1 & y_2 & & y_n \\ y_1' & y_2' & & y_n' \\ \vdots & \vdots & & \vdots \\ y_1^{(n-1)} & y_2^{(n-1)} & \cdots & y_n^{(n-1)} \end{vmatrix}.$$

When $n = 2$ this formula reduces to the familiar formula $W(y_1, y_2) = y_1 y_2' - y_1' y_2$ of Chapter 3. This Wronskian is either never zero or else is identically zero over the interval J. The set $\{y_1, \ldots, y_n\}$ is a fundamental set of solutions of (H) if and only if $W(y_1, \ldots, y_n)(x) \neq 0$ for some x on J.

EXAMPLE 1.6   Consider again Example 1.5. The Wronskian of the given set of solutions is

$$W(y_1, y_2, y_3)(x) = \begin{vmatrix} e^x & xe^x & e^{2x} \\ e^x & e^x + xe^x & 2e^{2x} \\ e^x & 2e^x + xe^x & 4e^{2x} \end{vmatrix} = e^{4x} \neq 0$$

for $-\infty < x < \infty$. Hence the set $\{e^x, xe^x, e^{2x}\}$ is a fundamental set of solutions of the given equation. A general solution of this differential equation is

$$y = c_1 e^x + c_2 x e^x + c_3 e^{2x}. \quad \blacksquare$$

EXAMPLE 1.7   It is not hard to verify that $y_1 = e^{-x}$, $y_2 = xe^{-x}$, and $y_3 = x^2 e^{-x}$ are solutions of the equation

(1.4) $$(D^3 + 3D^2 + 3D + 1)y = 0.$$

The Wronskian of this set of solutions is

$$W(y_1, y_2, y_3)(x) = \begin{vmatrix} e^{-x} & xe^{-x} & x^2 e^{-x} \\ -e^{-x} & e^{-x} - xe^{-x} & 2xe^{-x} - x^2 e^{-x} \\ e^{-x} & -2e^{-x} + xe^{-x} & 2e^{-x} - 4xe^{-x} + x^2 e^{-x} \end{vmatrix}.$$

We may check $W(y_1, y_2, y_3)(x)$ at any point x in J. For ease of computation we will use $x = 0$, where we find that

$$W(y_1, y_2, y_3)(0) = \begin{vmatrix} 1 & 0 & 0 \\ -1 & 1 & 0 \\ 1 & -2 & 2 \end{vmatrix} = 2 \neq 0.$$

Thus these solutions are linearly independent. A general solution of (1.4) is

$$y = c_1 e^{-x} + c_2 x e^{-x} + c_3 x^2 e^{-x}. \quad \blacksquare$$